QUESTIONS & ANSWERS

From the Bible

Dirk Waren

QUESTIONS & ANSWERS From the Bible

Other translations are listed in the **Bibliography**.

All underlining, italics and bracketed notes in scriptural quotes are added by the author.

Pronominal references to Deity in this work may not always be capitalized.

Edited by KEEII with special thanks to Raquel J. for assistance.

ISBN: 979-8-218-26274-7
PUBLISHED BY SOARING EAGLE PRESS
Youngstown

Printed in the United States of America

A wise man has great power,
and a man of knowledge increases
strength.

- Proverbs 24:5

CONTENTS

Introduction

Life Is Full of Mysteries

I was listening to a song where the singer asked, *"Why is life this mystery?"* Let's face it, life in this messed up world is a big mystery, filled with never-ending questions. Some common ones are *Why do I exist? What's my purpose?* and *Is there a God?* The purpose of this book is to answer such questions from a *biblical* perspective. In other words, what do the Judeo-Christian Scriptures say on the subject?

While 170 questions are listed in the Contents Page, dozens of others, probably hundreds, are addressed *within* the answers to those questions. For instance, the question of whether or not believers are under the Mosaic Law is not directly asked, but the answer is provided in a couple of spots. This prevented the already-long Contents Page from being way longer.

The answers given are stated as brief as possible without being so shallow they're worthless. Sometimes, however, a long answer is necessary, like with the question *Does the Bible Offer a Plan to Spiritual Maturity?*

Please understand that this is a *non-sectarian* guide to what the Bible teaches on the various topics. It does not represent a particular sect or camp in the body of Christ and therefore doesn't speak according to the doctrinal parameters of a specific group. If something is taught in the Bible, I'll convey it; if not, I won't. If something's vague or hinted at, I'll say so.

While such an approach might turn-off rigid sectarians—seeing as how they tend to put God and truth in a box—it should be a breath of fresh air to those honestly seeking biblical answers to life's most vital questions.

If you disagree on some point, that's okay, just make sure you disagree based on actual scriptural grounds and not simply because your pastor or sect teaches differently. Whatever the truth is on a topic, the clearest and most detailed passages trump the more ambiguous and sketchy verses. Speaking of which, the methodology used in acquiring answers in the work is based on these four common sense hermeneutical guidelines:

1. **Scripture interprets Scripture** with the plainest, most detailed verses taking precedence.
2. **Context is king** in which passages are interpreted according to the obvious meaning within the surrounding text.
3. **Literalize rather than spiritualize**, unless it's obvious that the text is using figurative language. In which case, the literal truth the symbolism intends to convey is looked for.
4. **If the plain sense makes sense—and is in harmony with the rest of Scripture—don't look for any other sense, lest you end up with nonsense.** This is basically the other 'rules' combined.

I wanted to include more details and scores of other questions (like on Noah's ark and the curious exploits of Samson), but there just wasn't space. For answers to those other questions, as well as further info on the ones provided, see the articles at the Fountain of Life site or pick up the corresponding book listed on the final page. If you still disagree on some point, please write Fountain of Life and we'll hammer-out the issue on the anvil of honest criticism and balanced scriptural dialogue.

This work is a celebration of my 40 years as a believer. I accepted the message of Christ at the age of 20 and I'll be turning 60 in a couple months. What better way to celebrate this milestone than to share some of the most important bits of knowledge I've acquired over these past four decades?

Feel free to jump around to the questions that interest you. If some answers are too complex, put them on the back burner and maybe return later.

1

Life's Most Fundamental Questions

Does God Exist?

There are two basic options concerning how human life originated and life in general, not to mention the Earth & Universe: They're either the result of mindless, nonliving matter or there is a Creator. Which one is more logical and scientific? The reason you can read a book or hear a song is because someone created them. The reason you can live in your abode is because someone designed it and someone built it.

The Bible teaches that everything you see and experience—living and un-living—did not just accidently manifest. There is an Intelligent Designer of all that exists. Belief in God is simply a part of the make-up of human beings; it's in our spiritual DNA because we were made in God's image and likeness.

The Earth & Universe and all living things inspire belief in a Creator; more than that, creation *screams out* God's existence (Psalm 19:1-4 & Romans 1:18-20). To suggest that everything in the Universe came about through accident and that there's no Intelligent Designer behind it all is like expecting a Boeing 747 to emerge out of a metal scrapyard after millions of years. It's absurd. The hypothetical scrapyard can't even produce a simple table or chair let alone a jet airplane!

Furthermore, the scientific axiom of biogenesis notes that **life only proceeds from life**. In other words, living things cannot manifest from something unliving. Only conscious life can produce conscious life. It's a scientific fact, obvious to a simpleton. As such, there *is* some kind of God—a Creator—from which all life proceeds.

So, the question is not *if* there is a God, but rather…

Who Is God?

The very first verse of Holy Scripture authoritatively states that "In the beginning God created the heavens and the earth" (Genesis 1:1). The original Hebrew word for 'God' is *Elohim (uh-LOW-him)*, which is a generic term for God or supernatural beings or even a human authority. However, the next chapter more precisely reveals what Genesis 1:1 means by 'God':

> **This is the account of the heavens and the earth when they were created, when the LORD God made the earth and the heavens.**
>
> **Genesis 2:4**

The Hebrew for "LORD" is YHWH (transliterated), which is pronounced *YAH-way* (or *YAH-hoo-way* for devout Hebrews). Some English speakers say Jehovah. In any case, God *is* Yahweh.

When God was revealed to Moses in the burning bush and said "I AM WHO I AM," the LORD was giving the translation of what Yahweh means (Exodus 3:13-15). In other words, God's proper name, Yahweh, was formed from "I AM WHO I AM." The LORD was saying in effect, "My name is the fact that I exist." Isn't that a perfectly fitting name for the Creator—I AM?

This explains why the religious Hebrews wanted to stone Christ to death when he said “Very truly I tell you, before Abraham was born, **I Am**” (John 8:58)—he was making himself *equivalent* with Yahweh, the Great I AM, which is why he testified “I and the Father are one” (John 10:30).

How Did God Create People?

The Bible offers details about the LORD’s creation of human beings:

> **Then God said, “Let us make mankind in our image, in our likeness, so that they may rule over the fish in the sea and the birds in the sky, over the livestock and all the wild animals, and over all the creatures that move along the ground.”**
> **27 So God created mankind in his own image,**
> **in the image of God he created them;**
> **male and female he created them.**
>
> **Genesis 1:26-27**

As you can see, the LORD—Father/Son/Holy Spirit—decided to make humankind in their image/likeness and then did so. The Hebrew for ‘image’ is *tselem (SEH-lem)*, which simply means image, representation, copy or duplicate whereas the Hebrew word for ‘likeness’ is *demuth (dem-OOTH)*, which means similitude, that is, something that *resembles* another; it’s something that is a, *match* or *counterpart* to another.

As such, human beings *resemble* the Almighty; you could say that **we’re God’s *counterpart* in the physical realm**. Whereas the LORD is triune in the sense of Father/Son/Holy Spirit we are also triune in the sense of spirit, mind & body.

Despite this, the Scriptures stress the difference between the Creator and those created in God’s image:

Know that <u>the LORD is God</u>. It is he who made us, and we are his; we are his people, the sheep of his pasture.
Psalm 100:3

While the LORD's way is perfect and God's word is flawless (Psalm 18:30) this is not the case with people, which brings us to our fourth fundamental question…

Why Are People Separated From God?

The Scriptures are frank that "all have sinned and fallen short of the glory of God" (Romans 3:23) and "There is no one righteous, not even one… All have turned away" (Romans 3:10-12). Turned away from whom? Our Creator, which is why the Bible puts it like this: "your iniquities have *separated* you from your God; your sins have hidden his face from you, so that he will not hear" (Isaiah 59:2).

To 'sin' means to "miss the mark" in the sense of morally failing. The penalty for sin is death (Romans 6:23) and the first thing sin kills is communion with God.

How Have People Tried to Solve This Problem?

Through the creation of **religion**. Humanity inherently *knows* there's a Creator God because we're created in the LORD's image, but also senses that a separation of sorts exists, which has given birth to religion. The Latin root word for 'religion' is *re-ligare*. *Ligare* means "to bind" or to "connect" and so adding *re* before *ligare* brings about the thought of "re-binding" or "re-connecting."

Thus religion is **the human attempt to reconnect with God**, which usually involves things like good works, certain rituals or adherence to the supposedly correct doctrine. However, Christ pointed out the failure of religion when his disciples asked him who could be saved:

> **"<u>With man this is impossible</u>, but not with God; all things are possible with God."**
>
> **Mark 10:27**

You see? Salvation through the flesh—through religion—is **impossible**. Yet, with God, salvation is not only possible, it's available to all, regardless of race, culture or social status. This is Christianity—*real* Christianity, not the counterfeit legalism, which is religious "Christianity."

Is Forgiveness of Sins and Reconciliation Possible?

Humanity's problem is that we have a sin nature, which separates us from our holy Creator and puts us on a collision course with eternal death. The LORD's conundrum is that God is love and thus loves humanity (1 John 4:8 & John 3:16), but God is also just and must therefore issue out the just wages of sin, which is death (Romans 6:23 & Matthew 10:28).

The LORD is willing to *forgive* sin, but cannot *ignore* sin. So the Almighty came up with an ingenious plan to save humanity from eternal death by engineering a way to forgive a person's sin through providing someone without sin willing to die in his/her place (2 Corinthians 5:21, Hebrews 4:15 & 1 John 3:5).

Consider this parable: An entomologist lived by some woods where he studied the various insects and became particularly fond of a huge ant hill. When news came that the nearby road would be extended through the woods and it was on a collision course with the ants, the entomologist longed to save his beloved insects, but it was impossible to communicate the dangers to them. The only way he could do so would be to become an ant!

This is the Christian message in a nutshell: God became a human being in the form of Jesus Christ to warn us to **repent or perish** (Luke 13:1-9) and, more than that, die in our place as a sin sacrifice (1 Peter 3:18 & Hebrews 9:14, 9:26). Think about it, God could've just kicked back in Heaven and destroyed us all for our sin, which would've been a just act. Instead, the

LORD was born into this humbling, brutal planet to suffer and die for us (Philippians 2:5-11).

Thankfully, it doesn't end there, Christ was also raised from the dead for our justification (Romans 4:25).

Hence, the penalty of sin—death—is paid for and those who **believe & repent** are saved from eternal death (Mark 1:15 & Acts 20:21), as well as reconciled to their Creator (Romans 5:10 & 5:11). Belief, by the way, simply means you *believe* the message while repentance means to "change your mind" in response to that particular truth, which naturally has an impact on your actions or lifestyle.

How Can I Escape Bondage to Sin?

'Gospel' literally means "good news." The good news of the message of Christ isn't just that we escape the penalty of eternal death, but that we escape the power of sin through spiritual regeneration (Titus 3:5 & 1 Peter 1:3) and the ensuing renewing of the mind (Romans 12:2).

Along with spiritual rebirth, believers receive the indwelling Holy Spirit, who is our helper, teacher and advocate (2 Timothy 1:14 & John 14:26).

On top of all of this, the LORD has provided believers with the baptism of the Holy Spirit and the benefits that come with this awesome gift (*shh*, Christians aren't supposed to talk about spiritual gifts these days).

If you're struggling with some kind of life-dominating sin—whether it's something sexual, or drugs, alcohol or whatever—I understand. Freedom is available for you through Christ and the benefits of the gospel. To walk free of any sin bondage simply put into practice the 3-point plan detailed in Chapter **5** under the heading *What's the Key to Walking Free From Sin?*

Can I Know and Walk With My Creator?

While atheists like to make fun of believers for having a relationship with their "invisible friend," people were created to have a relationship with their Creator. In other words, **fellowship with God is perfectly normal and is actually the first order of life**. This explains Christ's statement "seek first God's kingdom and his righteousness" (Matthew 6:33).

As far as personal relationship goes,

- Adam communed with God in the Garden of Eden, even after his fall (Genesis 3:8-13);
- Enoch "walked with God" and they were so close that the LORD simply "took him away," presumably so they could be together in Heaven (Genesis 5:22-24), but also as a type of the future Rapture;
- Moses communed with God in the Tent of Meeting where the LORD dwelt on the mercy seat of the Ark of the Covenant between the two gold-sculptured cherubim (Exodus 33:11);
- Asaph walked with his Creator so closely that they figuratively held hands (Psalm 73:23-25); and…
- David, of course, was "a man after God's own heart" (1 Samuel 13:14 & Acts 13:22).

All of these people from the Old Testament had a **relationship with the LORD** despite the fact that they had an inferior covenant with God. Today a vastly *superior* covenant is available to all people through Jesus Christ (Hebrews 8:6-7). This is the awesome message of the gospel—we can reconcile with our Creator, be forgiven of sin, have a relationship and receive eternal life & immortality (2 Timothy 1:10).

So how do you develop a relationship with God? We have to get away from this erroneous idea that we only encounter the LORD when we go to church gatherings once or twice a week. The Bible speaks of "praying without ceasing" (1 Thessalonians 5:17 KJV) and the "fellowship of the Holy Spirit" (2 Corinthians 13:14), which suggests developing a 24/7 rapport with God. You can have conversations with your Creator throughout the day, every day—when you wake up in bed, when you're in the shower, when you're driving, when you're walking down the hall, in the evening, etc. Just remember prayer protocol. You pray:

1. **To** the Father (Matthew 6:9)
2. **In** the name of Jesus Christ (John 16:23)
3. **By** the Holy Spirit (John 16:13)

As far as more 'official' personal prayer sessions go, start with "Be still, and know that I am God" (Psalm 46:10). **Turn off the gadgets and get away from the noise of the crowd.** Instead of glancing at God while gazing at your needs, learn to gaze at God while glancing at your needs.

There's a difference between the 24/7 fellowship noted above and personal prayer sessions. Christ said "when you pray, go into your room, close the door and pray to your Father, who is unseen. Then your Father, who sees what is done in secret, will reward you" (Matthew 6:6). He was talking about finding a solitary place for prayer sessions, known only to you and the LORD.

This is in contrast to religious hypocrites who love to pray in front of others, which really isn't communion with God, but rather putting on a show to impress people, which is fakeness (Matthew 6:5). 'Hypocrite' literally means "actor." This isn't to say, by the way, that it's wrong to pray with other believers, as is depicted in the Bible (Acts 12:12), just that it's wrong to pray in front of others *for the purpose of* impressing them with one's supposed devoutness.

When the Messiah said to "go into your room, close the door and pray" he was simply talking about finding a solitary place where it's just you and the LORD. It's interesting that Jesus often went to solitary places in the wilderness to pray "as was his habit," as observed in Mark 1:35, Matthew 14:23 and Luke 22:39-41. Why did he do this? Because there's something about nature that's conducive to encountering the Creator.

I think this is why people are attracted to outdoor activities—like hiking, kayaking, fishing, hunting and so on—because on some primal level they encounter God who is revealed in creation (Psalm 19:1-4, 97:6 & Romans 1:20). Paul and his ministry companions understood this:

> **On the Sabbath we went outside the city gate to the river, where we expected to find a place of prayer.**
>
> **Acts 16:13**

Does God Have a Purpose for Me?

While salvation from eternal death and relationship with God are core to Christianity, something naturally proceeds from that salvation & relationship, as noted here:

> **For it is by grace you have been saved, through faith—and this is not from yourselves, it is the gift of God—[9]not by works, so that no one can boast. [10] For we are God's handiwork, created in Christ Jesus to do good works, which God prepared in advance for us to do.**
>
> **Ephesians 2:8-10**

The LORD has works for you to do regardless of which season in life you are in, as well as an ultimate calling. For instance, Jesus Christ was called to be a fulltime minister for 3.5 years and to ultimately lay his life down for the salvation of humanity but, before that, he had regular assignments while earning a living as a carpenter up to the age of 30, such as drawing close to God, growing in knowledge/understanding/wisdom, learning how to minister and serving specific people in various ways.

Christians tend to think that if they're not called to be a pastor, they're of no value to God. This is a lie straight from the enemy. The LORD is very interested in your life. In fact, you're God's *child* through spiritual rebirth (1 John 5:1 & 3:9). Any normal, healthy parent is intensely interested in the life of his/her son or daughter; how much more so your *heavenly* Father? You must get a hold of the fact that God has strategic purposes for every believer, including YOU.

Keep in mind that any work you do for the LORD must *proceed from* your relationship and not be a *substitute for* your relationship. For instance, when Christ came to Martha & Mary's abode Martha focused on running around in a frenzy trying to **work for** the Lord whereas Mary focused on relationship, quietly **receiving from** the Lord. Martha was so misled that she arrogantly barked orders at the mighty Christ. Naturally Mary's actions where commended by the Lord rather than Martha's works (Luke 10:38-42).

So, focus on relationship with the LORD and seek to discern your purpose in each season of life, as well as specific works within that context. Then use the mind God gave you to *plan* your way and *act* according to that plan with the leading of the Holy Spirit. This will give you a sense of purpose in life and will build invigorating momentum. As Jesus said, "My food [sustenance, energy] is to do the will of him who sent me and to finish his work" (John 4:34).

For a biblical 3-point strategy that's easy as pie see *How Can I Obtain My (Righteous) Desires?* in chapter **10**.

What Is the Promise of Eternal Life All About?

Christianity at its core is the answer to humanity's ultimate quest. Think about it, what is humanity's greatest desire—a desire greater than wealth, fame, true love or sexual gratification? From the ancient epic of Gilgamesh to Ponce De Leon's obsession with the fountain of youth to our modern-day compulsion to be youthful-looking as long as possible, humanity is obsessed with the idea of immortality, the idea of living forever.

The answer is revealed clearly in the Holy Scriptures and this is further reason why the message of Jesus Christ is the "good news." Religionists may have obscured this truth over the centuries with their tangled web of life-stifling half-truths and lies, but the truth is still there, it cannot be quenched: "The wages of sin is death, but **the gift of God is eternal life in Christ Jesus our Lord**" (Romans 6:23).

In other words, **Christianity is about receiving immortality & eternal life**, which is plainly stated in passages like 2 Timothy 1:10, John 3:16 and John 3:36. And eternal life involves enjoying a purposeful life in a wondrous new Universe without the curse of sin & death, which the Scriptures call "the new heavens and new earth":

> **But in keeping with his promise we are <u>looking forward to</u> a new heaven and a new earth, where righteousness dwells.**
>
> **2 Peter 3:13**

Unfortunately, most believers aren't looking forward to their eternal life beyond this fallen Earth. Why? Because most ministers rarely teach or preach on this amazing topic and, if they do, they pretty much limit it to "spending eternity in Heaven," which naturally gives the impression of sitting on a cloud playing a harp forever. This, needless to say, seems fantastical and is hardly invigorating.

But what exactly are the "new heaven and new earth"?

The "new heaven" does not refer to the spiritual abode where God's throne is located—Heaven (Psalm 103:19 & 11:4)—because Heaven is already perfect and therefore doesn't need restored. After all, how can you restore perfection? Understand that the term 'heaven' or 'the heavens' can also refer to the physical Universe and everything in it.

For example, Psalm 19:1 states: "<u>The heavens</u> declare the glory of God; <u>the skies</u> proclaim the work of his hands." This is an example of Hebrew poetry known as synonymous parallelism in which the second part of the verse simply repeats the first in different words. In this case "the heavens" in the first part is confirmed as "the skies" in the second.

So, the "new heaven" refers to a divinely renovated physical Universe. Likewise, "new earth" refers to a renovated Earth.

Has this piqued your attention? Go to chapter **<u>16</u>** for amazing details on the nature of eternal life in the New Heavens and New Earth.

2

Questions About the Nature of God

Is God Father/Son/Holy Spirit?

The LORD is revealed in the Scriptures as Father/Son/Holy Spirit but, interestingly, the word 'Trinity' does not appear in the Bible, which explains why I don't use the term in my teachings. After all, if the LORD doesn't use it, why should I?

So, what is the biblical evidence to support the tri-unity of God?

Let's start with the very beginning of the Bible where the Creator is plainly referred to *in the plural:*

> **Then God said, "Let us make mankind in our image, in our likeness…"** **Genesis 1:26**

> **And the LORD God said, "The man has now become like one of us, knowing good and evil. He must not be allowed to reach out his hand and take also from the tree of life and eat, and live forever."**
>
> **Genesis 3:22**

Yet the LORD's plurality doesn't indicate the false notion of polytheism because the Bible emphasizes that God is **one** (Deuteronomy 6:4 & Isaiah 45:5,6,18). Rather, it's an indication of **one God in three parts**: **Father**, **Son** and **Holy Spirit**. Here are *ten* plain passages to illustrate this:

> **Then Jesus came to them and said, "All authority in heaven and on earth has been given to me. [19] Therefore go and make disciples of all nations, baptizing them in the name of the Father and of the Son and of the Holy Spirit, [20] and teaching them to obey everything I have commanded you."**
>
> **Matthew 28:18-20**

> **May the grace of the Lord Jesus Christ, and the love of God, and the fellowship of the Holy Spirit be with you all.**
>
> **2 Corinthians 13:14**

> **For through him** [Christ] **we both have access to the Father by one Spirit.**
>
> **Ephesians 2:18**

> **As soon as Jesus was baptized, he went up out of the water. At that moment heaven was opened, and he saw the Spirit of God descending like a dove and alighting on him. [17] And a voice from heaven said, "This is my Son, whom I love; with him I am well pleased."**
>
> **Matthew 3:16-17**

> **There is one body and one Spirit, just as you were called to one hope when you were called; [5]one Lord, one faith, one baptism; [6]one God and Father of all, who is over all and through all and in all.**
>
> **Ephesians 4:4-6**

> **But when the kindness and love of God our Savior appeared, [5] he saved us, not because of righteous**

things we had done, but because of his mercy. He saved us through the washing of rebirth and renewal by the Holy Spirit, [6] whom he poured out on us generously through Jesus Christ our Savior

Titus 3:4-6

There are different kinds of gifts, but the same Spirit distributes them. [5] There are different kinds of service, but the same Lord. [6] There are different kinds of working, but in all of them and in everyone it is the same God at work.

1 Corinthians 12:4-6

"All this I have spoken while still with you. [26] But the Advocate, the Holy Spirit, whom the Father will send in my name, will teach you all things and will remind you of everything I have said to you."

John 14:25-26

Peter, an apostle of Jesus Christ,
To God's elect, exiles scattered throughout the provinces of Pontus, Galatia, Cappadocia, Asia and Bithynia, [2] who have been chosen according to the foreknowledge of God the Father, through the sanctifying work of the Spirit, to be obedient to Jesus Christ and sprinkled with his blood:
Grace and peace be yours in abundance.

1 Peter 1:1-2

For the kingdom of God is not a matter of eating and drinking, but of righteousness, peace and joy in the Holy Spirit, [18] because anyone who serves Christ in this way is pleasing to God and receives human approval.

Romans 14:17-18

It might help you to grasp the concept of the tri-unity of God by considering that human beings are triune in nature—**spirit, mind & flesh**.

For anyone who thinks it's wrong to relate human nature to God's nature, the New Testament does this very thing:

> **For who knows a person's thoughts except their own spirit within them? <u>In the same way</u> no one knows the thoughts of God except the Spirit of God.**
>
> **1 Corinthians 2:11**

Also, there are items in nature that reflect the **three-in-one** principle, like the shamrock. Or consider water, which is one element that can manifest as fluid, ice or vapor.

In any case, these passages clearly prove the notion of God as **Father**, **Son** & **Holy Spirit**.

Why Is There Ire Toward the Tri-Unity of God?

The enemy *hates* any teaching that relays the truth of God as Father, Son & Holy Spirit because the kingdom of darkness desperately wants people—including believers—to think less of Christ and the Holy Spirit, rather than view them as equal to the Heavenly Father.

In other words, the devil wants to trick people into thinking Jesus Christ and the Holy Spirit are less important and have less power than God and, therefore, what they say or do is just not as important. This is a LIE.

As the Messiah said, "The truth shall set you free" (John 8:31-32).

Can You Be Saved if You Reject the Tri-Unity of God?

It should be stressed that believers who don't understand or accept the tri-unity of God are genuinely saved and therefore brother & sisters in the LORD. After all, you don't have to properly understand someone's nature in order to have a relationship with him/her. For instance, does a person have to grasp my physical/psychological/spiritual make-up to have fellowship with me? Of course not. Just the same, you don't have to have a perfect understanding of God's nature to have a genuine relationship.

Furthermore, no passage on salvation thru Christ, like John 3:16 or Romans 10:9-10, includes a clause about how one *must* embrace the tri-unity of God in order to be saved. In other words, while the nature of the LORD is an important topic in Scripture, it's not essential to salvation. Put another way, to be a genuine Christian—a sincere learner of the Anointed One—you don't have to have a perfect understanding of God's nature.

What Is God's Name?

While we breached this subject in chapter **1**, let's go into a little more detail. In the Hebrew Scriptures, God's name is transliterated as **YHWH**. This is the Tetragrammaton *(teh-truh-GRAM-uh-tawn)*, which is the actual name of God in the Bible.

YHWH is typically rendered "LORD" in English versions of Holy Scripture (all capitals) and stems from "I AM WHO I AM" (Exodus 3:13-15). In other words, the LORD's name is the fact that God exists.

From the 2nd or 3rd century BC, The Name was considered too holy to speak in Jewish culture and therefore substitute words for YHWH were used, like *Adonai (AH-doh-NAHY)* and *Elohim (uh-LOH-him)*. *Adonai* is a title of reverence for God and *Elohim* is a generic term for "god" or "gods."

Since YHWH became ineffable, the actual pronunciation was lost over time, although *YAH-way* is the likely articulation (or *YAH-hoo-way* to some Jews). "Jehovah" is merely the English form of the Tetragrammaton (JHVH) with the vowels of *Adonai* inserted. By being a combination of YHWH and *Adonai*, Jehovah means, in essence, the LORD God.

What Name Do We Call On à la Romans 10:13?

Let's read this particular passage with the surrounding verses:

> **Moses writes this about the righteousness that is by the law: "The person who does these things will live by them." 6 But the righteousness that is by faith says: "Do not say in your heart, 'Who will ascend into heaven?' " (that is, to bring Christ down) 7 "or 'Who will descend into the deep?' " (that is, to bring Christ up from the dead). 8 But what does it say? "The word is near you; it is in your mouth and in your heart," that is, the message concerning faith that we proclaim: 9 If you declare with your mouth, "Jesus is Lord," and believe in your heart that God raised him from the dead, you will be saved. 10 For it is with your heart that you believe and are justified, and it is with your mouth that you profess your faith and are saved. 11 As Scripture says, "Anyone who believes in him will never be put to shame." 12 For there is no difference between Jew and Gentile—the same Lord is Lord of all and richly blesses all who call on him, 13 for, "Everyone who calls on the name of the Lord will be saved."**
>
> **14 How, then, can they call on the one they have not believed in? And how can they believe in the one of whom they have not heard? And how can they hear without someone preaching to them? 15 And how can anyone preach unless they are sent? As it is written: "How beautiful are the feet of those who bring good news!"**
>
> **Romans 10:5-15**

Paul was quoting the prophet Joel in verse 13 and the Hebrew word translated as "LORD" in that Old Testament passage is YHWH. Hence, **we are to call upon the name of YHWH**. But the verses before and after reveal that Paul was talking about calling upon the name of the Lord *Jesus* and believing in Him. "Jesus" is the Greek rendition of the Hebrew Yeshua (or Joshua), which means "Yahweh saves" or "Yahweh is salvation."

Christ is the topic of this section of Scripture, as verified by verses 6, 7 and 9; and Jesus is even referred to as "Lord" in verse 9. This is the Greek word *kurios (KOO-ree-os)*, which is the very same word used to translate the Hebrew YHWH from Joel 2:32 in verse 13! In other words, **the same Greek word for "Lord"—*kurios*—is used to translate the Hebrew YHWH and is used as a reference to Jesus Christ in the same context**. Plus, keep in mind what Christ said: "Anyone who has seen me **has seen the Father**" and "I and the Father **are ONE**" (John 14:9 & John 10:30).

How Do I Respond to JWs on God's Name?

Keep this data in mind for the next time a Jehovah's False Witness tries to scam you about the Father and the Son who, as you can plainly see, **are both YHWH**. Romans 10:5-15 (above) is strategic in proving this.

Speaking of the Jehovah's Witnesses, they make this big deal about referring to God by His proper name YaHWeH, which they pronounce as "Jehovah." The problem with this is threefold:

1. YHWH is pronounced Yahweh *(YAH-way)*, not Jehovah.
2. The Tetragrammaton—YHWH—actually does not appear in the New Testament, at least not in any extant text. As noted above, the Greek word *kurios* is used to translate it (Joel 2:32 & Romans 10:13). *Kurios,* by the way, means "Lord, master, sir."
3. When Christ instructed us how to pray, he said we are to address Yahweh as "heavenly **Father**" or "**Father** in heaven" (Matthew 6:9-13). This corresponds to *familial* relation where we're Yahweh's ***children*** through spiritual rebirth (1 John 3:9, 1 Peter 1:23 & John 1:12-13). As such, we are to naturally refer to Yahweh as *"abba* Father" (Romans 8:15). The Aramaic *abba* is a term of *tender endearment* by a beloved child for his/her father; it's an *affectionate* word akin to "Daddy" or "Papa." Think about your relationship with your earthly father. Do you call him by his proper name or do you use a term of endearment, like "Dad," "Pa" or "Father"? This is why Christ said we are to address YHWH as

"Father" when we commune, which isn't to say we *can't* refer to Him as Yahweh (more on this in a moment).

What Does It Mean to Misuse God's Name?

As noted above, *YAH–way* is the accepted pronunciation of YHWH (or *YAH-hoo-way*), but proper pronunciation has nothing to do with the commandment—"You shall not misuse the name of the LORD your God" (Exodus 20:7)—especially in light of varying dialects. For instance, people of northern and southern Israel pronounced *Adonai* and *Elohim* differently, with the accent on different syllables. The idea that the LORD would reject someone merely because he or she put the accent on a different syllable than someone else is silly. God looks to the heart not to whether or not one pronounces a word perfectly (1 Samuel 16:7).

As far as YHWH becoming ineffable, that didn't happen until the Hellenistic period, which coincided with the intertestamental era (i.e. "between testaments"—approximately 400 BC to the time of Christ). And it's actually unbiblical in light of David—"a man after God's own heart"—**utilizing YHWH frequently in his prayer time, as seen throughout the Psalms, which shows that God *approves* of people using YHWH in our communion together.**

In short, to exclusively use substitute names and titles on the grounds that we might severely offend God by mispronouncing YHWH is unbiblical.

Lastly, taking the LORD's name in vain refers to **the wrongful use of The Name**, not mispronunciation based on one's dialect or what have you; unless, of course, someone was to *intentionally* mispronounce it in a mocking sense.

God of course has many secondary names, such as the Almighty, the Most High, the Ancient of Days, the First and the Last (Alpha and Omega), and so on.

3

Questions About Sin and Redemption

Why Is This World So Messed Up?

You don't have to live long or be an Einstein to realize that we live in a really messed up world plagued by lies, pain, disease, aging, death, grief, immorality, confusion, corruption, injustice, abuse, hostility and war. How did humanity and the Earth get to where we are? What is God's answer in the Bible? The explanation, in short, is **the great war of the Three Realms**. What is this war and how did it begin?

The three realms are **Heaven**, **Earth** and the **Underworld** (Philippians 2:9-11 & Revelation 5:2-3). Heaven is the spiritual abode where God's throne is located. The physical Universe, which includes the Earth, was created from the LORD's invisible realm (Hebrews 11:3). After satan & his corrupt angels rebelled and were kicked out of Heaven, it resulted in the Underworld. The Underworld is simply the dark heavenlies that parallel the Earth & Universe from which the devil & his demons operate (Ephesians 6:12).

Once satan fell, he focused on taking humanity down with him and he was successful in misleading the first man, Adam, by duping his wife, Eve

(Genesis 3). Ever since, there has been a cosmic war between Heaven and the Underworld with humanity & the Earth caught in between these two forces of good and evil.

Before satan's fall from Heaven along with a third of the angels, he was originally Lucifer—aka "Morning Star" or "Shining One"—the most attractive, talented and honored angel the LORD had created (Isaiah 14:12). Lucifer was a guardian cherub and archangel handpicked by God for the privilege of guarding—covering—God's throne in Heaven, similar to the cherubim who were assigned to guard the Garden of Eden after Adam & Eve were banished (Genesis 3:24).

Ezekiel 28:12-19 shows that Lucifer had an intrinsic musical anointing and dwelt in the presence of the Almighty. When God created the Earth & Universe the angels "sang together" and "shouted for joy." Satan's rebellion occurred sometime after this because there had to be an Earth and the corresponding undergirding spiritual realm for him to fall to and inhabit (Luke 10:18). Again, the "Underworld" is simply the spiritual dimension that undergirds the Earth & Universe. Not being physical beings, the devil & his fallen angels function from this spiritual realm to negatively influence the natural world.

Job 38:4-7 shows that "all the angels shouted for joy" when the Earth was created. The word 'all' is *kol (kohl)* in the Hebrew, meaning "the whole." The Hebrew for 'angels' in this verse literally means "the sons of God," a phrase used to describe angels elsewhere in Scripture, including the devil & his filthy angels (Genesis 6:2-4 & Job 1:6, 2:1). My point is that all the angels rejoiced when God created the Heavens and the Earth (Genesis 1:1), which would include Lucifer and his subordinates *before* their rebellion and ouster from Heaven.

Yet in Genesis 3:1-15 we observe satan, after his fall, possessing a serpent-with-legs in order to tempt the first woman. This shows that Lucifer and his cohorts rebelled and were cast from Heaven sometime *after* the creation of the Earth & Universe, but *before* the devil's duping of Eve, which means sometime between Genesis 1:31 and Genesis 3:1.[1] We don't know the exact expanse of time between these two events, but it could've been years. In any case, this shows that **satan's rebellion occurred shortly after the creation of human beings**.

We know that Lucifer's insurgency was due to pride:

> **13You said in your heart,**
> **"<u>I will</u> ascend to the heavens;**
> **<u>I will</u> raise my throne**
> **above the stars of God;**
> **<u>I will</u> sit enthroned on the mount of assembly,**
> **on the utmost heights of Mount Zaphon.**
> **14<u>I will</u> ascend above the tops of the clouds;**
> **<u>I will</u> make myself like the Most High."**
> **Isaiah 14:13-14**

These five "I will" statements reveal satan's arrogance—he wanted to be God rather than be God's servant. This was the first sin ever committed; and with far-reaching negative impact. Observe that sin is traced to what's going on in one's heart, which is corroborated by Christ in the New Testament (Mark 7:20-23). No wonder the Lord emphasized this in the Sermon on the Mount (Matthew 5:21-22, 27-28).

Lucifer was not satisfied with his extraordinary blessings and privileges. Instead, he wanted to be God and so, after his defeat, he naturally tempted Adam & Eve with the same basic sin which led to his downfall (Genesis 3:1-5). But there's more to this story, *way* more…

Lucifer was possibly having problems with the concept of serving before God created Adam & Eve, but once humans were created and he caught wind of the fact that angels were commissioned to serve people (Hebrews 1:14) his pride couldn't handle it, particularly when he found out that

---

[1] This is the young Earth perspective. Gap theorists, who embrace the old Earth model, place the fall of Lucifer & his fallen spirits sometime between Genesis 1:1 and 1:2. For details, see *How Old Is the Earth?* in chapter **<u>13</u>**.

human beings were created in the likeness of God. And, worse (to him), that they were expressly created to be co-heirs with Christ, seated with Him at the right hand of the Father, a privilege and position not granted to angels (Romans 8:17, Hebrews 1:13 & Ephesians 2:6). Lucifer's envy went into overdrive and so he orchestrated his doomed revolt.

Lucifer thus became satan, which means "adversary" or "enemy." Knowing God's character, the LORD gave satan & his cronies time to repent, but they were incorrigible. Since angelic spirits possess intrinsic immortality (Luke 20:34-36), God couldn't annihilate satan & his fallen angels and so sentenced them to eternal separation from God's kingdom, which necessitated the creation of the lake of fire as their eternal habitation (Matthew 25:41).

Theoretically, this is when the devil—which means "slanderer"—accused the LORD of being unloving and unjust. God consequently allowed a universal demonstration to all the angels—faithful and fallen—to prove both His great love and perfect justice by allowing the enemy to tempt human beings, which would result in humanity's fall. This would pave the way for God to implement his wonderful plan of redemption through the suffering & sacrifice of Christ, which offered forgiveness, reconciliation and eternal life for any human being who humbly repented—receiving God's graciousness (Acts 20:21)—which was something the devil & his cronies were foolishly unwilling to do.

Hence, God's sentence on the fallen angels was temporarily suspended until this universal demonstration was completed. In the meantime, the devil & his underlings are doing everything they can to thwart God's demonstration. For anyone who might object to the idea of a dispute between God and the devil and the corresponding exhibition on Earth, the Bible details just such a scenario on a smaller scale in the book of Job (1:8-12 & 2:3-7).

Satan's top priority, of course, is to keep as many people from eternal salvation as possible (2 Corinthians 4:3-4). Apparently, he thinks that if he can prevent enough people from acquiring redemption, the Creator will be forced to bend his justice, which would set a precedent and thus grant satan & his demons an acquittal.

I know this is heavy, but it reveals the big picture of what's going on behind the scenes and explains our messed-up Universe with its ongoing war between good and evil. All the pieces of the puzzle fit. Mull over the data and decide for yourself.

In any case, this is a temporary war and God's kingdom wins in the end. Thus all the humbly repentant are looking forward to "the new heavens and new earth, the home of righteousness" (2 Peter 3:13), which is addressed at length in Chapter **16**.

Can You Offer Details on God's Plan of Redemption?

The Bible is all about **1.** the LORD creating the Heavens & Earth and all living things, **2.** the rebellion and expulsion from Heaven of satan & his foul underlings, **3.** humanity's fall, **4.** satan's usurpation of authority over creation and, most of all, **5.** God's brilliant, loving plan of **redemption**.

The events of Genesis 3 are history, but involve the staples of great drama:

- **The stage** is a beautiful garden roughly the size of California or Iraq (according to the dimensions specified in Genesis 2:8-15) on a planet called Earth in a solar system in one galaxy of an estimated 200 billion galaxies in the Universe.
- **The players** are: **1.** The Almighty Creator, **2.** His nemesis who was kicked out of Heaven and dwells in the dark spiritual dimension that parallels the Earth and Universe, **3.** Adam & Eve (and the human race in their loins), the only beings created in the likeness of God and called to be co-heirs with Christ, and **4.** a harmless, beautiful animal that satan uses to dupe Adam & Eve and usurp their authority over the Earth and Universe.
- **The prop** is a tree with the forbidden fruit thereof.

- **The suspense** concerns whose word Adam & Eve will believe—God's word or satan's—which will determine their destiny and the destiny of the human race.
- **The tragedy** is their fall, the cursing of creation and the ensuing pathos of life in a fallen world.
- **The challenge** is how the Creator can possibly set things aright without compromising perfect justice.
- **The story** contains elements of all great dramas—a noble hero, a wicked villain, protagonists, deceit, the testing of character, tragedy and potential redemption, which brings us to…

God's Plan of Redemption

To 'redeem' means "to liberate through payment of ransom" or "to clear of debt through proper payment." In the 1st century nearly half the people on Earth were slaves in one form or another. The Greek word for 'redeem' was used back then in reference to purchasing freedom for a slave.

While slavery still exists today, it's less widespread and usually hidden. However, spiritual slavery is rampant because everyone born from Adam is a slave to sin and captive to the kingdom of darkness. The awesome news is that God has purchased our freedom from this spiritual slavery through the precious blood of Christ.

> **For you know that it was not with perishable things such as silver or gold that you were redeemed from the empty way of life handed down to you from your ancestors, 19 but with the precious blood of Christ, a lamb without blemish or defect.**
>
> **1 Peter 1:18-19**

We've been liberated through the death and resurrection of Christ, which is the gospel (1 Corinthians 15:1-4). Peter summarizes what we've been freed from as "**the empty way of life**" handed down to us from our ancestors. This refers to people's empty existence separate from God as slaves to sin with satan as slave master. Such bondage was handed down to us by our ancestors, Adam & Eve.

Some will argue that it's unfair for sin and spiritual slavery to be passed from our primordial parents to the rest of us. This is what theologians refer to as **federal headship**, which simply means that Adam was the human race's spiritual, moral and physical fountainhead, our lone representative. The entire race was in his loins when he deliberately sinned and thus a sin nature was passed on to all descendants (Romans 5:12). Think about it in terms of genetics: We naturally inherit characteristics of our fore-parents, such as facial features, skin color and height; the same principle is at play in a spiritual sense.

To be set free from this generational curse of sin we'd have to be born of a *new* Adam—a second Adam—who doesn't transfer sin and death, but rather life, because he was *not* born of the seed of Adam, but of the seed of God. Believe it or not, this is the core message of the gospel. Christ is the second Adam (1 Corinthians 15:45-49). Let me explain…

Our freedom was purchased through the precious blood of Yeshua:

> **For He has rescued us from the dominion of darkness and brought us into the kingdom of the Son he loves,**
> **14 in whom we have redemption, the forgiveness of sins.**
>
> **Colossians 1:13-14**

God has rescued us—*liberated us*—from bondage to the kingdom of darkness through Christ. We're no longer slaves to satan, as long as you've accepted the awesome gospel.

This great salvation corresponds to the LORD's prophecy after the fall of Adam & Eve:

> **"And I** [God] **will put enmity**
> **between you** [satan] **and the woman,**
> **and between your offspring and hers** [Christ]**;**
> **he** [Christ] **will crush your head,**
> **and you will strike his heel."**
>
> **Genesis 3:15**

The offspring of the woman—Christ—would eventually deal satan a fatal blow. The best the devil could do to circumvent this was to try to thwart the coming of the Messiah—which he repeatedly tried to do, but failed.

The satanic attempt to pollute the bloodline through the "sons of God" copulating with women was one such occasion (Genesis 6:1-4). Once Yeshua was born, the devil moved upon Herod to murder the child (Matthew 2:16). And, ultimately, manipulated his puppets in the Roman/Hebrew governments to have Jesus unjustly captured, tortured and executed, which amounted to "striking his heal." Of course, this played into God's genius plan as the death and resurrection of Christ was key to our redemption.

Why Is Humanity Separated From God?

Adam's sin and the passing of a sin nature to his descendants built an impenetrable wall between God and the human race. Yet the ministry of the second Adam—Jesus Christ—tore that wall down so that we can reconcile with our Creator.

This "great wall" is a barrier consisting of four figurative blocks:

1. **The holy character of God**
2. **The debt of sin**
3. **Slavery to satan**
4. **Spiritual death**

Let's look at all four:

The holy character of God. Have you ever known people who were so 'good' that you felt uncomfortable around them, perhaps inferior? This is magnified when you know they're aware of some of your more hideous "skeletons in the closet." The reason you felt uncomfortable is because their moral standards were so high that you assumed they'd be judgmental of you, which created a sense of alienation.

Now relate this to the human race and God. All humanity is born of Adam's seed and therefore has an inherent sin nature, which stands in stark contrast to the LORD's flawlessness—absolute purity, righteousness, justice, love, immutableness (unchangeableness), and veracity. Thus God's holy character became a barrier after the fall.

Is it any wonder that the Bible says "all our righteous acts are like filthy rags" (Isaiah 64:6)? Notice it doesn't say that our *bad* deeds are like filthy rags, but rather our *righteous* acts! God is so holy—so absolutely perfect—that even what we would consider good works by human standards are offensive by comparison. In short, there's an infinite gap between fallen humanity and the LORD due to God's holy character.

The debt of sin. Back in the Roman Empire when criminals were judged they were given a Certificate of Debt, which was placed on the door of their cells. This document cited how they failed to live according to the law of Caesar and denoted the corresponding sentence. When the penalty was fulfilled, their Certificate of Debt was stamped "Paid in Full" so that they would not be punished again for their crimes. Of course, if the penalty was death this was irrelevant, yet if the consequence was *time,* it was valuable: If someone tried to accuse them of a past offense all they had to do was show their canceled Certificate of Debt. Until that debt was paid, however, it stood between them and freedom.

Let's relate this to the human race and the perfect moral Law of God, summed up in the Ten Commandments and the Sermon on the Mount. All of us have sinned against God's Law because the infection of sin passed from our Federal Headship to us. We're all infected with a sinful nature and have missed it one way or another; actually, we've transgressed *innumerable* ways, not just "one," particularly when you consider the so-called "little sins," like arrogance, envy, jealousy, rivalry, greed, carnal lust and the like. Since the "wages of sin is death" (Romans 6:23), we've all been assigned a Certificate of Debt, which cites the penalty of our offenses as death (Colossians 2:14). This is why the Bible says "whoever does not believe stands *condemned already*" (John 3:18).

Humanity's debt of sin means that we're in a state of criminality apart from Christ, the second Adam. We're thus "objects of wrath" (Ephesians 2:3). It's an impassable barrier between us and God and can only be removed if a qualified individual paid the penalty of death in our place.

Slavery to satan. This third block in the great wall that separates God and humanity refers to satan apprehending power-of-attorney over physical creation and hence becoming the "god of this age" (2 Corinthians 4:4) or, as Christ called him, "the prince of this world" (John 12:31, John 14:30 & John 16:11). 'Prince' in the Greek is *archon (AR-kohn)*, which means "ruler, governor, leader." The devil is the dark spiritual ruler of this planet and thus the world is one big slave market where everyone born of the seed of Adam is legally a slave to satan, whether they know it or not.

This explains why the Messiah said the conservative religious leaders of Israel where children of the devil, to their astonishment (John 8:33-44). It's why the New Testament proclaims in no uncertain terms that "the whole world is under the control of the evil one" "who leads the whole world astray" (1 John 5:19 & Revelation 12:9). It explains Christ's commission to Paul to turn people "from the dominion of satan to God" (Acts 26:18). It explains why satan is referred to as "the ruler of the kingdom of the air, the spirit who is now at work in those who are disobedient" (Ephesians 2:2).

Unredeemed humanity may be God's creation, but they're *not* God's children. They lawfully belong to their slave master, the devil. The only person born into this world that was not born in subjugation to satan is our Mighty Savior, Jesus Christ, because he was *not* born of the seed (sperm) of a human father and therefore was not tainted with Adam's sin infection (Luke 1:34-35). To be set free of slavery to satan, a person has to be born of God's seed and thus become a child of God (1 John 3:2,9 & 5:1).

Spiritual death. God warned Adam & Eve not to eat of the tree of the knowledge of good and evil because "in the day" they did so they would "surely die" (Genesis 2:17). The Hebrew word for 'death'—*muwth (mooth)*—is actually used *twice* in this statement and therefore could be rendered "in dying you will die." In short, something died in Adam & Eve the moment they sinned, which led to their eventual physical decease. Theologians refer to this as spiritual death, which doesn't mean that their spirit ceased to exist, but rather that their spirit became dead to God because Adam & Eve lost their spiritual life or eternal life. Their relationship with their Creator was thus short-circuited; it died. This condition was passed on to everyone born into this world ever since.

Of course, God does not hold children accountable until they reach the "age of accountability," which refers to the age that youths are held responsible for their sins (Isaiah 7:16). Theologians typically place this age at 13 based on the Jewish custom that a child becomes an adult at 13, but the Bible doesn't actually say this. Interestingly, God only held Israelites 20 years-old and older accountable for serious sins of unbelief committed during the Hebrews' desert journey to the Promised Land (Numbers 14:29-30). No doubt the age of accountability varies according to the maturity level of the individual and the severity of the sin in question.

In any case, before the age of accountability children are spiritually alive; after the age of accountability, they're spiritually dead (Paul implied this in Romans 7:9). Yet all people inevitably sin—assuming they mature—and therefore they spiritually die due to the sin infection passed from Adam.

Because of this condition of spiritual death there's a great wall between God and humanity. It's impossible for unredeemed people to do anything to change this condition and reconcile to the LORD *by their own efforts*. As such, no human-made religion can reconcile people to their Creator and grant forgiveness of sins or eternal life. This explains a statement Jesus made when the disciples asked him who could be saved. He responded:

> **"<u>With people it is impossible</u>, but not with God; for all things are possible with God."**
>
> **Mark 10:27**

Eternal salvation and everything that goes with it—reconciliation with the LORD, the forgiveness of sins and acquisition of eternal life—are only available through God and not human-made religion, including religious "Christianity," which isn't actual Christianity. These wonderful things are available exclusively from God through the gospel, which explains why 'gospel' literally means "good news."

Paul said that God gives "**all men** life" (Acts 17:25). The word 'life' here is the Greek word *zoe (ZOH-ay)*, which in this context refers to the temporal life *(zoe)* that God grants all people and is acquired simply by being born of the perishable seed of Adam. Consequently, everyone born into this world has temporal life *(zoe)*. To receive eternal life *(zoe)* people must be born-again of the imperishable seed of Christ, the second Adam. For support, see 1 John 3:9, 1 Peter 1:23, Romans 5:16-17 and 1 Corinthians 15:45. This is what the message of Christ is all about and it's all summed up nicely in the Bible's most famous passage:

> **"For God so loved the world that he gave his one and only Son that whoever believes in him shall not perish but have eternal life."**
>
> **John 3:16**

This is the gospel in a nutshell.

Summing all of this up, the "great wall" that separates God and fallen humanity consists of four impenetrable blocks—**1. God's holy character**, **2. our debt of sin**, **3. slavery to satan** and **4. spiritual death**—and no amount of human effort, religion or philosophy can bring it down. We can't even get over the wall with God's aid; the barrier *must* be destroyed.

This is precisely what Jesus Christ—the second Adam—did. As noted in chapter **1**, the only way an entomologist can save his precious ants from a road being built on a collision course with the huge ant hill would be to become an ant and communicate the danger to them.

I'm sure you see the parallel to God's concern for the human race. Yet there's one huge difference: God didn't just become a human being to warn us to repent or perish (Luke 13:1-9), the Creator sacrificed Himself for us by dying in our place.

How Did Christ Demolish the 'Great Wall'?

Let's look at the four works that the Lord did to demolish the great wall between God and humanity:

Propitiation. This somewhat intimidating theological term simply means that Yeshua's sacrifice turned away God's wrath by satisfying violated justice. In other words, propitiation appeased the offense to God's holy character and rendered us favorable to the LORD—reconciling the wrongdoer with the affronted. Thus the Messiah's act of propitiation—his atoning sacrifice—demolished the block of God's offended character:

> **He is the atoning sacrifice** [aka propitiation] **for our sins, and not only for ours but also for the sins of the whole world.**
>
> **1 John 2:2**

Christ is the "atoning sacrifice" for our transgressions. These two words are one word in the Greek: *hilasmos (hil-as-MOSS)*, which means "a propitiation" or "atoning sacrifice." You'll usually see *hilasmos* translated as one or the other in English Bibles. To atone means to make amends or reparations for an offense or a crime. That's what the Messiah did for us.

Redemption. This is the work of Christ that **1.** canceled our debt of sin and **2.** freed us from slavery to satan. In other words, redemption demolished the next two blocks that separates God and humanity.

Concerning canceling our debt of sin, when Yeshua was nailed to the cross darkness fell for three hours whereupon He bore the sins of the world. It was at this time that the Son was utterly forsaken by the Father (Matthew 27:45-46). The Father perhaps allowed the pitch blackness so that no one could see the horror of what happened as the Son was engulfed by Divine wrath when the sins of humanity were put on him.

For the first time Christ experienced the aloneness of being wholly separated from the Father & Holy Spirit with the corresponding sense of emptiness and meaninglessness.

Right before he died, Jesus cried out a single potent word, *teleó (tel-AY-oh)*, which means “It is finished” or “Paid in full” (Matthew 27:50 & John 19:30). This was the same Greek word stamped on a Roman prisoner’s Certificate of Debt when his or her sentence was completed. In other words, the price was paid for our sins and thus *our* Certificate of Debt was essentially stamped “Paid in Full.”

Concerning freeing us from satanic slavery, this passage best details our redemption through Christ’s sacrifice:

> **For there is one God and one mediator between God and mankind, the man Christ Jesus, [6] who gave himself as a ransom for all people.**
>
> **1 Timothy 2:5-6**

Again, to ‘redeem’ means “to liberate through payment of ransom; to clear of debt through proper payment.” We’ve been liberated from slavery to the kingdom of darkness through the sacrifice of the Creator. Jesus was qualified to do this because **1.** He wasn’t himself a slave to satan since He wasn’t born of Adam’s seed, but rather God’s seed (Luke 1:35); and **2.** He was a *willing* redeemer. You see, a slave doesn’t have the clout to order someone to pay for his/her ransom. The liberator had to do so *voluntarily*, which explains why Christ stressed this (John 10:17-18).

Yet what was the motivation? Love. Love sent the Lord to the cross to cancel our debt of sin and liberate us from slavery to the devil (John 3:16).

Substitutionary death. Whereas propitiation concerns God and appeasing his offended character; and redemption concerns sin and paying our debt of sin, as well as liberating us from satan’s slave market; substitutionary death concerns the penalty of death, which is “the wages of sin” (Romans 6:23). All “substitutionary death” means is that Christ died in our place, the innocent for the guilty, which we observe here:

> **But we do see Jesus, who was made lower than the angels for a little while, now crowned with glory and**

> **honor because <u>he suffered death</u>, so that by the grace of God <u>he might taste death for everyone</u>.**
>
> **Hebrews 2:9**

By dying in our place, Yeshua removed the barrier of spiritual death and all that goes with it—being dead to God, the loss of eternal life, physical death and, ultimately, the dreaded second death (Revelation 20:11-15).

Because death is the wages of sin, substitutionary animal sacrifice was implemented immediately by God to reestablish fellowship after Adam & Eve's fall. Thus an innocent animal had to die when the LORD killed a mammal to cover their nakedness (Genesis 3:21). This established the principle that a guiltless substitute needed to perish in order for sin to be forgiven or, at least, temporarily covered.

This blood sacrifice at the beginning of human history was prototypical and therefore cultures in ensuing generations utilized the concept, some staying close to the pattern and others devolving into perverse variations.

It's interesting to observe in Scripture how substitutionary sacrifice applied to **1.** one lamb for one person (Genesis 4:4 & Leviticus 4:32), **2.** one lamb for one family (Exodus 12:3-14), **3.** one lamb or bull for a nation (Leviticus 16) and **4.** one "lamb" for the world, which refers to Christ and explains why John the Baptist exclaimed: "Look, the Lamb of God, who takes away the sin of the world!" (John 1:29). The Lord's great sacrifice fulfilled the need for one lamb for one person, one lamb for one family and one lamb for one nation.

It was no coincidence that Christ's crucifixion took place on the Day of Passover because he was the world's Passover lamb. Just as the blood of a lamb placed on the doorframes of the homes of the Hebrews allowed the death angel to "pass over" their abodes (Exodus 12:7,12-13), so the blood of Christ sprinkled on the doorposts of our hearts prompts God to "pass over" us, as far as the damning judgment of eternal death goes.

I want to stress again the Lord's motivation for dying for us. Jesus said, "Greater love has no one than this: to lay down one's life for one's friends" (John 15:13). Christ died in our place because **He loved us**!

While the Messiah's propitiation, redemption and substitutionary death demolished the four blocks of the great wall which alienated God from humanity, a final work was necessary to unite us by reestablishing *relationship:*

Reconciliation. To 'reconcile' means to change from a state of enmity to friendship. Reconciliation therefore neutralized hostility between God and humanity and this explains something Paul said:

> **Once you were alienated from God and were enemies in your minds because of your evil behavior. [22] But now he has reconciled you by Christ's physical body through death to present you holy in his sight, without blemish and free from accusation—[23] if you continue in your faith, established and firm, and do not move from the hope held out in the gospel.**
>
> **Colossians 1:21-23**

At its core the gospel is about reconciling to our Creator, which is why the "good news" is also referred to as "the message of reconciliation":

> **All this is from God, who reconciled us to himself through Christ and gave us the ministry of reconciliation: [19]that God was reconciling the world to himself in Christ, not counting people's sins against them. And he has committed to us the message of reconciliation. [20]We are therefore Christ's ambassadors, as though God were making his appeal through us. We implore you on Christ's behalf: Be reconciled to God.**
>
> **2 Corinthians 5:18-20**

The conditions for reconciling with God are repentance and faith (Acts 20:21). Repentance seems to have a negative connotation today, but it simply means to change your mind for the positive, which therefore changes your direction. It means turning from rebellion to compliance, from dark to light, from destructivity to productivity. While it's possible to repent and not believe, it's not possible to *truly* believe and not repent.

A person's embracing of the message of reconciliation is the first stage of what Christ called the "**restoration of all things**," which refers to the liberation of the Earth and all creation from satan's dominion and the bondage to decay (i.e. entropy).

What Is the "Restoration of All Things"?

Peter spoke of "the period of **restoration of all things**" when preaching to a crowd after the miraculous healing of a lame beggar (Acts 3:21 NASB). God's great restoration of creation takes place in four stages:

1. **Spiritual rebirth of people** who accept the gospel.
2. **The redemption of our bodies**, which is when we'll receive glorified bodies and (primarily) takes place at the Rapture.
3. **Christ's millennial reign on Earth** after the seven-year Tribulation.
4. **The establishment of the New Heavens and New Earth**, the eternal home of righteousness.

Let's consider these stages and the scriptural support for each…

STAGE ONE: Spiritual Regeneration Through the Gospel

The Messiah noted the restoration of all things here:

> **Jesus said to them, "Truly I tell you, at <u>the renewal of all things</u>, when the Son of Man sits on his glorious throne, you who have followed me will also sit on twelve thrones, judging the twelve tribes of Israel."**
>
> **Matthew 19:28**

The Greek word for 'renewal' in this verse is *paliggenesia (pal-ing-hen-es-EE-ah)*, which means "new birth, regeneration or renewal." It's only used twice in Scripture. The other occasion is Titus 3:5, where it refers to the ***regeneration*** *of the human spirit*, which occurs when a believer accepts the gospel through repentance and faith (John 3:3,6 & Mark 1:15).

Spiritual regeneration is **the first stage** of God's "renewal of all things." You see, the restoration of all things is jump-started in our current age through the spiritual rebirth of believers. When a person experiences divine regeneration they are transferred from the dominion of satan to the kingdom of God (Acts 26:18). In terms of physical appearance, it doesn't look like anything has changed with the person, although their new attitude undoubtedly changes their demeanor. This is because, spiritually, they've swapped kingdoms and are **no longer slaves to satan**, which naturally has an impact on one's disposition.

Think about it in terms of those sci-fi flicks based on Jack Finney's book *The Body Snatchers*; the first two were called *Invasion of the Body Snatchers*. The same basic principle is at play except that the extraterrestrials are wholly good because they're God—Father, Son & Holy Spirit—who want to snatch people from satan's dominion. The way they do this is through inward regeneration.

STAGE TWO: The Rapture

Spiritual rebirth culminates with Christ's return for His Church, which is **the second stage** of the restoration of all things. All believers are promised this blessing providing they persevere in faith (Colossians 1:22-23 & 1 Corinthians 15:2).[2]

This second stage concerns Jesus' return for the Church wherein **believers' bodies are finally redeemed**:

[2] This is just common sense; after all, if it takes faith to be saved, a person can no longer be saved if they give-up at some point and no longer believe.

> **We know that <u>the whole creation has been groaning as in the pains of childbirth right up to the present time</u>.**
> **23 Not only so, but we ourselves, who have the firstfruits of the Spirit, groan inwardly as we wait eagerly for our adoption to sonship, <u>the redemption of our bodies</u>.**
>
> **Romans 8:22-23**

The "redemption of our bodies" occurs when Christ snatches up His Church, as detailed in 1 Thessalonians 4:13-18. When this 'Rapture' takes place, living believers will be translated to Heaven with new, glorified bodies while believers who physically died previously will be bodily resurrected with the same kinds of awesome bodies. How awesome will these bodies be? The Bible describes them as **imperishable**, **glorified**, **powerful** and **spiritual** in nature (1 Corinthians 15:42-44). Chew on that.

While some claim that the word 'Rapture' isn't biblical, it is. It refers to a phrase used in the main passage detailing this event:

> **After that, we who are still alive and are left will be <u>caught up</u> together with them in the clouds to meet the Lord in the air. And so we will be with the Lord forever.**
>
> **1 Thessalonians 4:17**

'Caught up' in the Greek is *harpazó (har-PAD-zoh)*, which means to "snatch up" or "obtain by robbery." It's translated in Latin as *rapio* in the Vulgate, which is where we get the English 'rapture.' With this understanding, when the Bridegroom, Yeshua, comes for His bride, the Church, He's going to obtain us by **robbing us off the Earth**!

If you'd like further scriptural support for the Rapture, see Luke 17:24-35, John 14:1-3, 1 Corinthians 15:50-54, 1 Thessalonians 1:10 and Revelation 3:10. We'll address this topic further in chapter <u>7</u> in the section *What Is "The Resurrection of the Dead"?*

STAGE THREE: Christ's Millennial Reign on Earth

The restoration of all things continues after the seven-year Tribulation when Christ returns to Earth and establishes His millennial kingdom, which is what Jesus was specifically referring to in Matthew 19:28 (quoted three pages earlier). This is **the third stage** of the restoration of all things at which time Old Testament saints will be resurrected while Tribulation martyrs will be bodily resurrected. Both will receive their immortal bodies at this juncture. As for the mortal humans that Christ allows to enter the Millennium after The Judgement of Living Nations (aka The Sheep and Goat Judgment detailed in Matthew 25:31-46), their lifespans will return to the lengthy ones of people before the flood of Genesis 6.

Glorified believers will be priests of God and will reign with Christ during the Millennium. Such believers will not be able to propagate because, as Messiah taught, "they will neither marry nor be given in marriage… for they are like the angels" (Luke 20:34-36). This doesn't mean, by the way, that we'll *be* angels; simply that we'll be *like* angels in the sense of not marrying and that we'll attain intrinsic immortality, which we don't currently possess (Romans 2:7 & 2 Timothy 1:10).

Isaiah 11:6-9 shows what life will be like during the Millennium: Carnivorous animals will become herbivorous and therefore wolves will live with lambs and leopards will lie together with goats; calves and lions will 'hang out' and be led by little children. Cows and bears will feed together and formerly carnivorous beasts, like the lion, will eat straw like an ox. Furthermore, children will play by the cobra's den and the viper's nest without fear because poisonous creatures will no longer be poisonous.

At the end of the Millennium satan will be released and deceive the nations, inciting a mass attack on the righteous government of Christ in Jerusalem. This rebellion is easily defeated and the devil is cast into the lake of fire forever. Revelation 20:1-10 details these events.

STAGE FOUR: The Eternal New Heavens and New Earth

As wonderful as the thousand-year reign of Christ will be, it's just another stage in the "restoration of all things." **The fourth and final stage** takes place when God wholly renovates the Earth & Universe and the heavenly city, the New Jerusalem, comes "down out of heaven from God" to rest on the New Earth (Revelation 21:1-4). Thus the renewal of all things climaxes with the renewing of the Earth & Universe. This is the New Heavens and New Earth, the eternal "home of righteousness" (2 Peter 3:13).

The Greek word for 'restoration' in the phrase "the final restoration of all things" is *apokatastasis (ah-pok-ah-TAS-tah-sis)*, which appears only once in the Bible:

> **For he** [Jesus] **must remain in heaven until the time for <u>the final restoration</u>** *(apokatastasis)* **<u>of all things</u>, as God promised long ago through his holy prophets.**
>
> **Acts 3:21**

The root word for *apokatastasis* is *apokathistémi (ah-pok-ath-IS-tay-mee)*, which means "to set up again" and "restore to its original position or condition." That's what the "restoration of all things" is about—**restoring the Earth and Universe to its original condition before the fall, which is the way God originally intended it to be**.

What About "Creation Waits in Eager Expectation"?

The Bible stresses that creation itself *yearns* for the redemption provided in the restoration of all things:

> **For <u>the creation</u> waits <u>in eager expectation</u> for the children of God to be revealed.**
>
> **Romans 8:19**

What does creation "wait in eager expectation" for? The children of God to be revealed, which is part of the restoration of all things.

What exactly is "the creation" in this verse? It refers to the Earth and Universe and all living things thereof, including the animal kingdom and even the plant kingdom. They will all be partakers in this redemption of the physical Universe. Why else would all creation "wait in eager expectation" for this great restoration if they were not included in it? Of course, animals and trees aren't literally yearning for this renewal, but they yearn for it in a figurative sense because *they're included in it.*

Consider something interesting: When the high priest sprinkled animal blood on the cover of the Ark of the Covenant once a year to atone for the sins of the Hebrews, the blood covered God's Law, which was represented in the Ark via the tablets of the Ten Commandments. This ritual resulted in God's mercy year to year, covering the Israelites' sins. But the blood of animals could only temporarily cover sin, not cleanse it away forever (Hebrews 10:1-4).

The good news is that Jesus Christ, who is the believer's High Priest, offered his *own* blood when he went to the Most Holy Place in Heaven, which is different from merely offering the blood of animals (Hebrews 9:23-28). Interestingly, Leviticus 16:15 shows the high priest sprinkling blood *on the ground in front of the Ark* after sprinkling it on the cover. The Ark was housed in the tent Tabernacle at the time and so the blood was literally poured **on the ground**. This is significant because the entire ceremony pointed to Christ's blood atonement in Heaven and the high priest didn't just sprinkle blood on the lid of the Ark for the redemption of humanity, but also on the ground for the restoration of all creation.

So "**the final restoration of all things**" (Acts 3:21) refers to **the LORD** ***restoring everything in creation to the condition it was originally intended***. The Greek word for 'all things' is *pas (pass)*, which means "all, the whole, every kind of." So, God is going to restore *all* creation to its initial condition, as originally intended before satan duped Adam & Eve and usurped power-of-attorney over physical creation. Revelation 21:5 adds an interesting insight in that God will be "making everything new" and not making new things. There's a difference. Chew on it.

Of course, the LORD *won't* restore those condemned to the lake of fire. This includes damned human beings, the devil & his filthy angels or anything else cast into the lake of fire, such as death and Hades (Revelation 20:10-15 & Matthew 25:41). The lake of fire is basically God's garbage dump. The good news of the gospel of Christ is all about escaping this eternal condemnation and partaking of "the restoration of all things."

Needless to say, make sure YOU are a partaker and do everything in your power to get those linked to you to be partakers as well. As "Christ's ambassador," YOU are a "minister of reconciliation" called to share the "message of reconciliation" (2 Corinthians 5:18-20).

Here's a diagram of the restoration of all things to help you visualize it:

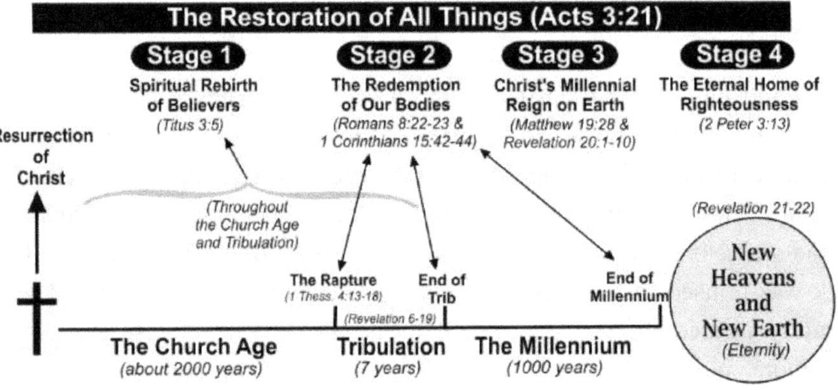

What Is God's Purpose for the Millennium?

The Millennium is basically a transitional phase between this present evil age (Galatians 1:4) and the eternal righteous age-to-come (Luke 18:29-30). But what exactly is God's purpose for the Millennium? It's simple:

The Millennium is the LORD's irrefutable proof to humanity that the religion of secular humanism is a lie. As you may or may not know, secular humanism is atheistic in nature and therefore anti-God. To those who embrace this godless religion there's no sin problem because there's no God for whom to sin against. To them, the problem of evil isn't humanity's sin nature and the corresponding alienation from our Creator, but rather a negative environment.

As such, they believe corruption, crime, poverty, war and other ailments will largely be eradicated when the right government is in place and every person is provided an education, a decent job, a nice living environment, protection from crime, and so on. While these things are good, they don't actually remedy the sin problem or reconcile people to their Creator. They cannot set us free from satan's dominion and the slavery thereof. After all, a white collar man living in a upscale suburb is still perfectly able to commit fraud due to a greedy heart, not to mention be a drunkard, drug addict, wife-beater, slanderer, hypocrite, adulterer, murderer, blowhard, oppressor, porn addict or practicing homosexual.

In the Millennium the LORD is going to provide the perfect government and environment for nations of mortals. It will be a veritable worldwide utopia. Since Jesus will be the King over all the Earth and his assistants will be glorified believers who don't have a sin nature there will be zero corruption in the government (imagine that!). Yet, as the population increases over the course of the thousand years, many of the offspring of the original "sheep"—the mortals whom Christ allows to enter into the Millennium (Matthew 25:31-46)—will just go through the motions of being faithful to the Lord while their hearts aren't in it. This is legalism—putting on the airs of godliness without the heart of godliness.

Because legalism is an "outward job" it's decidedly inauthentic. As such, when the devil is unleashed at the end of the thousand years these covert rebels will naturally embrace the lies of the kingdom of darkness and unite for war in a harebrained attempt to take over the completely righteous government of Christ! (This, by the way, shows that satan is thoroughly incorrigible—he never learns from his mistakes).

Of course, the rebellion is quickly quelled and, after the Great White Throne Judgment, the eternal age of the New Heavens and New Earth will manifest (Revelation 20:9-15 & Revelation 21-22).

So, at heart, the Millennium is the Most High's eternal showcase in disproving the religion of secular humanism. (There's more to it than that, of course, but we don't have space for further details).

4

Questions About the Son/ Jesus Christ

What Do the Names "Jesus" and "Christ" Mean?

Christ is not the last name of Jesus. 'Christ' is translated from the Greek word *Christos (khris-TOS)*, which means "anointed one" and comes from the Hebrew *mashach (maw-SHAKH),* meaning "anointed" or "chosen one." A good example of this Hebrew term used in reference to Jesus in the Scriptures is Psalm 45:7.

As for Jesus, aka Yeshua in the Hebrew (also spelled Y'shua or Yehoshua), this was simply the name the angel Gabriel gave to Mary, as shown in Luke 1:31. The name was specifically given because 'Jesus' is the transliteration of a Hebrew term meaning "Yahweh [God] saves" (or "Yahweh is salvation"). So 'Jesus' is the Lord's God-given proper name while 'Christ' is His title, signifying that Jesus was sent from God as humanity's King and Deliverer—our "salvation" and, hence, our Savior.

While the meaning of *mashach*—"anointed"—literally refers to the pouring of oil, it can also refer to one's separation unto God, even if literal oil is not actually used (Hebrews 1:9). You see, when someone was promoted to a position of authority in the Old Testament, oil was smeared on the person's head to signify being consecrated (separated) for God's work. First Samuel 10:1 is a good example. Anointing was a ritualistic act indicating God's choosing (e.g. 1 Samuel 24:6). Kings, priests, and prophets were all set apart for the LORD's ministry in this manner.

With this understanding, 'Jesus Christ' means "Jesus the Anointed One" and could be translated as "God saves through His Anointed One." It's "the name above all names," as revealed in Scripture:

> **9Therefore God exalted him to the highest place**
> **and gave him <u>the name that is above every name</u>,**
> **10that at the name of <u>Jesus</u> every knee should bow,**
> **in heaven and on earth and under the earth,**
> **11and every tongue acknowledge that <u>Jesus Christ</u> is Lord,**
> **to the glory of God the Father.**
>
> **Philippians 2:9-11**

What Are the Main Proofs That Jesus Christ Is God?

Here are seven of the most glaring proofs in Scripture:

1. Christ Plainly Said He and the Father Are One

This can be observed here:

> **"I and the Father <u>are one</u>"**
>
> **John 10:30**

And is implied here:

> **"...Anyone who has seen me has <u>seen the Father</u>..."**
>
> **John 14:9**

2. Christ Plainly Said He Was "I AM"

This can be observed in the Messiah's debate with some Pharisees:

> **56"Your father Abraham rejoiced at the thought of seeing my day; he saw it and was glad."**
> **57"You are not yet fifty years old," they said to him, "and you have seen Abraham!"**
> **58"Very truly I tell you," Jesus answered, "before Abraham was born, I am!" 59At this, they picked up stones to stone him, but Jesus hid himself, slipping away from the temple grounds.**
>
> **John 8:58-59**

Christ wasn't just saying that he existed prior to Abraham since, if that were the case, he would've said, "Before Abraham was born, I was." Instead, he boldly said, "before Abraham was born, I Am!" This was:

1. A statement of eternal self-existence.
2. A reference to the name that God gave to Moses at the burning bush to describe Himself, "I Am Who I Am" (Exodus 3:14). Jesus just shortened it to the first and last Hebrew words, "I Am."

Since Yeshua was clearly claiming to be God, the Pharisees & their followers responded by trying to stone him to death for blasphemy.

There are, incidentally, seven times total where Christ said "I AM" linked to specific things in a figurative sense, like "I AM the bread of life" (John 6:35,48). The six others are: "I AM light of this world" (8:12), "I AM the gate" (10:7 & 10:9), "I AM the good shepherd" (10:11 & 10:14), "I AM the resurrection and the life" (11:25), "I AM the way, the truth and the life" (14:6) and "I AM the vine" (15:1 & 15:5).

3. Christ Is the Living Word of God, Who Was With God in the Beginning and IS GOD

This is plainly chronicled here:

> **<u>In the beginning was the Word</u>, and <u>the Word was with God</u>, and <u>the Word was God</u>. [2]He was with God in the beginning. [3]Through him all things were made; without him nothing was made that has been made.**
>
> **John 1:1-3**

Additional proof that Yeshua is the "Word of God" can be observed in Revelation 19:13 and 1 Peter 1:23.

4. Christ Is Immanuel, Meaning "God With Us"

One of the Messiah's names is Immanuel (Isaiah 7:14 & Matthew 1:23), which means "**God with us**." Yeshua's deity couldn't be stated clearer.

You see, Christ is "the Word" who was "with God" "in the beginning" and the Word "*was* God" (John 1:1). This Word was made flesh when Mary was impregnated by the Holy Spirit (Matthew 1:18 & Luke 1:35) and gave birth to Jesus, which is the incarnation as also pointed out in the first chapter of John:

> **<u>The Word became flesh</u> and made his dwelling among us. We have seen his glory, the glory of the one and only Son, who came from the Father, full of grace and truth.**
>
> **John 1:14**

5. YHWH Is the First and the Last, Both Father and Son

Notice what the LORD (YHWH) says in the book of Isaiah:

> **"This is what the LORD says—**
> **Israel's King and Redeemer, the LORD Almighty:**
> **<u>I am the first and I am the last</u>;**
> **<u>apart from me there is no God</u>."**
>
> **Isaiah 44:6**

The same terminology is used in reference to Jesus Christ in the New Testament:

> **When I saw him, I fell at his feet as though dead. Then he placed his right hand on me and said: "Do not be afraid. I am the First and the Last."**
>
> **Revelation 1:17**

> **"To the angel of the church in Smyrna write: These are the words of him who is the First and the Last, who died and came to life again."**
>
> **Revelation 2:8**

This next verse from the final chapter of Revelation says the same thing, but adds that Christ is the "Alpha and Omega," which refer to the first and last letters of the Greek alphabet:

> **"I am the Alpha and the Omega, the First and the Last, the Beginning and the End."**
>
> **Revelation 22:13**

Compare this with who is said to be the "Alpha and Omega" in the first chapter of Revelation:

> **"I am the Alpha and the Omega," says the Lord God, "who is, and who was, and who is to come, the Almighty."**
>
> **Revelation 1:8**

Wow, you'd have to be spiritually blind to not see Christ's deity!

6. Angels Refused Worship While Christ Accepted It

Because angels are supernatural beings, they're fascinating creatures and we should appreciate them and take advantage of their services, but we must not entertain any temptation to worship them. 'Worship' is *proskuneó (pros-koo-NAY-oh)* in the Greek, which literally means "to acknowledge and adore via prostration." The apostle John was tempted to do this twice with an angel while he was receiving the revelation of Jesus Christ imprisoned on the Island of Patmos. Notice what this angel says to John on these occasions:

> **So I fell at his feet to worship to him. But he told me, "Do not do that! I am a fellow servant with you and your brothers who rely on the testimony of Jesus. Worship God!"**
>
> **Revelation 19:10**

> **But he said to me, "Don't do that! I am a fellow servant with you and with your fellow prophets and with all who keep the words of this scroll. Worship God!"**
>
> **Revelation 22:9**

It's important to understand this because the Bible warns us that **the worship of angels stems from an "unspiritual mind" and it is an identifying mark of those who try to mislead believers** (Colossians 2:18). Cults thus put undue emphasis on either heavenly angels or fallen spirits. Do not be misled by such false teachers. Let your worship be reserved for God alone, as this particular angel instructed John.

The angel's corrective response shows that these spiritual beings are adamant about our attention being focused on the Lord, their 'employer,' not them. They prefer to stay in the background and let the Mighty LORD have the throne. As created beings, they know their rightful place and their purpose: To worship and serve the Creator, not be worshipped themselves.

Also, notice how this angel described himself in each of his responses to John: He said "I am **a fellow servant with you**". We must get ahold of this fact: **Angels are "ministering spirits"—*serving* spirits—sent by God** (their 'Boss') **to serve people** (Hebrews 1:14). People, by contrast, do not serve angels; they serve us. In fact, we will *judge* angels in the age-to-come (1 Corinthians 6:3).

The Lord Christ is not an angel in the commonly understood sense, but since 'angel' means "messenger," the Son is The Angel of the LORD because he's the Living Word of God—**God's message to humankind**. In contrast to angels, Jesus Christ allowed himself to be worshipped as observed with this man, born blind, that he healed:

> **[35]Jesus heard that they had thrown him out, and when he found him, he said, "Do you believe in the Son of Man?"**
> **[36]"Who is he, sir?" the man asked. "Tell me so that I may believe in him."**
> **[37]Jesus said, "You have now seen him; in fact, he is the one speaking with you."**
> **[38]Then the man said, "Lord, I believe," and he worshiped him.**
>
> **John 9:35-38**

This is the same Greek word for 'worship' noted above.

Later, when doubting Thomas met the resurrected Lord, he exclaimed, "My Lord and my God!" (John 20:28), which reveals Christ's nature and bespeaks of worship (reverence, honor, submission). The Greek word for 'Lord' here is explained in chapter **2** under the question *What Name Do We Call On à la Romans 10:13?*

Lastly, worship has to do with adoration and reverence, as well as honoring someone greater than yourself and the corresponding submission. Notice what Christ said about honor:

> **[22]Moreover, the Father judges no one, but has entrusted all judgment to the Son, [23]that all may honor the Son just as they honor the Father. Whoever does not honor the Son does not honor the Father, who sent him.**
>
> **John 5:22-23**

In short, the same honor that we are to bestow on the Father, we are to offer the Son. Why? Because *both* Father and Son are the Almighty LORD, YHWH. Speaking of which…

7. The Hebrew Word for 'LORD' in the Old Testament, YHWH, Is Cited in Reference to Christ in the New Testament

This is explained in chapter 2 in the sections *What Is God's Name?* and the following *What Name Do We Call On à la Romans 10:13?*

Isn't Yeshua Referred to as God's "Firstborn"?

This question is based on these two verses:

> **And again, when God brings his firstborn into the world, he says,**
> **"Let all God's angels worship him."**
>
> **Hebrews 1:6**

> **The Son is the image of the invisible God, the firstborn over all creation.**
>
> **Colossians 1:15**

The Jehovah's False Witnesses use these texts to support their belief that Jesus was the first created being of the LORD; and then Father God used Yeshua to create everything else. However, Scripture interprets Scripture and so we know from other passages that Jesus *is* Yahweh (YHWH), albeit the Son, not the Father.

So, what do these verses mean by describing Yeshua as the "firstborn." The apostles, like Paul, borrowed this term from their Hebraic upbringing in which "firstborn" meant especially honored. For instance, the nation of Israel was referred to as God's "firstborn," but this obviously didn't mean Israel was the first nation that ever existed (Exodus 4:22).

Similarly, God referred to David as His "firstborn" when he was hardly the first male God created, not to mention David was the youngest of Jesse's eight sons (Psalm 89:20 & 89:27). Furthermore, David was the *second* divinely-appointed king of Israel. In light of all this, when Christ is referred to as the "firstborn" it simply means that the Son has a place of honor before the Father, shared by no one else; as well as a place of honor over all creation.

There are several other reasons for rejecting the idea that Christ was God's first created being. Here are two obvious ones:

1. Jesus cannot be both "first created" and "one and only Son" (John 1:14 & 1:18, 3:16 & 3:18, 1 John 4:9).
2. John 1:3 says that "Through him [Christ] **all things** were made; **without him nothing was made that has been made**." If Yeshua is the Creator of **all things**, he cannot also be the first created. It's simple logic.

Doesn't the Bible Say God Is ONE?

Yes, the Scriptures emphasize that God is **one** (Deuteronomy 6:4 & Isaiah 45:5, 45:6, 45:18), but there's obviously a *triunity* within that oneness consisting of **Father**, **Son** and **Holy Spirit**, as detailed in chapter 2.

Does Jesus Christ Appear in the Old Testament?

The LORD, the Son, does appear repeatedly in the Old Testament, just not by the name Jesus Christ since Jesus didn't exist until the incarnation. Yet the Son is God and is eternal, which can be observed in this prophecy:

> **For to us a child is born,**
> **to us a son is given,**
> **and the government will be on his shoulders.**
> **And he will be called**
> **Wonderful Counselor, Mighty God,**

> **Everlasting Father, Prince of Peace.**
>
> **Isaiah 9:6**

This is yet further proof that the Son *is* God and is one with the Father!

Now look at the first two lines: When the Son was incarnated, Jesus Christ was born into this world; I'm talking about Yeshua, the Anointed One. By contrast, the Son was *given* because He already existed from eternity. Are you following?

Here's an interesting insight on the Living Word of God:

> **<u>No one has ever seen God</u>, but the one and only <u>Son</u>, who is himself God and is in closest relationship with <u>the Father</u>, <u>has made him known</u>.**
>
> **John 1:18**

If no one has ever seen God then how do we explain Hagar seeing the LORD in Genesis 16:7-13? The answer lies within the second part of this verse: No one has ever seen God, the Father, but the Son—who also is God—has made Him known. How did the Son make God known?

1. Christ made the Father known through His incarnation, which is confirmed by Jesus' statements: "Anyone who has seen me has seen the Father" (John 14:9), "whoever sees me sees him who sent me" (John 12:45 ESV) and "If you knew me, you would know my Father also" (John 8:19).
2. The Messiah also made the Father known in Old Testament times *before* his incarnation, as illustrated when Hagar saw God via The Angel of the LORD.

There are quite a few appearances of the pre-incarnate Christ in the Old Testament, whether as "the Angel of the LORD" or otherwise. I'm not talking about *types* of Christ, like Joseph, but rather what theologians call theophanies or Christophanies. Here are several examples:

- The aforementioned occasion where the Angel of the LORD appeared to Hagar in Genesis 16:7-13. Verse 13 makes it clear that this "angel" (messenger) was, in fact, the LORD, Yahweh.
- The Angel of the LORD appeared to Moses in the burning bush in Exodus 3:1-8. Verse 7 plainly identifies this "angel" as the LORD, Yahweh.
- The Angel of the LORD appeared to Gideon in Judges 6:11-16 where verses 14 & 16 verify him to be the LORD.
- The Angel of the LORD appeared to the parents of Samson in Judges 13 and he is identified as God in verse 22.
- Jacob wrestled with God in Genesis 32:22-31 and the latter is identified as the Angel of the LORD in Hosea 12:3-4.

Why is the pre-incarnate Christ repeatedly referred to as the Angel of the LORD? Because the work of the Son is to make known the Father to people in this lost & dying world. In short, the Son is the Father's message to humanity and that's what 'angel' means—messenger.

The Son makes another pre-incarnate appearance prior to the sack of Jericho where he's not identified as The Angel of the LORD, but rather as the Commander of the Army of the LORD:

> **Now when Joshua was near Jericho, he looked up and saw a man standing in front of him with a drawn sword in his hand. Joshua went up to him and asked, "Are you for us or for our enemies?"**
> **[14] "Neither," he replied, "but as commander of the army of the Lord I have now come." Then Joshua fell facedown to the ground in reverence, and asked him, "What message does my Lord have for his servant?"**
> **[15] The commander of the LORD's army replied, "Take off your sandals, for the place where you are standing is holy." And Joshua did so.**
> **[1]Now the gates of Jericho were securely barred because of the Israelites. No one went out and no one came in.**

> [2] **Then <u>the LORD</u> <u>said to Joshua</u>, "See, I have delivered Jericho into your hands, along with its king and its fighting men."**
>
> **Joshua 5:13-6:2**

It didn't take long for Joshua to realize that this mysterious man with a drawn sword wasn't merely a "man" because Joshua fell facedown to the ground in worship. Keep in mind that both the Hebrew and Greek words for 'worship' literally mean to prostrate oneself in adoration or reverence. This was likewise Abraham's response to the LORD, as observed in Genesis 17:3 and 18:1-2, which document two other appearances of the pre-incarnate Christ.

Joshua then called this curious man "Lord" and referred to himself as his "servant" (verse 14).

Further evidence that this Commander of the Army of the LORD is deity can be observed in that he immediately commanded Joshua to remove his sandals because he was standing on holy ground. This recalls what The Angel of the LORD instructed Moses at the burning bush (Exodus 3:5).

Lastly, the Commander of the LORD's Army is identified at the end of the passage simply as "the LORD" (verse 2) wherein He supplies Joshua with the strategy he needed to conquer the pagan city. Keep in mind that there were no chapter divisions in the original manuscripts; these were added 2600 years *after* the book of Joshua was written.

So, the Commander of the Army of the LORD is the pre-incarnate Christ.

Now, let me ask you: Does this Commander come across as a milksop or does he strike you as a mighty warrior that commands respect and awe? Notice what he says when Joshua asks him if he's on Israel's side or Jericho's side: "Neither, but as commander of the army of the LORD I have now come." This response is simple and succinct, but it speaks volumes: Jesus Christ is so magnificent, so great—so incredibly awesome—he's above the mundane conflicts of this world and the politics thereof.

Bringing this home for us today: The Mighty Christ is above the perpetual squabbling of the Leftwing and Rightwing factions of our governments. That said, supporting a Conservative candidate may sometimes be questionable, no doubt, yet voting for a **LIE**beral is unthinkable.

Is Jesus Christ a Milksop?

In the modern day, the Messiah is largely portrayed and perceived as timid, weak, ineffectual, even effeminate. In colloquial terms, this means a wimp, pantywaist, sissy or wuss. You don't have to look far to find support for this. I saw a T-shirt that blatantly said "Jesus is a ****." I can't say the word but it essentially meant "Jesus is a wuss." Sterile religion and worldly culture has fostered this false image to the point that it's the general perception of most people, spoken or unspoken. So, when the average person thinks of Jesus Christ they think of "gentle Jesus meek and mild" rather than the awesome Lion of Judah. I'm not saying that Yeshua didn't have a gentle side, but how about some balance?!

When I was a lost teenager my impression of Jesus Christ wasn't good. I perceived him as a wimpy doormat when nothing could be further from the truth. I turned to the LORD at the age of 20 and immediately started consuming God's Word voraciously. Something really blew me away—the spectacular and powerful depictions of both Father God and Jesus Christ, who are One (John 10:30). I was like, "Whoa! Who is this?" What I saw totally contradicted what religion and culture had taught me.

Simply put, the widespread image of Jesus Christ is a lie concocted by the enemy to deceive people and prevent them from following the Lord of Lords, particularly men who refuse to follow someone they don't respect. And it's impossible to respect a weakly milksop.

We've already considered powerful examples of the Son plainly *not* being a pansy in His pre-incarnation days, how about after His incarnation and, specifically, during His earthly ministry?

Let's start with the fact that Christ was brilliant in argumentation (Matthew 22:15-22). He astonished and silenced his enemies (Luke 20:26) to the point that "no one dared ask him anymore questions" (Mark 12:34). Does this sound like an impotent pantywaist? Furthermore, Jesus was dynamic—full of energy, power, passion and life. He had aura of pizzazz, not stultifying dullness. Want evidence?

- Christ said he *was* life and could therefore offer abundant life to anyone who chose to follow him (John 14:6 & 10:10).
- Because the Messiah possessed abundant life, he had a vibrant spirit of joy; he was not always ultra-solemn and sorrowful; and he certainly wasn't boring.
- He had wholehearted conviction about what he knew—he truly believed what he taught & preached and His aura of authority was palpable (Matthew 7:28-29).

Yeshua was incredibly bold, outspoken and had no qualms about offending people who were deserving of correction:

- He was invited to a dinner party with some Pharisees and immediately began insulting the host and honored guests, not because He was abusive but because they *needed* rebuked (Luke 11:37-53). This is tough love.
- He was forthright and honest—He got straight to the point and didn't beat around the bush with overly diplomatic language (Matthew 15:1-20 & 18:7).

One of the most amazing examples of Christ's incredible boldness and power can be seen when he cleared the Temple of ungodly fools:

> **On reaching Jerusalem, Jesus entered the temple area and began driving out those who were buying and selling there. He overturned the tables of the money changers and the benches of those selling doves, [16]and would not allow anyone to carry merchandise through the temple courts. [17] And as he taught them, he said, "Is it not written: 'My house will be called a house of prayer for all nations, but you have made it a den of robbers.' "**

[18]The Chief priests and the teachers of the law heard this and began looking for a way to kill him, for they feared him, because the whole crowd was amazed at his teaching. Mark 11:15-18

Notice that Christ radically threw over tables and benches and would not allow anyone to carry merchandise through the Temple courts. Does this sound like "gentle Jesus meek and mild" or the bold Lion of Judah? Can you imagine Jesus *not allowing* men to carry goods into the Temple?

Believe it or not, the Messiah cleared the Temple in this manner *twice* during his earthly ministry. This account took place near the end of his ministry, but he also cleared the Temple near the beginning—three years earlier—as detailed in John 2:13-17. On the earlier occasion he made a whip and utilized it in driving out the animals, yelling and scattering coins!

And notice the response of the legalists in Mark 11:18: They *feared* him! They feared him so much that they decided to kill him and remove him from the scene altogether. Let me tell you something, impotent milksops don't inspire fear and they certainly don't provoke VIPs to plot murder. Also, notice how the people who witnessed him clear the Temple responded: They were *amazed!* Dull sissies don't inspire amazement, but people who are dynamic, courageous and authoritative do! (And by "authoritative" I *don't* mean authoritarian, which is abusive. 'Abuse' is the misuse of power).

All over the gospel accounts we see evidence of Christ being bold, amazing, imposing and even frightening! Just look up these passages: Matthew 7:28-29, 14:26, Mark 1:27, 2:10-12, 4:37-43, 7:37, Luke 5:8-11, 7:14-16, 20:20-26 and 20:40, as well as the aforementioned John 2:13-17. People who imply that the Messiah was some effeminate weakling evidently don't know how to read.

What about Yeshua's agonizing crucifixion? Any of us who have seen *The Passion of the Christ* realize that no pansy could face that horrible challenge, let alone bear it.

Although He came to this world as a lamb to be sacrificed, He shall return as a mighty warrior, as shown in Revelation 19:11-16. Please check out this passage and you'll see that the mighty Messiah is anything but a pitiful weakling.

Speaking of being a lamb, Yeshua was a sheep only in the sense that he was a sacrificial lamb for the sins of the world (Revelation 13:8). In truth, He was and is "the good shepherd" or "Chief Shepherd" (John 10:11,14 & 1 Peter 5:4), a powerful leader who leads not only by word, but by example and service.

'Christ' means "Anointed One" and 'Christian' means "little anointed one" or "like the Anointed One." Hence, Christians are to be like their leader, Jesus Christ.

This certainly means walking in love, kindness, peace, gentleness and humility, but these traits have been emphasized at the expense of the Messiah's more dynamic qualities noted above. It goes without saying that the body of Christ needs to cultivate Yeshua's more masculine attributes as well as the softer ones. It's simply a matter of *balance.* Christians are sheep in the sense that they follow the "good shepherd" not in the sense that they're weak pushovers.

Furthermore, followers of the Mighty Lord possess abundant life and *dunamis* power. *'Dunamis'* is the Greek word for power, which is where we get the English words dynamic and dynamite. This power is available to every believer but we have to "fan it into flame" (2 Timothy 1:6-7). Tell me, does "abundant life" and "dynamite power" sound boring and weak? No, they're exciting and explosive and believers will walk in them more and more as they take hold of the eternal life—the life-of-the-age-to-come—to which they're called (1 Timothy 6:12).

Let me leave you with a passage to chew on:

> **The wicked flee though no one pursues,**
> **but the righteous are as bold as a lion.**
> **Proverbs 28:1**

5

Questions About Human Nature: Spirit, Mind, Body

How Does the Bible Define a Human Being?

The simplest definition for a person—a human—is a "living soul," which is in accordance with the hermeneutical law of first mention. In other words, what does our Creator say about human beings the first time they're defined in Holy Scripture? Here's what Genesis says:

> **And the LORD God formed man of the dust of the ground, and breathed into his nostrils the breath of life; and man became a living soul *(nephesh)*.**
>
> **Genesis 2:7** (KJV)

> **The LORD God formed the man from the dust of the ground and breathed into his nostrils the breath of life and the man became a living being *(nephesh)*.**
>
> **Genesis 2:7** (NIV)

As you can see, the first book of the Bible describes precisely how God created human beings: The LORD formed the human **body** out of "the dust of the earth,"[3] breathed into it "the **breath of life**," and so man became a "**living soul**" (KJV) or "**living being**" (NIV). Notice the three key facets of the human being. The Bible mentions other parts of human nature, of course, like the heart, which we'll look at as we progress for a fuller understanding.

Isn't the Use of "Man" for Humanity Sexist?

No, the term 'man' in the Bible refers to *both* male and female, unless the context tells otherwise, as observed here:

> **Then God said, "Let us make <u>mankind</u> in our image, in our likeness, so that they may rule over the fish in the sea and the birds in the sky, over the livestock and all the wild animals, and over all the creatures that move along the ground."**
> **[27]So God created <u>mankind</u> in his own image,**
> **in the image of God he created them;**
> **<u>male and female he created them</u>.**
>
> **Genesis 1:26-27**

The Hebrew word translated "mankind" is the same word for "man" in Genesis 2:7 (quoted in the previous section). Notice in verse 27 that 'man' in this generic sense refers to *both* male and female. That said, I regularly use 'human' for man, and 'humankind' (or 'humanity') for mankind, so that there's no misunderstanding and no one's needlessly offended.

Isn't a 'Soul' the Immaterial Part of a Person?

It depends on the context. To explain, we saw in Genesis 2:7 above that *nephesh (neh-FESH)* is the Hebrew word for "soul." The equivalent New

---

[3] It's a scientific fact that the human body is made up of the same essential chemical elements that are in the soil. Humanity did not discover this until relative recent times, but the Creator revealed it here *thousands of years ago*.

Testament word is the Greek *psuché (soo-KHAY)*, which can be observed when the creation text—Genesis 2:7—is partially quoted in 1 Corinthians 15:45 where *nephesh* is translated by the Greek *psuche.* Of course, *psuche* is where we get the English words psyche, psychology and psychiatry.

So, *nephesh* and *psuche* are the respective Hebrew and Greek words for 'soul' in the Bible.

Sometimes these words are used in reference to the *whole* person, such as Genesis 12:5, Jeremiah 52:30 and 1 Peter 3:20. In other words, 'soul' (*nephesh*/*psuche*) in its broadest sense refers to the *entire* person—spirit, mind and body—and not just the immaterial part of the human being. This is hidden from the English reader because most translations render *nephesh* & *psuche* as "persons" or "people" in such cases.

However, 'soul' can also refer to one or more of the three main parts of human nature—spirit, mind and flesh. For instance, *psuche*—"soul"—refers specifically to the **mind** in this passage:

> **May God himself, the God of peace, sanctify you through and through. May your whole spirit, soul and body be kept blameless at the coming of our Lord Jesus Christ.**
>
> **1 Thessalonians 5:23**

Nephesh & *psuche* also refer specifically to the **mind** in 1 Chronicles 28:9 and Acts 14:2 respectively.

Meanwhile *nephesh* refers explicitly to the **body** in Leviticus 21:11 and Numbers 19:11. And *psuche* refers specifically to the human **spirit** in Luke 1:46-47. In the latter case, Mary was employing synthetic parallelism. She says her "soul"—*psuche*—glorifies the Lord in verse 46, but specifies in verse 47 that it is her spirit that rejoices in God. Thus "soul," a broad term for the whole human being, refers specifically to the spirit on this occasion.

Nephesh & *psuche* can also refer to *both* **spirit and mind** in some contexts, such as Psalm 31:9 and Revelation 6:9-10.

Minutia like this is tedious to most readers, but the reason it's important is because it reveals the Bible's definition of human beings. **People are <u>living souls</u> comprised of <u>spirit</u>, <u>mind</u> and <u>flesh</u>**, as illustrated here:

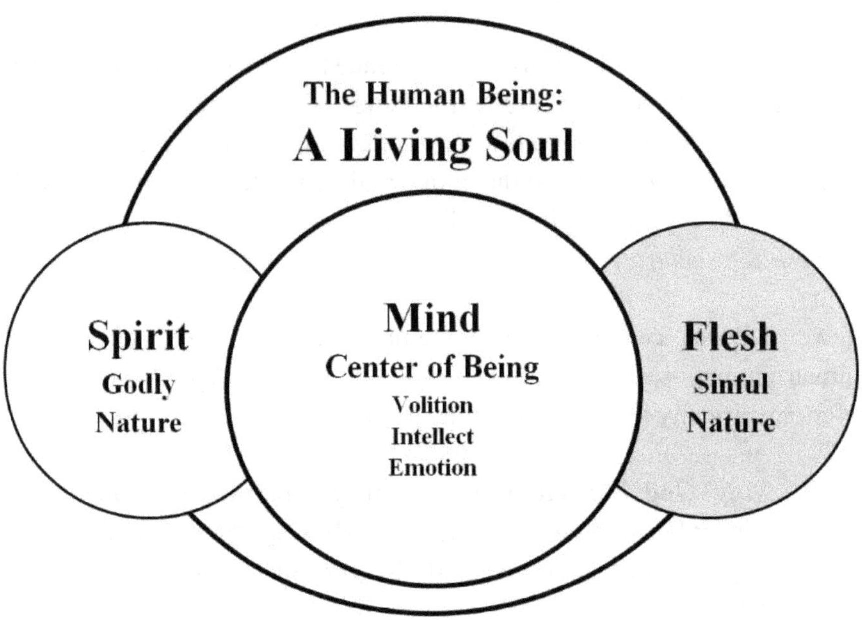

How Is the Mind the "Center of Being"?

First Thessalonians 5:23 (cited in the previous section) describes human nature as having three basic facets—spirit, mind and body. This can also be observed in this passage:

> **For I know that nothing good dwells within me, that is, in my <u>flesh</u>. I can will what is right, but I cannot do it. [19] For I do not do the good I want, but the evil I do not want is what I do. [20] Now if I do what I do not want, it is no longer I that do it, but sin that dwells within me.**

> [21] **So I find it to be a law that when I want to do what is good, evil lies close at hand.** [22] **For I delight in the law of God in my inmost self** [i.e. spirit], [23] **but I see in my members another law at war with the law of my mind, making me captive to the law of sin that dwells in my members.**
>
> **Romans 7:18-23** (NRSV)

Paul speaks of three facets of human nature. In verse 18 he mentions his "**flesh**" (or "sinful nature" in the NIV) and states that "nothing good dwells within" it.

In verse 22 he mentions his "inmost self" and says that this part of his being delights in God's law, which is a reference to his **spirit**.

In verse 23 he mentions his "**mind**" and the "war" that it is fighting. The nature of this "war" is made clearer just a few verses later:[4]

> **For those who live according to the flesh set their minds on the things of the flesh, but those who live according to the spirit[5] set their minds on the things of the spirit.** [6] **To set the mind on the flesh is death, but to set the mind on the spirit is life and peace.**
>
> **Romans 8:5-6** (NRSV)

---

[4] Keep in mind that Paul's original letter to the Romans had no chapter and verse divisions. These divisions were added well over a thousand years later for convenience in scriptural study and citation.

[5] Since there is no capitalization in the biblical Greek, translators must determine if "spirit" should be capitalized, in reference to the Holy Spirit, or not capitalized, in reference to the human spirit. Many translations capitalize "spirit" in these passages and some do not (for example The New English Bible). Since these passages (and other such passages) are plainly referring to the human spirit, "spirit" should not be capitalized. A good example of this is Matthew 26:41. In a way it makes no significant difference since the believer's reborn spirit is **indwelt and led by the Holy Spirit**.

These divinely inspired words reveal two truths: **1.** That there are three basic facets to human nature—flesh, mind and spirit; and **2.** that the mind is caught in a struggle between the other two facets—flesh and spirit. This is the "war" Paul is talking about in verse 23.

What exactly is the **mind**? The mind is your **center of being**. The Greek for "mind" is *nous (noos)* meaning "The intellect, i.e. the mind (divine or human; in thought, feeling or will)" (Strong 50). This reveals the three qualities of the human mind: **volition, intellect** and **emotion**:

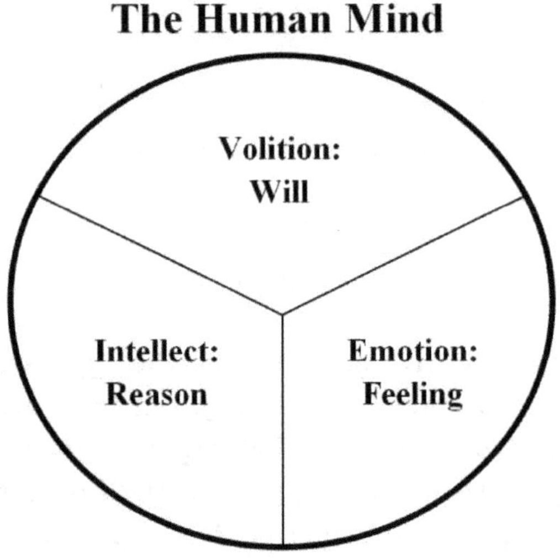

Since the mind is the center of volition and will, it is the mind that *decides* whether to live according to the flesh or according to the spirit.

What Are Flesh and Spirit?

The flesh and spirit are **the opposing facets of your being**. In Romans 7:18 above Paul describes the flesh as the part of his being where "**nothing good dwells**." In verse 22 he describes his spirit as the side of him that **delights in God's laws**. We could therefore define flesh and spirit as follows: **The "flesh" is that part of you that veers toward what is negative, destructive and carnal. The "spirit" is that part of you that inclines toward what is positive, productive and godly.**

These contrasting facets are repeatedly mentioned in Scripture:

> **"Watch and pray, lest you enter into temptation. The spirit indeed is willing, but the flesh is weak.**
>
> **Matthew 26:41** (NKJV)

> **I say then: Walk in the spirit, and you shall not fulfill the lust of the flesh. [17] For the flesh lusts against the spirit, and spirit against the flesh; and these are contrary to one another, so that you do not do the things that you wish.**
>
> **Galatians 5:16-17** (NKJV)

It's interesting to note that the formulator of psychoanalysis, Sigmund Freud, was able to discover these three basic facets of human nature through his research. The mind is comparable to Freud's "ego"; likewise, the flesh coincides with his "id"; and the spirit corresponds to the "superego." I'm obviously not an advocate of Freud, but pointing this out may help readers who are familiar with secular theories to better understand the biblical model of human nature—spirit, mind and body.

Where Does the Heart Fit Into This Model?

Many verses speak of the human "heart," such as Mark 7:6,21. The Greek word for "heart" is *kardia (kar-DEE-ah),* which is where we get the English 'cardiac.' Like the English "heart," *kardia* literally refers to the blood-pumping organ but figuratively to the **core thoughts or feelings of a person's being or mind** (Strong 39). E.W. Bullinger describes the heart as "**the seat and center** of man's personal life in which the distinctive character of the human manifests itself" (362). The heart could therefore be described as the core of the mind, the center of your being. It is part of the mind, but specifically the most central part, i.e. **the core**.

What is *in* a person's heart is determined by whether **your mind has *decided*** to live by the flesh or by the spirit. Christ said, "The good man brings good things out of the good stored up in his heart, and the evil man brings evil things out of the evil stored up in his heart. For out of the overflow of the heart the mouth speaks" (Luke 6:45). If you, in your mind, ***decide*** to dwell on carnal thoughts, then carnal, negative, destructive things will naturally store-up in your heart. If, on the other hand, you ***choose*** to dwell on spiritual thoughts, then good, positive, productive things will grow in your heart. Proverbs 4:23 puts it like this (in the NCV): **"Be careful what you think for your thoughts run your life."**

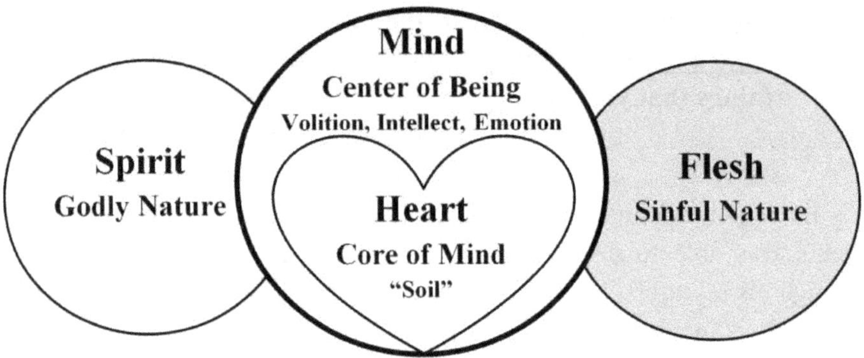

The bottom line is that **you** *decide* what's stored up in your heart depending on whether you're governed by flesh or spirit.

I think it's important to point out that carnal and crazy thoughts will at times flash through your mind; yet this doesn't mean these thoughts are stemming from your heart. Having carnal, crazy thoughts flash through your mind is natural to the human experience; in other words, if you're human, it happens. Sometimes you may even be bombarded with such thoughts. These thoughts may originate from the flesh, unclean spirits, ungodly people, the environment you're exposed to, or otherwise, but just because they flash through your mind it does not mean they're *in* your heart. These thoughts *are not you*, and *are not originating from your heart;* but **they can become *you* if you allow them to get lodged in your heart by dwelling on them and giving them life**.

Such thoughts should just be ignored or, if that doesn't work, taken "captive" and made "obedient to Christ," the Word of God (2 Corinthians 10:3-5). Otherwise, they will become a weed with the potential of growing into a big, ugly tree of destructive bad fruit (e.g. bitterness, immorality, frustration, sloth, depression, arrogance, abuse, gossip/slander, rage, etc.).

What's the Key to Walking Free From Sin?

The first step to freedom from the flesh is turning to the LORD in repentance & faith (Mark 1:15 & Romans 10:9-10) wherein you'll receive **spiritual regeneration** (John 3:3-6 & Titus 3:5). This means you'll acquire the spiritual hardware necessary to overcome any sin bondage, not to mention the help of the indwelling Holy Spirit (1 Corinthians 3:16).

Secondly, it's necessary to learn how to be spirit-controlled. This just means being spirit-driven rather than flesh-ruled. In other words, your being controlled by your higher self as opposed to the lower self. To do this you simply have to learn to put *off* the old self and put *on* the new:

> **You were taught with regard to your former way of life, to put off your old self, which is being corrupted by its deceitful desires; [23] to be made new in the attitude of your minds; [24] and to put on the new self, created to be like God in true righteousness and holiness.**
>
> **Ephesians 4:22-24**

The "old self" is the flesh or sin nature and we are instructed to put it off. Why? Because the old self is corrupted by "deceitful desires." Your flesh has desires, which means it has a 'voice,' but these desires are deceitful. They promise happiness but don't deliver. They can only ultimately bring death and all that goes with it. We are told to "put off" these fleshly desires, which involves stripping off the old way of thinking in favor of a new way.

Verse 23 tells us how to do this: We need to be made new in the attitude of our minds. What is the new attitude we should have? We are to count ourselves dead to the old self and alive to God in Christ Jesus (Romans 6:11). Counting yourself alive to God includes accepting everything God says you are **in Christ**, that is, who you are in your new self, the spirit.

This results in what verse 24 calls "putting on the new self," which refers to a believer living out of his/her spirit as led of the Holy Spirit. When you do this, you'll be spirit-controlled and produce the fruit thereof. The Bible describes this in different ways. When you are spirit-controlled…

- you "live by the spirit" (Galatians 5:16),
- you "clothe yourself with the Lord Jesus Christ" (Romans 13:14),
- you "participate in the divine nature" (2 Peter 1:4), and
- you "put on the new self" (Colossians 3:10).

How can putting on the new self be described as clothing yourself with Christ or participating in the divine nature? Because the "new self" refers to your regenerated spirit, which was "created to be *like God* in true righteousness and holiness" (verse 24).

If there's a *true* righteousness and holiness there's also a *false* righteousness and holiness, which is religious legalism. True righteousness and holiness can only be attained by, first, being born-again spiritually and, second, living out of your spirit rather than the flesh. The latter is a learning process, of course, and takes time, but the more you do it, the easier it is, and the more fruit you'll produce.

The fruits of the spirit are the fruits of God's nature. Hence, those who live by their spirit, which is guided by the Holy Spirit, will be "like God" because the spirit naturally produces the fruits of God's nature:

> **The acts of the sinful nature are obvious: sexual immorality, impurity and debauchery; [20]idolatry and witchcraft; hatred, discord, jealousy, fits of rage, selfish ambition, dissensions, factions [21] and envy; drunkenness, orgies, and the like. I warn you, as I did before, that those who live like this will not inherit the kingdom of God. [22] But the fruit of the spirit is love, joy, peace, patience, kindness, goodness, faithfulness, [23] gentleness and self-control. Against such things there is no law.**
>
> **Galatians 5:19-23**

This list of the fruit of the spirit isn't exhaustive any more than the list of the works of flesh is exhaustive. God has many other character traits, like righteousness (Philippians 1:11), truth (Ephesians 5:9), power (2 Timothy 1:7), righteous anger (Mark 3:1-6) and boldness (Mark 11:15-18).

The awesome news is that believers can walk free of the works of the flesh and the two ways they manifest in the Church—legalism and libertinism—simply by putting off the flesh in favor of participating in the divine nature. If this were not possible, Paul would've never instructed us to "be imitators of God" in Ephesians 5:1.

Christians are usually blown away by this verse. They ask, "How can *I* possibly imitate God?" It's simple: Put off the flesh and learn to live out of your spirit and you'll automatically participate in the divine nature and produce the very fruit of God's character!

So how exactly do you walk in the spirit like this? There are **three things** necessary to do, all corresponding to the three parts of your nature—mind, body and spirit. These are the three keys to walking in the spirit:

1. **Renew your mind.** Make it your mindset that you are dead to sin but alive to God in Christ Jesus. This includes making it your confession. Say: "I [state your name] am dead to sin and alive to God in Christ Jesus." Renewing your mind effectively includes lining up your thoughts and words with who God's Word says you already are in Christ. For instance, the Bible says that you're dead to sin, holy, righteous and more than a conqueror in covenant with the Lord. These all describe who you are in your spirit as opposed to the flesh. You may not feel like you are these things, but you *already are* in your spirit. By accepting these positional truths by faith you're being spirit-focused rather than flesh-focused. Do it.
2. **Offer the parts of your body to God as instruments of righteousness.** This includes serving the Lord—doing what God wants you to do (both general instructions from the Scriptures and specific instructions from the Spirit)—but also praise & worship. Each of these puts into motion the law of displacement. By moving forward in the spirit, you aren't slipping backwards in the

flesh. By spending time in the light of God's presence through regular praise & worship, darkness flees. How do you get the darkness out of a room? You simply turn on the lights!

3. **Pray (and sing) in the spirit regularly.** This will keep you charged up and built-up in faith. It'll produce the power you need to walk in the full life Christ came to give us (John 10:10). It'll empower you to *agape* love people you don't have warm feelings toward, including your enemies who hate you without cause. It'll enable you to walk in *tough* love when necessary, including righteous radicalness, like when Paul rebuked an arrogant sorcerer and temporarily cursed him with blindness to humble him, as led of the Holy Spirit (Acts 13:8-12). It'll provide the self-discipline necessary (2 Timothy 1:7) to overcome personal weaknesses, including lack of confidence, depression and various sin issues, like alcoholism, drugs, lying, gossip/slander and sexual lust.

Practicing these three principles is simply a matter of wisdom and love. The first and greatest command is to love God with all your heart and the second is to love people as you love yourself (Matthew 22:34-39). This is the New Covenant law of Christ or law of love (Galatians 6:2 & 1 Corinthians 9:21), which is different from the Mosaic law that believers are *not* under (Romans 7:6 & Galatians 5:18).

In a sense there are three commands in the law of Christ since we are commanded to **love God** and **love others** *as* we **love ourselves**, which means you have to love yourself first. I mean that in a healthy sense, of course, and not a narcissistic way. If you genuinely love yourself, you'll put these principles into practice on a regular basis. After all, if you fail to implement them you won't have a victorious Christian life and you won't be intimate with God. You'll be encumbered and limited by personal weaknesses or areas of the flesh. This will not bless you; it won't bless those linked to you; and it won't bless God.

Practicing these three principles is the key to walking in the spirit. It's the key to producing the fruit of the spirit and, therefore, being *spiritual* rather than *carnal*. Simply put, it's the key to being spirit-controlled rather than flesh-ruled. The former gives life while the latter brings death.

What Are "Positional Truths"?

A positional truth is a truth that reveals your *position* in Christ and therefore *how God sees you* because of this position. For instance, Colossians 1:22 declares that we are "holy **in His sight**, without blemish and free from accusation." This is **how God sees you** because this is ***who you are*** in Christ. A good example from the Old Testament is Gideon, who viewed himself as the weakest and least, but God saw him as a "mighty warrior" (Judges 6:12-16). He had to change his thinking to fulfill his call.

Here are ten positional truths to chew on and renew your mind:

1. You are **holy** (Colossians 1:21-22).
2. You are a **child of God** (John 1:12-13).
3. You are a **new creation** (2 Corinthians 5:17).
4. You are the **righteousness of God** (2 Corinthians 5:21).
5. You are **dead to sin** (Romans 6:11,14,18).
6. You are **more than a conqueror** (Romans 8:37).
7. You are a **temple of the Holy Spirit** (1 Corinthians 6:19-20).
8. You are **rich** (2 Corinthians 8:9).
9. You are **healed** (1 Peter 2:24).
10. You are a **royal priest** of the Most High God (1 Peter 2:9).

What Does It Mean to be Created in the Image of God?

Here's the first reference to being created in God's image and likeness:

> **Then God said, "Let us make mankind in our image, in our likeness, so that they may rule over the fish in the sea and the birds in the sky, over the livestock and all the wild animals, and over all the creatures that move along the ground."**
> **27 So God created mankind in his own image,**
> **in the image of God he created them;**
> **male and female he created them.**
>
> **Genesis 1:26-27**

The LORD—Father, Son & Holy Spirit—decided to make humankind in 'their' image and likeness and then did so. The Hebrew word for "likeness" is *demuth (dem-OOTH)*, which means likeness or similitude—that is, something that *resembles* another; it's something that is a *match* or *counterpart* to another. As such, human beings *resemble* the Almighty; you could say that **we're God's *counterpart* in the physical realm**.

The Hebrew for "image" is *tselem (SEH-lem)*, which simply means representation, copy or duplicate. For instance, the LORD instructed Moses to drive out the inhabitants of the Promised Land and "destroy all their carved images *(tselem)* and their cast idols" (Numbers 33:52). Also, the false god Baal was perceived as a man with the head and horns of a bull; hence, the carved images of the Canaanites depicted this—the carving (idol) was a physical *image* of the mental concept.

So, humankind—male and female—is the physical image of God. This shows that, while "God is spirit," as Christ said (John 4:24), the LORD is not some amorphous cloud entity in the spiritual realm. God has a shape, similar to people, with a head, torso, arms and legs. It has been argued that God has no *physical* body, which is obvious, but the Creator certainly has a *spiritual* form or "body." For instance, the Bible repeatedly says that the LORD sits enthroned in Heaven (Psalm 47:8, 103:19 & Isaiah 40:22). Does this refer to a shapeless cloud-being sitting on a throne in Heaven? No, the Creator has a central presence and spiritual form, parallel to the body of human beings, who were created in God's image and likeness.

Consider Ezekiel's awesome vision of an incredible craft in which God sits on a throne that rests on a sparkling ice-like platform propelled by four cherubim with the aid of four giant wheels within intersecting wheels:

> **Above the expanse over their heads was what looked like a throne of lapis lazuli, and high above on the throne was a figure like that of a man. [27] I saw that from what appeared to be his waist up he looked like glowing metal, as if full of fire, and that from there down he looked like fire; and brilliant light surrounded him. [28] Like the appearance of a rainbow**

> **in the clouds on a rainy day, so was the radiance around him.**
> **This was the appearance of the likeness of the glory of the LORD. When I saw it, I fell facedown, and I heard the voice of one speaking.**
>
> **Ezekiel 1:26-28**

I realize this is a vision, but it's **describing God's form**—"the appearance of the likeness of the glory of the LORD"—which is chronicled as "a figure like that of a man." This is *how* the God-breathed Scriptures describe the Creator's appearance and it is the Scriptures that we are to use to formulate accurate doctrine; they're the basis for correcting error (2 Timothy 3:16-17). Sure, the references to "glowing metal" from the waist up and "fire" from there down are figurative, but Ezekiel was simply using items he was familiar with to describe the indescribable—God.

Genesis 1:26 (cited above) provides further insight on what it means to be created in God's image and likeness: It means to possess authority of some sort, like that which humankind holds over the Earth and its creatures. This explains why people have zoos for animals and not vice versa.

Being created in God's likeness further means to possess volition, which is the power to consciously choose. It also means to distinguish good and evil. People have a conscience, an inward moral compass. Only those who harden their hearts are bereft of this sense (1 Timothy 4:2). Animals, by contrast, are instinctual and do not comprehend such concepts.

Being created in the LORD's image moreover means having the ability to create in a *sophisticated* sense, like the Creator. Hence, human beings create cities, vehicles, highways, languages, literature, art, music, movies, computer systems and so on. Animals, of course, lack such aptitude.

While the same Hebrew & Greek words for 'soul'—*nephesh*/*psuche*—are used in reference to animals (e.g. Genesis 1:20,24 and Revelation 8:9 & 16:3) and animals are animated by a "breath [spirit] of life" from the Creator (Genesis 7:15), they are not created in God's image and therefore lack these human attributes.

6

Questions About the Holy Spirit

Is the Holy Spirit God or a Divine Force?

Scripture reveals that God is One (Deuteronomy 6:4 & Isaiah 45:5-6,18) but also that there's a *tri-unity* within that Oneness, as proven by multiple plain-as-day passages in chapter **2**.

The most popular verse, John 3:16, clearly shows the distinction of God and the Son with Philippians 2:11 more plainly distinguishing the former as God **the Father**. Both the Father and Son are the LORD, aka YaHWeH.

But the Holy Spirit is the LORD too, as observed when Christ gave the Great Commission: "Therefore go and make disciples of all nations, baptizing them in the name of **the Father** and of **the Son** and of **the Holy Spirit**" (Matthew 28:19).

The fact that the Holy Spirit is part of the Divine tri-unity is also observed in Matthew 3:16-17 (and the parallel Mark 1:10–11), as well as the fact that Peter said Ananias "lied **to the Holy Spirit**" followed by "You have not lied just to human beings but **to God**" (Acts 5:3-4). Bear in mind that

Christ plainly distinguished the Spirit from both the Father and Himself (John 16:7).

For those who argue that the Holy Ghost is merely the "force from God" and not a person, the Holy Spirit…

- is referenced with personalized pronouns (John 16:13),
- has a will (1 Corinthians 12:4-7),
- an intellect (1 Corinthians 2:10-13),
- personally guides/directs people (John 16:13 & Acts 16:6),
- speaks (Acts 13:2)
- and can be grieved (Ephesians 4:30).

For those who argue that the Holy Spirit is simply the *spirit of* the Son or the *spirit of* the Father, Christ said "Anyone who speaks a word against **the Son of Man** will be forgiven, but anyone who speaks against **the Holy Spirit** will not be forgiven, either in this age or in the age to come" (Matthew 12:32) and something similar in Luke 12:10. This obviously *distinguishes* the Son from the Holy Spirit as separate persons within the Divine oneness or Godhead.

Father God is also clearly distinguished from the Holy Spirit, like when Christ said: "But **the Advocate**, **the Holy Spirit**, whom **the Father** will send in **my name**, will teach you all things and will remind you of everything I have said to you" (John 14:26). The Father sends the Holy Spirit to teach believers, not Himself. Please note the tri-unity of God detailed in the verse—**Holy Spirit**, the **Father** and **Christ** ("my name").

Now observe how Paul differentiates Father God and the Spirit: "And he [our heavenly Father] who searches our hearts knows **the mind of the Spirit**, because **the Spirit intercedes for God's people** in accordance with **the will of God**" (Romans 8:27). The Holy Spirit has a *mind*—thoughts, purposes—and *intercedes* for believers, both of which bespeak of a ***person***, albeit Divine.

Also, consider Paul's blessing that he spoke over believers: "May the grace of **the Lord Jesus Christ**, and **the love of God**, and **the fellowship**

of the Holy Spirit be with you all" (2 Corinthians 13:14). This plainly bespeaks of a **Divine tri-unity**. Observe the stress on the *"fellowship of"* the Holy Spirit. One does not fellowship with a force or radar, but rather a person.

Hence, the Holy Spirit is not merely a force, but a Divine being, coequal with the Father & Son, revealed in the opening verses of Scripture (Genesis 1:1-2). Of course, one could argue that the Spirit is *both* a **person** within the triunity of God as well as a Divine **force**. For instance, we say "So & so is a force to be reckoned with," which means the *person* is powerful or influential. It's the same with the Spirit except to the nth degree.

Whilst Father/Son/Holy Spirit are equally the LORD, Yahweh, there is subordination in an economical or relational sense. For instance, the Scriptures clearly show that the Father is the head over the Son and this is explicitly stated (1 Corinthians 11:3 & 15:27-28). While the Father and Son are equal in being, the Son is subordinate to the Father in function or relationship. Hence, Christ would never contradict the Father; in fact, He *can't* contradict the Father because, as He said, "I and the Father are one" (John 10:30) (see also John 14:9, 8:19 & 12:45). Meanwhile the Holy Spirit is the third person of the triunity of God.

What Is the Holy Spirit's Role in Redemption?

Most people understandably think of the Son when the topic of human redemption comes up, and understandably so, since Christ obediently became a lowly human in order to greatly suffer & die for our sins so that we might be reconciled to the Creator and have eternal life (Philippians 2:5-11 & John 3:16). Yet the Holy Spirit plays a strategic role as well.

For instance, the Holy Spirit:

- **Convicts** us of our need of salvation (John 16:7-11),
- **Draws** us to the Lord (John 6:44),
- Gives us **spiritual rebirth** (John 3:6 & John 1:12-13)…

- …which **baptizes** us into Christ (1 Corinthians 2:11),
- **Circumcises** our hearts (Romans 2:29),
- **Indwells** us (1 Corinthians 3:16 & 2 Corinthians 6:16),
- **Empowers** us (Romans 8:11 & Acts 1:8),
- **Guides** us (John 16:13),
- **Teaches** us (John 14:26),
- **Helps, comforts** and **intercedes** for us (John 16:17) (the Greek word *paraklétos—par-AK-lay-tos—*means all three),
- **Sanctifies** us (1 Peter 1:2),
- And **Seals** us for salvation (Ephesians 1:13).

So, the Holy Ghost's role in human redemption is quite significant. Chew on these passages for greater understanding & appreciation of the awesome Spirit of God.

How Does the Holy Spirit Convict People?

Here's what Christ said about the Holy Ghost convicting the lost:

> **But very truly I tell you, it is for your good that I am going away. Unless I go away, the Advocate will not come to you; but if I go, I will send him to you. [8] When he comes, he will prove the world to be in the wrong about sin and righteousness and judgment: [9] about sin, because people do not believe in me; [10] about righteousness, because I am going to the Father, where you can see me no longer; [11] and about judgment, because the prince of this world now stands condemned.**
>
> **John 16:7-11**

The Spirit of God convicts the world in three ways:

- In regards to **sin**, which means to miss the mark morally and whose wages is eternal death (Romans 6:23);

- In regards to **righteousness** because our righteousness is filthy rags (Isaiah 64:6) and we desperately need the *gift* of righteousness thru Christ (Romans 5:17 & 2 Corinthians 5:21);
- In regards to **judgment** because, apart from the Anointed One, people will have to stand before the LORD at the Great White Throne Judgment (Revelation 20:11-15).

(When you intercede for those who are lost & dying in this world, pray accordingly).

Of course the Holy Spirit also convicts *believers* of sin, which is part of the process of sanctification and keeps one in fellowship with the LORD along with God's grace/favor flowing into his or her life (1 John 1:7-9).

Is the Holy Spirit the Feminine Side of God?

This is one of those "controversial" questions where answering it is sure to offend someone, except to those open to what the Scriptures teach.

The creation account states:

> **So God created man in his own image, in the image of God he created him; male and female he created them.**
> **Genesis 1:27**

There are a few things I'd like to point out about this verse: "man" in the Hebrew is *adam*, which is how Adam got his name. Secondly, "man" in the generic sense refers to humankind in general, *both* male and female. And, thirdly, "man"—male *and female*—was created in the image of God. With this understanding, **the feminine nature originated with the LORD**.

Of course, God has a "feminine" side in that Scripture gives evidence of His softer traits (feminine), as well as His sterner side (masculine). Some good examples include Psalm 103:8, 1 John 4:8 and Matthew 11:28-30.

Also consider this verse:

> **As the eyes of slaves look to the hand of their master,**
> **as the eyes of a female slave look to the hand of her <u>mistress</u>,**
> **so our eyes look to <u>the LORD our God</u>,**
> **till he shows us his mercy.**
>
> **Psalm 123:2**

The LORD is ***compared*** with both a master (male) and a mistress (female). And the Creator has no problem including such a passage in the God-breathed Scriptures (2 Timothy 3:16-17). Think about that.

Yet when it comes to Father, Son and Holy Spirit, which one especially suggests the feminine nature? Obviously not the Father or Son because, after all, they're the **Father** and **Son**—both clearly masculine.

I would offer that the Holy Spirit generally reflects the feminine nature. For instance, the symbol for the Holy Spirit is a dove, which suggests gentleness and harmlessness (Luke 3:22). Also, the Holy Spirit is referred to as a "Helper" of believers in John 14:16,26 (also translated as "Comforter" and "Counselor"). One of Eve's main purposes was to be Adam's "helper" (Genesis 2:18, 20). In addition, the Holy Spirit is shown to be sensitive—easily grieved—in Ephesians 4:30 and Hebrews 10:29.

The most glaring evidence of the Holy Spirit's feminine nature can be observed in John 3:6 where the Messiah pointed out that "Flesh gives birth to flesh, but **the Spirit gives birth to spirit**." Christ was comparing natural birth with spiritual regeneration. Just as a woman gives birth to a child ("flesh gives birth to flesh") so the Holy Spirit gives rebirth to a person's spirit when s/he turns to God through the gospel. Giving birth clearly bespeaks of the feminine nature.

By contrast, in 1 Peter 1:23 believers are said to be "born again" of the imperishable **seed** of the living Word of God, who is Jesus Christ. This is also conveyed in 1 John 3:9 where "seed" in the Greek is *sperma,* the

Greek word for sperm. You see, believers are born-again of the sperm of Christ, but given spiritual rebirth by the Holy Spirit (Titus 3:5).

Furthermore, this may spur chuckles, but when the Messiah said, “Anyone who speaks a word against the Son of Man will be forgiven, but anyone who speaks against the Holy Spirit will not be forgiven, either in this age or in the age to come” (Matthew 12:32), I can’t help but think of the way men get irate when someone says something insulting about their Momma.

In regards to the biblical instructions *not* to grieve the Holy Spirit (Ephesians 4:30 & Hebrews 10:29), I can’t help but think of the saying: “If Momma ain’t happy, no one’s happy.”

It is true that the Holy Spirit is referred to by the pronoun “he” in Scripture (e.g. John 16:13) and Mary was inseminated by the Holy Spirit (Matthew 1:18-20), but that seed was the seed of the Word of God, which is Jesus Christ; and the thrust of Scripture points to the Holy Spirit’s feminine nature, as detailed above. Besides, God transcends quaint masculine and feminine associations and there is neither male nor female in Christ (Galatians 3:28). Also, Jesus is the wisdom of God, as seen in 1 Corinthians 1:30, but wisdom is personified as a *woman* in Proverbs 8-9 and referred to with a *feminine* pronoun (e.g. Matthew 11:19).

This is not meant to be the all-and-end-all on the topic, but merely food for thought from the Scriptures to provoke further study.

7

Questions About the Church & Christianity

What Is *The* Church?

The word 'church' in the Greek is *ekklesia (ee-KLAY-see-ah)*, meaning "called out of" and thus "the called-out ones." It refers to people who have been called out of the darkness of this world and consecrated to the LORD via responding in faith & repentance to the good news of the message of Christ (Acts 20:21) and the ensuing spiritual rebirth (1 Peter 1:3,23 & James 1:18). The worldwide Church is synonymous with "the body of Christ" (Colossians 1:18) and is also called "God's household" or "the household of God" in Scripture (1 Timothy 3:15). **The Church includes every genuine believer who's experienced spiritual regeneration regardless of what sectarian tag they favor** (John 1:12-13 & 3:3,6).[6]

In its singular form, *ekklesia* is always used to describe all people across the globe who know Christ and not to a specific sect—like, in modern times, Southern Baptists, Nazarenes or Assemblies of God. When pluralized, *ekklesia* is used in reference to specific assemblies of believers

[6] Always remember this about tags: Putting a label of 'corn' on a can of beans doesn't make it a can of corn.

who meet together. In the 1st century this was often at a person's house (Acts 20:20 & Romans 16:3,5). It should be noted that the word 'church' is never used in the Scriptures to describe either a physical facility or a human-organized group—a sect or denomination—although the people of such an organization may, of course, be the Church ("called-out ones"); and usually are if it's a legitimate (biblical) ministry organization.

No *specific* assembly or denomination is necessarily the "one true church" because the body of Christ is not a human-organized institution, but rather **a spiritual entity comprised of those who have been reconciled to the LORD by grace through faith** (Ephesians 2:8–9 & 2 Corinthians 5:18-20). Such people—no matter where they meet, no matter what sect they're a part of, and no matter what nation they live in—are the true Church.

Any time you hear a minister or believer talk about his or her assembly/sect as the "one true church" it's an indication of the infection of staunch sectarianism, which is a spiritually immature mindset, as witnessed in Christ's disciples in Luke 9:49-50. Worse, it's actually a work of the flesh, as shown in Galatians 5:19-21 where "factions" is listed as one of the works of the flesh, also translated as "sects" (and sometimes dubiously as "heresies"). "Factions" or "sects" is a translation of the Greek word *hairesis (HAH-ee-res-is)*, which means "a religious or philosophical sect" and the resulting division, discord or contention in the body of Christ.

With the understanding of the above, **I** am the Church and **you** are the Church; that is, if you're a genuinely born-anew believer.

When Did the New Testament Begin?

When I was a young believer years ago, a brother in the Lord insisted that "the four Gospels are Old Testament not New Testament." This struck me as odd and inaccurate, but since I didn't have enough information at the time, I didn't contest his position. While what he said was understandable in light of the fact that the Church did not technically begin until the Day of Pentecost (more on this below), I've since discovered that what he said was patently false. Notice what Jesus Christ Himself said on the topic:

> **"The Law and the Prophets** [i.e. the Old Covenant] **were proclaimed until John. Since that time, the good news of the kingdom of God is being preached"**
>
> **Luke 16:16**

> **"From the days of John the Baptist until now, the kingdom of heaven has been subjected to violence, and violent people have been raiding it. [13]For all the Prophets and the Law prophesied *until* John."**
>
> **Matthew 11:12-23**

The Old Testament ended with John the Baptist who prepared the way for the Messiah via a baptism of repentance (Luke 3:2-19). **With the ministries of John and Jesus the kingdom of God was preached**, not the Law and the Prophets.

"The Law," incidentally, refers to the Torah, the first five books of the Bible—Genesis, Exodus, Leviticus, Numbers and Deuteronomy—whereas "the Prophets" refers to the prophetic books of the Old Testament. Combining "the Law and the Prophets" together, like Jesus did in Luke 16:16, was/is a reference to the Old Testament in general—the Old Covenant (contract) that God had with the Hebrews.

What Does "The Kingdom of God Is Near" Mean?

While the Old Covenant was proclaimed *until* the time of John the Baptist's public ministry, from that time forward "the good news of **the kingdom of God** is being preached" (Luke 16:16). "The "Good News" refers, of course, to the awesome message of Christ—the gospel.

Notice what John the Baptist, Jesus Christ, the 12 disciples and the other 72 disciples preached:

> **In those days John the Baptist came, preaching in the wilderness of Judea [2] and saying, "Repent, for the kingdom of heaven is near."** **Matthew 3:1-2**

From that time on Jesus began to preach, "Repent, for the kingdom of heaven is near."

Matthew 4:17

These twelve Jesus sent out with the following instructions: "Do not go onto the road of the Gentiles or enter any town of the Samaritans. [6] Go rather to the lost sheep of Israel. [7] As you go, preach this message: 'The kingdom of heaven is near.' "

Matthew 10:5-6

"If you enter a town and they welcome you, eat whatever is set before you. [9] Heal the sick who are there and tell them, 'The kingdom of God is near you.'"

Luke 10:8-9

John, Yeshua, the 12 disciples, and the other 72 disciples all preached that "the kingdom of God is near." Other translations say "the kingdom of God is at hand." The words "near" and "at hand" are translated from the Greek *eggizó (eng-ID-zoh)*, which means "extreme *closeness*, immediate imminence—even a *presence.*" Whether extremely close or even present to a degree, they preached the kingdom of God and not the Law and the Prophets, which agrees with Jesus' plain declaration in Luke 16:16 above.

The kingdom of God is essentially synonymous with the Church (Matthew 16:18-19), but only if "kingdom of God" is defined in a narrow sense, as in "a spiritual rule over the hearts and lives of those who willingly submit to the LORD's authority during this present age."

Those who rebel against God's authority and refuse to submit are obviously not part of the kingdom of God ("the kingdom of God" being the Church in this current era). By contrast, those who acknowledge the lordship of Christ and gladly surrender to the LORD's rule in their hearts are part of the kingdom of God and therefore part of the Church.

So, the Four Gospels Are NOT Old Testament?

Right, the four Gospels are the "prologue" to the New Testament and therefore **PART OF** the New Testament, even though the Church didn't technically start until the Day of Pentecost after the Lord's death & resurrection (Hebrews 9:17). Notice how Christ spoke **AS IF** the Church was already in function in this verse where he talks to his disciples about dealing with offending believers:

> **"If they still refuse to listen, tell it to the church; and if they refuse to listen even to the church, treat them as you would a pagan or a tax collector."**
>
> **Matthew 18:17**

As you can see, Jesus spoke ***as if*** **the Church was already in existence** even though He didn't die for our sins yet and was raised to life for our justification. You could say that the Church was alive but not birthed yet, like a baby in a mother's womb.

When Did the Church Begin?

The actual historical formation of the Church occurred in Jerusalem on the Day of Pentecost, which was 50 days after the Passover when Christ died and was resurrected three days later. Notice how Peter referred to the Day of Pentecost as "the beginning" as he testifies to Jewish believers about the Holy Spirit coming upon Gentile believers:

> **"As I began to speak, the Holy Spirit came on them** [the Gentile believers] **as he had come on us at the beginning.** [16] **Then I remembered what the Lord had said: 'John baptized with water, but you will be baptized with the Holy Spirit.' "**
>
> **Acts 11:15-16**

"The beginning" obviously refers to the Day of Pentecost when believers were empowered by the Holy Spirit (Acts 2:1-13). So, Pentecost marks the beginning of the Church as the spiritual reality of the body of Christ.

What About "On This Rock I Will Build My Church"?

The Messiah made this well-known statement after asking his disciples if they knew who he truly was. Simon Peter answered, "You are the Christ, the Son of the living God."

> **Jesus replied, "Blessed are you, Simon son of Jonah, for this was not revealed to you by man, but by my Father in heaven. [18] And I tell you that you are Peter, and on this rock I will build my church, and the gates of Hades will not overcome it.**
>
> **Matthew 16:17-18**

What is the "rock" on which Christ said He would build His Church? It's not Peter whose name in Greek, *petros*, means "stone." The "rock" on which Jesus will build His Church is *petra* in the Greek, meaning "large rock" or "bedrock." When you're driving a highway and pass through a section with sheer rock cliffs on either side it's obvious that the road-workers blasted through a big hill or mountain. When I see this, I marvel at the **solid mass of rock** underlying the topsoil. This is *petra* or **bedrock**. Christ figuratively said His Church would be built on such bedrock—an incredible mass of solid rock. What is this "rock"? It's the **revelation** that Yeshua is the Christ or Messiah, which literally means "anointed one." It's a revelation because Jesus said it was "**revealed**" to Peter by Father God.

When Peter replied "You are the Christ, the Son of the Living God" he was acknowledging that Yeshua was the anointed prophet that God would raise up as the savior of the world. This was prophesied repeatedly in the Hebraic Scriptures (e.g. Genesis 3:15, Deuteronomy 18:15,18, Isaiah 7:14 & 9:6). In short, Peter had a revelation that Jesus was humanity's Savior. And this revelation is the "bedrock" upon which Christ would build His Church, his "called-out ones." This makes perfect sense when you understand that it's this very revelation—this *belief* inspired by God—that prompts people to embrace the gospel and enables them to be reconciled to the Creator through spiritual regeneration and, hence, obtain eternal life (John 3:3,6,16,36). You can only be a "called-out one"—a member of Christ's Church—if you have this revelation, like Peter did. As such, it's the bedrock upon which Christ builds His Church. Anyone who doesn't have this revelation can't be a "called-out one" and the Lord cannot use that person to build His Church, which explains this passage:

> **Everyone who believes that Jesus is the Christ is born of God,**
>
> **1 John 5:1a**

Since you have to *believe* that Jesus is the Anointed Savior in order to **be** "born of God," this revelation is the rock upon which Christ builds His Church, His called-out ones.

Why did Yeshua emphasize Peter's name, *petros*? Because, although Peter was a little "stone," he would become a part of the bedrock of the Church of Jesus Christ, which is comprised of **all genuine believers** regardless of sectarian tag. We're all little "stones" that together make up the bedrock of the Church, Christ's body on Earth!

Yeshua adds in verse 18 that the "gates of Hades" would not overcome His Church. The "gates of Hades" was a colloquial Jewish phrase for death, which makes sense since *Hades* (or *Sheol* in Hebrew) is the **realm of the DEAD** and consequently a person would have to die to go there. Jesus was saying that even death, satan's ultimate weapon (Hebrews 2:14-15), could not stop the Messiah from birthing and unleashing His Church. And it didn't. He was raised to life and the rest is history (His story). Furthermore, death has no power to destroy the Church, period. Every satanic attempt to wipe out believers and stop the Church's spread has failed; in fact, the blood of martyrs has always served to advance God's kingdom rather than diminish it (e.g. Acts 7:59-8:4). In addition, when a spiritually-regenerated believer physically dies, their soul doesn't go to Hades/Sheol, the realm of the DEAD, but rather goes to be with the Lord in Heaven to await his or her bodily resurrection (Philippians 1:20-24, 2 Corinthians 5:1-10, 1 Thessalonians 5:10, Revelation 6:9-11 & 7:9-17).

So, Matthew 16:18 Doesn't Support the Idea of a Pope?

The God-breathed Scriptures simply do not support the idea of a supreme & infallible human leader of Christianity on Earth nor the doctrine of papal (apostolic) succession, which is the idea that the (supposed) supreme earthly authority of the papacy is transferred from pope to pope. The best biblical support Catholics can come up with is Matthew 16:18-19, which they milk for details that the rest of the New Testament refutes.

It is the Mighty Christ who is the worthy infallible **Head** of the worldwide Church (Colossians 1:18, 2:10 & 2:19), as well as the **Foundation** (Acts 4:11-12 & 1 Corinthians 3:11); and fivefold ministers—e.g. pastors and teachers—are *under*-shepherds who lead in a servant-like fashion (Galatians 2:1-14, Ephesians 2:19-20, 4:11-15 & 1 Peter 5:1-5).

Since this is so, some obvious questions surface: If Christ is the head of the worldwide Church, why do believers need a pope? If it is heresy to deny papal supremacy, as Catholics claim, then all early believers after Christ's death & resurrection were heretics seeing as how there was no pope. Since Christ had completed the work of reconciling believers to God, why would we need further mediation from a pope & his associates?

No where in the Bible are believers encouraged to follow some supreme & infallible bishop (aka Pope) in Rome. Other than Matthew 16:18-19, the best support Catholics can concoct is 1 Peter 5:13, which is pretty feeble evidence, to be honest. Whether or not Peter became the bishop of Rome, there's zero biblical evidence that this position was to have primacy over the worldwide Church. In other words, the doctrine of the earthly supremacy of the papacy is unscriptural, which is a huge problem when you consider that the God-breathed Scriptures are the LORD's blueprint for authentic Christianity. In short, the Bible is the basis for all Christian doctrine & practice and any **corrections** thereof (2 Timothy 3:16-17 & 1 Corinthians 4:6).

Isn't the Catholic Church the Original Church?

No, this idea is based on the erroneous premise of validation through physical lineage, which didn't wash in the 1st century when the Pharisees & Sadducees relied on the same argument to support their authority, which John and Christ refuted in no uncertain terms (Matthew 3:7-10 & John 8:39-44). It's *spiritual* lineage that counts (Galatians 5:6 & 6:15). And anyone spiritually regenerated by the Holy Spirit thru Christ can trace their lineal descent to the 1st century Church because those early believers were born-again of the *same* Spirit thru the *same* Lord (John 3:3,6 & Titus 3:5).

Did the New Testament Scriptures come through the fathers of Catholicism? Absolutely not because the Roman Catholic Church didn't even exist yet since its origins were forged at the Council of Nicaea in Asia Minor (Turkey) in 325 AD. At this council the dubiously-converted Roman Emperor Constantine, who mixed Christianity with paganism, attempted to unite Christendom because he envisioned Christianity unifying his deteriorating empire. While some good things came out of this historic council, like upholding the doctrine of Christ's divinity, it mixed Christianity with politics and the temptations of power & corruption thereof. Later in that century, Christianity became the official state religion of the Roman Empire, which is essentially when Catholicism was born.

The Roman church fell into increasing error. Christ & the apostles warned that this would happen (Matthew 7:15-23, Acts 20:28–32, 2 Corinthians 11:13, 2 Peter 2:1 & Jude 1:4). The acceptance of Augustine's false doctrines in 431 AD at the Council of Ephesus was the prologue to a thousand-year Dark Age where all kinds of absurdly unbiblical doctrines & practices were accumulated by the Roman sect. These heresies and corruptions are what prompted the great Protestant Reformation in the 1500s. The righteous dissenters were called "Protestants" because they righteously *protested* the glaring and damning errors of Catholicism.

The Muratorian Canon from around 170 AD *already listed* all the books of what is known as the New Testament except for Hebrews, James, 1 Peter and 2 Peter, plus the mini-epistles 2 John and 3 John. This was 155 years *before* the Council of Nicaea.

The Roman Catholic Church *claims* it began with Peter, whom they say was the first pope—bishop of Rome—but the proof is in the pudding of Scripture, which is **God's established pattern for authentic Christianity**. And nowhere in the God-breathed Scriptures will you find support for doctrines & practices like the papacy, apostolic succession, papal infallibility, equating traditions with Scripture, praying to dead saints, obsession with religious statues (which smacks of idolatry), regular confession to priests, infant baptism, celibacy mandated for ministers, transubstantiation, the absurd granting of indulgences, the immaculate conception, perpetual virginity, the assumption of Mary and mediatrix.

The Lord plainly said that you can recognize false ministers **by their fruit** (Matthew 7:15-23), which includes grossly unbiblical doctrines & practices (Matthew 16:11-12).

What Are the Leadership Positions of the Church?

There are five servant-leadership positions:

> **So Christ himself gave the <u>apostles</u>, the <u>prophets</u>, the <u>evangelists</u>, the <u>pastors</u> and <u>teachers</u>, [12] to equip his people for works of service, so that the body of Christ may be built up [13] until we all reach unity in the faith and in the knowledge of the Son of God and become mature, attaining to the whole measure of the fullness of Christ.**
>
> **Ephesians 4:11-13**

When people think of the term 'minister' they automatically think of a pastor, who oversees a local assembly. Yet this passage plainly shows that professional Christian ministry involves more than pastoring, as important as that service is.

These five callings in the body of Christ can be summed up briefly as follows:

- **Apostles**, like Paul and John, have an anointing & drive to go out and start assemblies, as well as oversee them. In order to start or oversee fellowships, an apostle obviously has to have the gift of pastoring. The Scriptures say that a true apostle is marked by "signs, wonders and miracles" (2 Corinthians 12:12), but this might be hard to come by in these days of gross unbelief, although I've seen modern apostles minister in this capacity; they're out there. In any case, apostles should at least have an anointing with the laying on of hands (Hebrews 6:1-2).
- **Prophets** are "interpreters or forth-tellers of the divine will" and should not be confused with that of occultist fortune tellers. The prophetic word is encouraging and able to touch believers in that specific area where they need ministered, as observed in Acts 15:32. The original Greek word for 'encourage' in this passage means "to cause to move forward." In other words, a prophetic word inspires believers and spurs them to go forward to fulfill God's call on their lives. This shows that prophets are more preachers than teachers. They see things in the spirit and proclaim God's will that's applicable to the situation or person, but they don't go into scriptural details on doctrine, like a teacher would.[7]
- **Evangelists** are "bringers of good news," which is what the Greek word means. Like prophets, they're preachers and not teachers. They proclaim by unction the truths of the gospel and the Word of God in general, but they're not effective at detail-oriented

---

[7] The gift of prophecy in the New Testament era was not given to the body of Christ for the purpose of leading and guiding God's people, as was the case with prophets in the Old Testament, whose prophecies often became Holy Scripture (which explains why their prophecies *had* to be 100% accurate, as observed in Deuteronomy 18:20-22). To explain, believers are born-again spiritually and have the Holy Spirit *within them* for this very purpose. As Jesus said, "But when he, the Spirit of truth, comes, he will guide you into all truth" (John16:13). Since it's the Holy Spirit's job to guide believers in the Church Age, we don't need the gift of prophecy for this function. So, when a prophet prophesies over you and says you're to do this or that and go here or there, don't receive it *unless* the Spirit has already been leading you in this direction. In other words, prophecies in the New Testament are to confirm what the Holy Spirit has already been leading you to do. You could say it's an external source to confirm or compliment the believer's internal source of direction from God.

teaching. Many hardcore missionaries would be examples of fivefold evangelists. Evangelists can certainly minister to believers at revivals and what have you, but their drive & focus is reaching the lost with the life-changing Good News of the message of Christ (2 Corinthians 5:17-21). Like apostles and prophets, evangelists cited in the New Testament operated in the gifts of the Spirit, such as Philip (Acts 8:4-7, 8:26-40 & 21:8).

- **Pastors** are shepherds in the sense of overseeing a 'flock' of people. Christ is the "Good Shepherd" of the worldwide Church (John 10:11,14,27) while pastors are under-shepherds of local assemblies, as observed in 1 Peter 5:1-4. This passage shows that pastors are responsible for **1.** Spiritually feeding the flock of God that is under their care, **2.** "watching over" them, that is, *overseeing* them, **3.** not pursuing dishonest gain, i.e. not being a lover of mammon (Luke 12:15), **4.** serving with gratefulness & enthusiasm and not "begrudgingly," **5.** not "lording it over" those entrusted to them but serving with a loving, humble *servant's* heart, and **6.** being examples to "the flock" in all they say and do. This shows that pastoring isn't just about "the ministry of the Word of God" (Acts 6:1-4), but also actually walking with the Lord and in newness of life. In short, it's not just talking the talk, it's walking the walk.
- **Teachers** have the anointing to carefully explain the Holy Scriptures in an understandable, enlightening way. They make the Scriptures come alive for people and help them to see things in God's Word they've never seen before. They give structure to knowledge and their potent insights often result in believers thinking, "I've never heard this, but it makes total sense. Where did s/he get his?!" This is the reaction people had to Christ when he taught (Mark 6:2). It is *teaching* from the Scriptures that feeds people spiritually (Matthew 4:4) whereas *preaching*—the passionate proclaiming of God's Word—motivates people to action (Acts 15:35 & 1 Timothy 5:17). Fivefold teachers differ from pastors (and apostles) in that they don't have the gift to oversee people. I'm a fivefold teacher. I have the gift to teach believers, but not oversee them. To be an effective pastor you have to want to watch over people. I have no such desire. I operate in

> the ministry of the word (Acts 6:1-4) and pray for my hearers/readers and then it's in the Spirit's hands, as well as the hands of their local pastors.

All fivefold ministers—whether apostles, prophets, evangelists, pastors or teachers—must **1.** walk with God on a daily basis, **2.** know the Holy Scriptures and **3.** be gifted to either teach or preach from them.

These five ministry gifts, by the way, are anointings or offices, they're *not* mandatory titles (2 Peter 3:15, Galatians 2:6-9 & Matthew 23:7-11).

What Characterizes an Abusive Minister?

We saw above that fivefold ministers are "to prepare God's people for works of service, so that the body of Christ may be **built up**" (Ephesians 4:11-13). In other words, genuine ministers—and believers in general—are to overflow with life, not death. Why? Because we're children of God and the LORD is the Fountain of Life (Psalm 36:9). This explains Christ's mission: **to give people life and life to the full**, not death (John 10:10).

Of course, there's a place for condemning sin and inspiring repentance when ministering. Capable ministers who are anointed of the Spirit will bring about a spirit of repentance via **the ministry of the Word**, but will also remove the weight of guilt, impart God's peace and spur people forward. In short, even though they condemn sin and encourage penitence, their ministry is inspiring and encouraging. This is the minister's job.

A good example of this can be observed in the Scriptures. After Christ's resurrection, he appeared to a couple of the disciples who were naturally disheartened in the wake of His undue execution. The Messiah suddenly joined them as they were traveling and they talked for a while, but they failed to recognize Him. After Yeshua left, the two reflected on this meeting: "Were not **our hearts burning within us** while he talked with us on the road and opened the Scriptures to us?" (Luke 24:32).

This is the kind of effect true ministers will have. You know you're at a fit fellowship when you depart with your heart burning with encouragement and you have fresh revelation from God's Word you never saw before.

If, on the other hand, you leave an assembly feeling beat up, weighed down and condemned, it's not good. It shows that the minister executing the service has become infected by a form of legalism and is spiritually toxic. Such a spirit of condo is at odds with the true ministerial spirit, which Paul summed up when he noted the authority ministers have for **building believers up and not tearing them down** (2 Corinthians 10:8 & 13:10).

What Are the Fundamental Doctrines of Christianity?

The Bible details six doctrines that will ensure a sound foundation:

> **Therefore let us move beyond the elementary teachings about Christ and be taken forward to maturity, not laying again the foundation of repentance from acts that lead to death, and of faith in God, [2] instruction about baptisms, the laying on of hands, the resurrection of the dead, and eternal judgment.** **Hebrews 6:1-2**

The writer of Hebrews was lamenting that the believers he was addressing needed to be taught these basic doctrines all over again when they should've been teachers by this point (see Hebrews 5:11-12). Notice that knowing these six elementary doctrines is conveyed in terms of "laying" a "foundation." In other words, these teachings are the **elementary understructure** for every Christian. They are as follows:

1. **Repentance from acts that lead to death**
2. **Faith in God**
3. **Instructions about baptisms**
4. **The laying on of hands**
5. **The resurrection of the dead**
6. **Eternal judgment**

The Greek word for "elementary" doesn't mean simple, but rather "the initial (starting) point." In short, these six doctrines come first and are therefore **the *chief* teachings of Christianity**. They're "basic" only in the sense that they're foundational and have priority over other doctrines.

The more fully you understand these preeminent doctrines, the more difficult it will be for anyone to lead you astray with false doctrine. For instance, some Christians falsely teach that it's not necessary for believers to keep in repentance, but the very first doctrine contradicts this. Some say that spiritual rebirth isn't biblical, but the third doctrine disproves this. Many insist that everyone will ultimately be saved regardless of the evil they chose to practice without repentance, but the sixth doctrine refutes this. Simply put, the six basic doctrines will protect you from doctrinal error, including traditional religious doctrines that aren't actually biblical.

What Is "Repentance From Acts That Lead to Death"?

The word 'repent' simply means to change one's mind for the positive. This means a change of mind with the corresponding actions, like the resolve to fulfill God's will (Acts 26:20) and turn from that which is opposed to God's will, meaning sin (Acts 8:22 & 2 Corinthians 12:21). Observe the connection between repentance and faith (belief):

> **I have declared to both Jews and Greeks that they must turn to God in <u>repentance</u> <u>and</u> <u>have faith</u> in our Lord Jesus.**
>
> **Acts 20:21**

Repentance and faith are two sides of the same coin and so, for repentance to be effective, it must be combined with faith, which is the second basic doctrine of Christianity. Otherwise, repentance is just a dead exercise.

John the Baptist referred to regularly confessing sin when he said, "Produce fruit in keeping with repentance." (Matthew & Luke 3:8). You see, the repentance/forgiveness dynamic is fundamental to your walk with the Lord because it enables you to **1.** get back up when you inevitably miss it, **2.** receive God's forgiveness, **3.** have your slate wiped clean, and **4.** continue to progress forward. It's difficult to bear fruit unto God while knowingly walking in impenitent sin, to say the least. The principle of "keeping with repentance" assures the continuing stream of the LORD's forgiveness and favor in your life as you faithfully 'fess up (1 John 1:5-9). Needless to say, don't allow unconfessed sin to block-up your spiritual arteries from the flow of God's grace.

Humbly 'fessing-up should become a regular activity in your life (Proverbs 28:13 & Psalm 32:5). It's particularly helpful for those who are in bondage to a certain sin. They want free, but keep falling back into the sin, which is a relapse. The principle of keeping-with-repentance ensures the flow of the LORD's forgiveness and favor into their lives. As they seek the Lord and continue in God's Word they will eventually walk free. Remember, you don't drown by falling in the water; you drown by *staying* in the water. This principle gets you *out* of the water when you fall.

What Is "Faith in God"

The Bible says "**without faith it is impossible to please God**, because anyone who comes to him must believe that he exists and that he rewards those who earnestly seek him" (Hebrews 11:6).

What exactly is faith? Faith is **the substance of things hoped for** and being certain of what we do not see (Hebrews 11:1). The Amplified Bible's translation of this verse calls faith the "title deed" of the things we hope for; that is, the things we righteously desire. In short, faith is the substance that brings the world of hope into reality! In the Gospels, for instance, people would come to Yeshua hoping for healing and, after receiving it, He would say something like "Your faith has healed you" (e.g. Mark 5:25-34). You see? Faith was the substance that brought them what they hoped for—healing. They were certain—convinced—that the Lord would heal them even though they couldn't yet see it physically.

Did you ever wonder why faith is so important to receiving salvation? Because **faith is nothing more or less than believing God**. That's precisely what Adam & Eve failed to do when they were tested in the Garden of Eden and that's why they fell (Genesis 2:15-3:24). In other words, **the fall of humanity came about due to unbelief and therefore humanity's restoration is dependent upon belief**.

It's interesting that repentance and faith are the first two basic doctrines of Christianity because these are the *conditions* to receiving God's gift of eternal salvation, as noted in the aforementioned Acts 20:21. We effectively "turn to God" via the gospel through **repentance** and **faith**. This was made clear in Christ's first sermon upon entering public ministry:

> **"The time is fulfilled, and the kingdom of God is at hand; repent and believe in the gospel."**
>
> **Mark 1:15** (ESV)

The Greek for "believe" here is the verb form of the Greek word for faith. The point is that repentance and faith are the keys to receiving the gospel—the message of Christ—and they are fittingly the first two basic doctrines of Christianity.

This doctrine is dubbed "faith **in God**" because genuine faith is the result of knowing the LORD—the result of relationship—as well as knowing God's word & promises. So, it's faith **in God**, not faith in faith.

In other words, the power in biblical faith stems from its object—God. It's not something in our flesh that makes faith work, but rather the character of the LORD combined with the faith that spring from our human spirit, as well as the indwelling Holy Spirit in the case of believers (Proverbs 20:27 & 1 Corinthians 6:19). Faith—belief—is simply the natural response to the truths (realities) of God, God's Word and God's creation. This prevents faith from becoming a human work and gives all the glory of our faith exploits to our Almighty Creator.

This is an encouragement to go deeper in your relationship with the Lord and to grow in the knowledge of God's Word and the promises thereof (2 Peter 3:18). The promises that your personal guide, the Holy Spirit, gives to you is another factor (John 14:26 & 16:13).

For more on how your faith can grow, see *Does the Bible Offer a Plan to Spiritual Maturity?* in chapter **10**.

What Is "Instructions About Baptisms"?

The Greek word for 'baptize' is *baptizó (bap-TID-zoh)*, which means "overwhelmed, covered or submerged." It was used in reference to being "baptized" by debts in ancient times. The noun form is in the plural in Hebrews 6:2 because **there are three baptisms in Christianity**. Most Christians only know about water baptism, which ironically is the least important (which is different than saying it's unimportant). Every believer should experience all three baptisms, but it's the first one that *must* be experienced in order to be a Christian. The three baptisms are:

1. Baptism into Christ
2. Water baptism
3. The baptism of the Holy Spirit

The baptism into Christ is the only baptism necessary for redemption (Galatians 3:26-27 & Romans 6:3) since it refers to a person being spiritually regenerated (1 Peter 1:23).

Water baptism is merely the symbolic testimony of what has *already occurred spiritually* through the baptism into Christ (e.g. Acts 10:47-48).

The baptism of the Spirit is distinct from being "born of the Spirit" (John 3:3,6), which is one-in-the-same as the baptism into Christ, although the two occasionally happen at the same time. When you're born of the Spirit, the Spirit is *in* you (Romans 8:9 & 1 Corinthians 6:19), whereas when you're baptized in the Spirit, the Spirit is *all over you* because you're immersed with the Spirit. It's the difference between drinking a glass of water and jumping into a pure, mountain lake.

Speaking in tongues is theoretically the initial physical evidence of the baptism in the Holy Spirit. While speaking in tongues is not the Holy Spirit and the Holy Spirit is not speaking in tongues, they go hand in hand. Here are five scriptural examples of people receiving this baptism:

1. **The believers in Jerusalem, as shown in Acts 2:1-4.** All of them spoke in tongues.
2. **The Samaritans, as shown in Acts 8:12-19.** The Samaritans were part Jew and part Gentile. Verse 18 shows that Simon the sorcerer "saw" that the Spirit was given to the Samaritans when the apostles laid their hands on them. In other words, he saw evidence that they received the Holy Spirit. What did he see? We must interpret Scripture with Scripture, which is a hermeneutical rule. Since the rest of the New Testament shows that speaking in languages the person doesn't know is the initial evidence of the baptism of the Holy Spirit, this must've been what Simon saw.
3. **Saul in Damascus, as shown in Acts 9:17-18.** Although speaking in tongues is not mentioned in this passage, the baptism of the Holy Spirit is, and we observe scriptural evidence elsewhere that Saul/Paul spoke in tongues on a regular basis, which is praying in the spirit (1 Corinthians 14:18-19).
4. **Cornelius' household in Caesarea, as shown in Acts 10:44-48.** This refers to the first Gentile believers. Verses 45-46 state: "The circumcised believers who had come with Peter were astonished that the gift of the Holy Spirit had been poured out even on the Gentiles. For they heard them speaking in tongues and praising God." Since believers who are not baptized in the Spirit can praise God, the evidence of the baptism is obviously speaking in tongues.
5. **The Ephesians, as shown in Acts 19:5-7.** This passage shows that all twelve spoke in tongues as a result of receiving the baptism, not just a select few.

As already noted, every Christian can and should receive this baptism and pray in the spirit to supplement prayer in his or her native language. This can be observed in 1 Corinthians 14:14-15, 18-19 and Ephesians 6:18. I have to emphasize this because there's this idea rampant in the body of Christ that speaking in tongues was done away with once the biblical canon was completed, which is known as cessationism. Don't believe it.

It's a colossal lie that has allowed the enemy to keep multitudes of sincere believers from the full empowerment and help of the Holy Spirit.

Praying in the spirit is important because it edifies the believer by building you up in faith and empowers you to love people, to walk free from sin, and to minister (Jude 1:20 & 2 Timothy 1:7).

That said, just because a Christian is baptized in the Spirit and can speak in tongues, it does not mean that he or she is walking in the spirit and producing the fruit thereof, like love, joy, peace, kindness, faith, humility and self-control (Galatians 5:16, 22-23). The baptism of the Holy Spirit and the corresponding gift of glossolalia should not be regarded as a badge of superiority wherein the believer becomes condescending toward those who don't (yet) have it. This would be arrogance and "God opposes the proud but shows favor to the humble" (James 4:6 & 1 Peter 5:5).

Lastly, if a believer can walk in the spirit to a good degree without the baptism of the Holy Spirit, how much more so if they *are*? In other words, just because you're doing well in your walk *without* glossolalia, don't let it rob you of this wonderful gift that God has provided all believers!

What Is "The Laying on of Hands"?

The doctrine of the laying on of hands refers to the transference of four things through physical contact: **1.** blessing, **2.** anointing and consecration for service, that is, ministry, **3.** the baptism of the Holy Spirit, and **4.** healing and deliverance. Let's briefly look at all four...

Blessing: Christ placed his hands on children and blessed them (Mark 10:13,16 & Matthew 19:13,15). To 'bless' someone means to speak positive words that have a productive impact. The priestly prayer supports this definition (Numbers 6:22-27) and you can find these types of blessings all over the Bible; for example, Romans 15:13 and Colossians 1:9-12.

Blessing in this manner is important because words "have the power of life and death" (Proverbs 18:21). Our words bring either life or death, blessing or cursing. “Reckless words pierce like a sword, but the tongue of the wise brings healing” (Proverbs 12:18). Words are powerful by themselves; adding the dimension of touch magnifies their impact.

Anointing/Separation for Ministry: Hands are to be lain on those called of God to special service. Biblical examples include the Levites (Numbers 8:10-11), Joshua, (Numbers 27:18-23), Stephen & six others (Acts 6:1-6) and Saul & Barnabas (Acts 13:2-3).

The people who qualify for such a rite of passage should *already* be full of faith, God’s Word and the Spirit, as was the case with Joshua and Steven. The laying on of hands simply provides a stronger anointing to fulfill their God-given assignment.

Paul instructed his protégé to not be “hasty in the laying on of hands” (1 Timothy 5:22) because ministers must be tested for character and there’s no test like the test of time. Those who hastily confirm untested ministers share responsibility for the damage they eventually do to people.

The Holy Spirit Baptism: Hands are to be laid on believers to receive the baptism of the Holy Spirit, detailed in the previous section.

While this powerful gift is typically received this way—that is, through someone who has it—a believer can also receive it simply through faith in God’s Word (Luke 11:9-13). In other words, believers don’t absolutely need a human conduit for this gift to be transferred.

Healing or Spiritual Deliverance: Christ prophesied that believers “will place their hands on sick people, and they will get well” (Mark 16:17-18).

The book of Acts says “God anointed Jesus of Nazareth with the Holy Spirit and power, and… he went around doing good and healing all who were under the power of the devil, because God was with him” (Acts 10:38). We see evidence of this throughout the Gospels:

- Christ laid hands on the sick and healed them or exorcized demons (Luke 4:40-41).

- A woman who was subject to bleeding for twelve years heard about Jesus' anointing to heal and therefore had faith to receive healing through him (Mark 5:25-34). When the woman touched his cloak Christ sensed "power had gone out from him" (verse 30).
- The Messiah had an anointing to heal, but His ministry was very limited in His hometown because of the people's lack of faith due to a "spirit of familiarity"—meaning they were so familiar with Jesus during His first three decades that they were hindered from acknowledging His Divine anointing and receiving from it (Mark 6:1-6). This example reveals that getting a healing is a matter of faith in regards to **1.** the person praying (i.e. the human conduit of God's power), as well as **2.** the recipient of the healing. So, receiving a healing via a human conduit involves a combination of faith. Needless to say, there's power in agreement (Matthew 18:20 & Leviticus 26:8). However…
- People with the **greatest faith** do not require hands to be laid on them for healing or deliverance. This type of faith **accepts the LORD at His Word**, like the centurion from Matthew 8:5-10,13. In other words, they don't require a human conduit to receive.

What Is "The Resurrection of the Dead"?

This doctrine means that everyone will be bodily resurrected—both the righteous and the unrighteous—as Jesus and Paul plainly declared (John 5:28-29 & Acts 24:15). This does not mean, however, that there will only be two resurrections in number, just that there are two *types* of resurrections: **1.** The resurrection of the righteous and **2.** the resurrection of the unrighteous. The former is called "the first resurrection" in Scripture (Revelation 20:5-6), which makes the latter the second resurrection.

The second resurrection takes place at the time of the Great White Throne Judgment (Revelation 20:11-15), which is addressed in chapter **14**.

The resurrection of the righteous, by contrast, concerns those in right-standing with God. While there's only one resurrection of the unrighteous, the resurrection of the righteous takes place in stages, which correspond to the analogy of a harvest in biblical times: **1.** the firstfruits, **2.** the main harvest, and **3.** the gleanings. The harvest began with the firstfruits, which concerned the first fruits & grains to ripen in the season and were offered to the LORD as a sacrifice of thanksgiving (Exodus 23:16,19). Later came the general harvest (Exodus 23:16) and, lastly, the gleanings, which were leftovers for the poor and needy (Leviticus 19:9-10).

Here are **the three stages** of the resurrection of the righteous:

1. The Firstfruits: Paul described Christ as the firstfruits in 1 Corinthians 15:21-23. Just as the firstfruits of the harvest were a sacrifice to the LORD, so Yeshua was sacrificed for our sins and raised to life for our justification (Romans 4:25). He's the firstfruits of the resurrection of the righteous.

2. The General Harvest: Verse 23 (of 1 Corinthians 15) shows that this main harvest takes place when Christ returns for the Church—His "bride"—which is the Rapture, detailed in 1 Thessalonians 4:13-18. Here are the key verses:

> **For the Lord himself will come down from heaven, with a loud command, with the voice of the archangel and with the trumpet call of God, and the dead in Christ will rise first. [17]After that, we who are still alive and are left will be <u>caught up</u> together with them in the clouds to meet the Lord in the air. And so we will be with the Lord forever.**
>
> **1 Thessalonians 4:16-17**

It was pointed out in chapter **<u>3</u>** that the phrase 'caught up' is one word in the Greek, *harpazó (har-PAD-zoh)*, which means to "snatch up" or "obtain by robbery." This word is translated in the Latin Vulgate as *rapio*, which is where we get the English 'rapture.' So the Lord is going to obtain His "bride" by snatching us up to Heaven!

As you can see, this general harvest includes *both* the bodily resurrection of physically-dead believers and the translation of physically-alive believers to Heaven. We'll receive our glorified bodies at this time, a fascinating topic covered in chapter **16**.

3. The Gleanings refer to the righteous who were not included in the main harvest and are, as such, "leftovers." This resurrection takes place at the time of Jesus' return to Earth to set up His millennial reign at the end of the Tribulation and is separate from the Rapture, which is when the general harvest occurs. Remember, when Christ comes for His Church, He won't return to Earth, but rather meets believers in the sky (1 Thessalonians 4:17). These gleanings include the resurrection of Old Testament saints (Matthew 19:28) as well as the bodily resurrection of believers who died during the Tribulation.

The "gleanings" will also include believers who physically die during the Millennium.

Someone might argue: How can *both* the resurrection of the righteous just before the Millennium and another resurrection at the end be "gleanings" since they're separated by a thousand years? Because the very word "gleanings" implies more than one gleaning; after all, the poor gleaned the harvested fields more than once in biblical times. Also, Psalm 90:4 and 2 Peter 3:8 show that a thousand years is like a day to the LORD, so the two gleanings occur only one day apart from the Divine perspective.

The resurrection of the righteous is called the "first resurrection" in reference to believers who die during the Tribulation (Revelation 20:4-6). But this is not saying that there were no resurrections prior to this since Christ was resurrected at the beginning of the Church Age and believers will be resurrected bodily at the time of the Rapture while living believers will be translated (1 Thessalonians 4:13-18). Then there's the resurrections of Enoch, Elijah and Moses as *types* of the different kinds of resurrections of saints. Their resurrections can be considered "taste-testing of the fruit" according to the harvest analogy.

Here's a diagram that helps visualize the first and second resurrections:

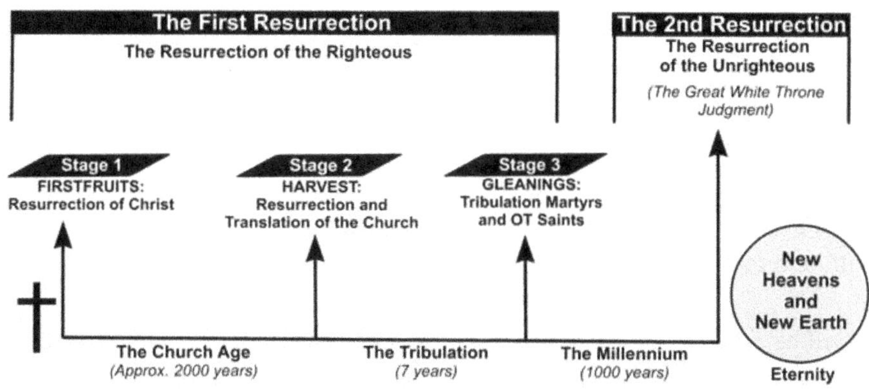

The diagram obviously supports the "pre-Trib" Rapture, which is substantiated by plain texts like this one:

> **For the Son of Man <u>in his day will be like the lightning, which flashes and lights up the sky from one end to the other</u>. 25 But first he must suffer many things and be rejected by this generation.**
> **26 "<u>Just as it was in the days of Noah, so also will it be in the days of the Son of Man</u>. 27 People were eating, drinking, marrying and being given in marriage up to the day Noah entered the ark. Then the flood came and destroyed them all.**
> **28 "<u>It was the same in the days of Lot</u>. People were eating and drinking, buying and selling, planting and building. 29 But the day Lot left Sodom, fire and sulfur rained down from heaven and destroyed them all.**
> **30 "It will be just like this <u>on the day the Son of Man is revealed</u>. 31 On that day no one who is on the housetop, with possessions inside, should go down to get them. Likewise, no one in the field should go back for anything. 32 Remember Lot's wife! 33 Whoever tries to keep their life will lose it, and whoever loses their life will preserve it. 34 I tell you, <u>on that night two people will be in one bed; one will be taken and the other left</u>.**
> **35 <u>Two women will be grinding grain together; one will be taken and the other left</u>." Luke 17:24-35**

As you can see, Christ cites two examples from history of God's people being warned/saved from the mass destruction of Divine wrath: Noah & his family escaped the destruction of the global flood via the ark while Lot & his kin were warned to leave the corrupted Sodom before God's judgment manifested. Yeshua says in verse 30 that "it will be *just like this* on **the day the Son of Man is revealed**." In other words, God's faithful will be removed *before* the LORD's wrath falls in the Tribulation.

It will be *just like* the days of Noah and Lot in which people were carrying on business as usual—eating, drinking, marrying, buying, selling, planting and building (verses 27-28). This is what people will be doing when Christ comes for His Church, not enduring a global upheaval wherein half the population of the planet is wiped out (Revelation 6:8 & Revelation 9:18), which disproves the post-Tribulation position.

Additional support for a "pre-Trib" Rapture can be observed in that the Lord says to the apostle John in Revelation 4:1, "Come up here [to Heaven]" before the 7-year Tribulation is detailed in chapters 4-19. John is representative of the Church and just before the Tribulation he is taken up into Heaven. Why? Because the Church itself will be delivered from the Tribulation via Jesus' return for His Church, which is the Rapture.

Another thing to consider is that the Church is referred to no less than nineteen times in the first three chapters of Revelation and not once on Earth in chapters 4-19. Why? Because the *existing* Church—all genuine believers—will be "snatched up" to Heaven before the Tribulation starts. Revelation 19 details Christ's return to the Earth at the end of the Tribulation. Who's riding with him? The Church (verse 14).

That said, it is true that millions of believers will go through the Tribulation. I'm referring to those who turn to the LORD *after* the Church is removed. Unfortunately, multitudes of these will be martyred, as observed in Revelation 6:9-11 and 7:9-17.

Also, consider that Yeshua spoke of His snatching up of the Church as "**the coming of the Son of Man**" (Matthew 24:27,37,39) and, within this context, are clear references to the Tribulation (verses 21-22 & 29). The

Greek for "coming" in these passages is *parousia (par-oo-SEE-ah)*, traditionally translated as 'advent' in Christian circles, as in "the Second Advent of Christ." This is the same word used to describe the Lord's coming at the *end* of the Tribulation in 2 Thessalonians 2:8. Messiah elsewhere referred to this latter coming as "**When the Son of Man comes** in his glory" (Matthew 16:27 & 25:31). Since the Rapture of the Church is clearly separate from the Lord's coming to the Earth and both the Rapture and Jesus' return to the Earth are described in terms of "coming" (*parousia*) then we must conclude that **they both represent His Second Coming**, albeit two phases.

You see, **to *believers,* the Rapture IS Christ's Second Coming** whereas, **to the unsaved, His return to Earth is the Second Coming**. So, *both* refer to the Lord's Second Coming depending upon the spiritual condition of the individual; they're just two different phases.

Lastly, Hebrews 9:28 states that Christ will appear "a second time"—clearly referring to His **Second Coming**—and then goes on to say that when He appears this "second time" He will "bring salvation to those who are waiting for him," which is an obvious reference to **the Rapture** and distinguished from His Return to Earth, as illustrated here:

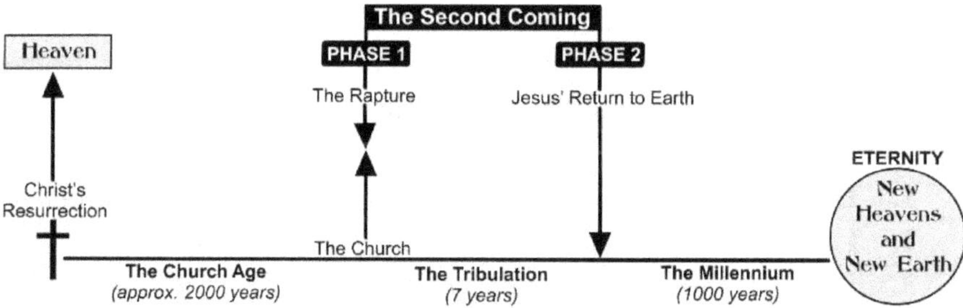

If anyone prefers to designate Christ's return to Earth *specifically* as his Second Coming, that's fine. I'm not going to argue. But this doesn't change the biblical fact that *parousia* is used to describe BOTH **1.** Christ's snatching up of the Church and **2.** His return to Earth shortly later. Since a thousand years is like a day to the Lord (Psalm 90:4 & 2 Peter 3:8), the seven years of the Tribulation would be akin to 10½ minutes!

It's the *timing* of the Rapture that believers disagree on and this is a secondary issue. Whether pre, mid or post, the Rapture *will* occur.

What Is "Eternal Judgment"?

This is the foundational doctrine that all persons will stand before the LORD for assessment and it will have eternal ramifications. Observe how this verse describes God:

> **There is only one Lawgiver and Judge, the one who is able to save and destroy.**
>
> **James 4:12**

This is a New Testament passage and it describes the LORD in terms of being a Judge, a Judge who's going to do one of two things with people depending on what they choose to do or not do on Earth. God's either going to **save** or **destroy**. Whether salvation or destruction, the judgment is eternal, meaning it applies to the never-ending age to come, which is the age of "the new heavens and new earth" (2 Peter 3:7,13).

There are four general judgments involving people and they apply to: **1.** the unredeemed who have died throughout history (i.e. the lost), **2.** New Covenant believers, **3.** the unsaved still alive when Christ returns to the Earth at the end of the Tribulation and **4.** Old Testament saints.

1. **The Great White Throne Judgment** applies to the first group.
2. **The Judgment Seat of Christ** applies to believers.
3. **The Sheep and Goat Judgment** applies to the third group.
4. **The Judgment of Matthew 19:28** applies to the fourth.

Since the Great White Throne Judgment (Revelation 20:11-15) is covered at length in chapter **14**, we'll only address the other three here…

The Judgment Seat of Christ

The Judgment Seat of Christ is detailed in these two passages:

> **For we** [believers] **must all appear before the judgment seat of Christ, so that each of us may receive what is due us for the things done while in the body, whether good or bad.**
> **11 Since, then, we know what it is to fear the Lord, we try to persuade others.**
> **2 Corinthians 5:10-11**

> **You, then, why do you judge your brother or sister? Or why do you treat them with contempt? For we** [believers] **will all stand before God's judgment seat…**
> **12 So then, each of us will give an account of ourselves to God. Romans 14:10, 12**

Paul is **addressing believers** in both passages and he says that *we* must all appear before the Judgment Seat of Christ. This is the judgment that believers will experience and is also called the *Bema (BAY-mah)* Judgment, named after the Greek word for "judgment seat."

The purpose of this judgment is obviously not to determine who will be granted eternal life, as all spiritually regenerated believers rightfully possess such. The exceptions would be those proven to be hypocrites, that is, fakes (e.g. Matthew 7:15-23, Luke 12:46 & 1 Corinthians 3:12-17). The purpose of this judgment is to acknowledge and reward Christians for the good things they did while in the body and to rebuke and penalize them for the bad, which will include an appraisal of our works. The "bad" will *not* concern sins already confessed because God forgives all such transgressions—*dismisses* them—and purifies accordingly (1 John 1:8-9).

The "bad" would include both unconfessed sins of commission and sins of omission. A sin of commission is something you *do*, like gossip/slander. A sin of omission involves something you *don't* do that you should have done, like God prompting a lady to give someone $100, but doesn't do it.

In the first passage above Paul adds something notable after stating that Christians will receive what is due them for the good or bad things they did: "Since then, we know what it is to fear the Lord." The King James

Version translates this as "Knowing therefore the terror of the Lord." This statement makes zero sense *if* believers just receive rewards at the Judgment Seat, as I've heard some ministers erroneously teach. Knowing that we will be held accountable for the bad things we do in this life can inspire some healthy "terror." It's spiritually healthy to regularly remind ourselves that we will one day stand before the throne of God and give an accounting of our lives, which is why the writer of Hebrews stressed it (Hebrews 4:13). The fear of the Lord inspires holy (pure) living. It inspires "keeping with repentance."

A minister argued that the Greek word for "bad" in 2 Corinthians 5:10 doesn't refer to moral evil and so, he claimed, believers won't be held accountable for unconfessed sins, including sins of omission. He contended that the word only means "worthless" in the manner of a piece of fruit that's rotten. Actually, the Greek term for "bad," *phaulos (FOW-los)*, *can* refer to moral evil, as plainly observed in John 3:20 and 5:29.

The good news is that God "is faithful and just and will **forgive us our sins** and **purify us from all unrighteousness**" whenever we humbly 'fess up (1 John 1:9), which means that we will *not* be culpable for these transgressions at the Judgment Seat. This is a spur to "keep in repentance."

The Greek word for 'judgment' in reference to the sixth basic doctrine—"eternal judgment" (Hebrews 6:2)—is *krima (KREE-mah)*, which means "judgment, verdict or lawsuit." The Greek for 'judgment seat' in the phrase "judgment seat of Christ" is a different word, the aforementioned *bema*, which refers to a platform from which justice is administered.

Because of this, some might suggest that the sixth basic doctrine—eternal judgment—doesn't apply to believers, but it does. For instance, James 3:1 says that "Not many of you should become teachers, my fellow believers, because you know that we who teach will be *judged* more strictly." James was addressing believers and says that those who teach will be judged more sternly. They will "receive a stricter judgment" (NASB and NKJV). The word "judgment" (or "judged" in the NIV) is the aforementioned *krima* used in the phrase "eternal judgment" in Hebrews 6:2. Where do you suppose those who teach God's Word will experience this stricter judgment? Not the Great White Throne Judgment, since that judgment applies strictly to *un*believers. No, these teachers will be judged at the Judgment Seat of Christ, where Christians are appraised.

Note what the Lord says in this verse:

> **"Anyone who speaks a word against the Son of Man** [Jesus] **will be forgiven, but anyone who speaks against the Holy Spirit will <u>not</u> be forgiven, either <u>in this age</u> or <u>the age to come</u>." Matthew 12:32**

The implication is that some sins—sins *not* confessed and forgiven **in this age**—must be dealt with and forgiven **in the age to come**. Believers will be held accountable for these sins at the Judgment Seat, penalized and ultimately forgiven. This does not in any way mean that the sufferings of Christ were insufficient to save us. All of our sins that are "under the blood" are forgiven; it's the sins that are not "under the blood" when we die that must be addressed at the Bema Judgment.

Someone might argue that Yeshua died on the cross for our past, present *and* future sins and therefore it's not necessary to keep in repentance to be forgiven of sins not yet committed. While it's true that Jesus died for our future sins along with our past and present ones, you can't very well confess something you haven't even done yet, which is why 1 John 1:8-9 is in the Bible, as well as similar passages, like Proverbs 28:13 (also see 2 Corinthians 12:21). Those who die with unconfessed sin will have to answer for these sins at the Judgment Seat since they were not confessed and forgiven *before* they physically died. Because these offenses weren't dismissed, they'll be accountable to them. While believers won't have to suffer the ultimate wage of sin since Christ paid the penalty of death in our place, they will be penalized as the Lord dictates at the Judgment Seat.

Some object to the notion of believers being judged on the grounds that Christ returns "to bring salvation to those who are waiting for him" and (supposedly) not to judge them (Hebrews 9:28). Yes, the Lord is returning to bring salvation to believers, but this does not negate the reality and necessity of the Bema Judgment.

I've known believers who routinely rip off people in business or readily engage in gossip & slander, usually due to hidden (but obvious) envy, rivalry and malice. The latter poisons listeners' minds against fellow believers—often believers they've never even met—and this naturally creates division in the body of Christ. The Enemy loves this! What doctrine of demons have these people embraced to cause them to walk in such blatant unrighteousness without penitence? Answer: The false doctrine that believers can sin all they want with no care of repentance and never be held accountable because Jesus is returning to bring rewards to believers and no judgment whatsoever. It's a wicked and thoroughly unbiblical doctrine! The Judgment Seat of Christ is part of the Six Basic Doctrines and is therefore a foundational teaching of genuine Christianity. It inspires God-fearing holiness and a spirit of humble repentance in believers. It protects us from false doctrine, like the idea that believers won't have to stand before the Lord at the Judgment Seat of Christ and give an account. Hebrews 4:13 says differently (look it up).

The Sheep and Goat Judgment

This particular judgment concerns non-Christians still alive on Earth *after* God's judgment falls on humanity during the 7-year Tribulation, which is detailed in Revelation 6-19. When the mighty Christ returns to Earth to set up His millennial kingdom He will judge the living nations, as shown in Matthew 25:31-46. They will be judged according to how they treated Tribulation saints, that is, those who embrace the gospel during the Trib.

You see, believers will be greatly persecuted during the Antichrist's worldwide reign of terror. When Christ returns, the surviving people of the nations will be judged according to how they treated these Tribulation saints. Those who had regard for believers—that is, the body of Christ on Earth—and acted accordingly will be designated as "sheep." They will be spiritually regenerated and allowed to enter the Millennium as born-again mortals (which is the condition of believers in this present evil age, including you and me). However, those who disregarded and persecuted believers will be cast into the lake of fire, God's garbage dump, to suffer the second death.

The Judgment of Old Testament Saints

These people will be judged at the time of their resurrection when the Lord returns to the Earth to establish His millennial reign, which takes place at the end of the Tribulation, as shown in the following two passages…

First, Daniel prophesied in Daniel 12:1-2 that the resurrection of the Israelites will not take place until after a "time of distress" so great that such a thing never occurred before in the history of humanity. This refers to the Tribulation detailed in the book of Revelation (chapters 6-19). Daniel speaks in general terms of the righteous who will be delivered or resurrected at this time. He refers to them as "your people"—i.e. God's people—and "everyone whose name is found written in the book," which would of course include more than just Old Testament holy people; it would include Christian martyrs during the Tribulation, as well as living believers who survived the Tribulation.

The Lord got more specific about the resurrection and judgment of Old Testament saints in this passage:

> **Jesus said to them, "Truly I tell you, at the renewal of all things, when the Son of Man sits on his glorious throne, you who have followed me will also sit on twelve thrones, judging the twelve tribes of Israel. [29]And everyone who has left houses or brothers or sisters or father or mother or wife or children or fields for my sake will receive a hundred times as much and will inherit eternal life. [30] But many who are first will be last, and many who are last will be first."**
>
> **Matthew 19:28-30**

Some might inquire why Old Testament saints are not resurrected at the time of Jesus' return for His Church—that is, the Rapture—which is when believers are either bodily resurrected or translated (1 Thessalonians 4:13-18), but this idea is negated by the obvious fact that the Rapture concerns the Lord's return for the Church—His bride—and not His return for people of the Old Testament period who were in covenant with God.

8

Questions About Angels and Demons

What Are Angels?

The word 'angel' is *angelos (ANG-el-os)* in the biblical Greek[8] and *malak (mal-AWK)* in Hebrew, both of which simply mean "a **messenger**." While the messenger in question *could* be human (1 Kings 19:2), it typically refers to a supernatural courier conveying news or directives from God.

Further insight can be observed in this fundamental description of angels:

> **Are not all angels ministering spirits sent to serve those who will inherit salvation?**
>
> **Hebrews 1:14**

As you can see, angels are defined as "ministering *spirits*." They are not people, nor are they people who have become angels; they are *spiritual* beings distinct from humanity.

---

[8] Biblical Greek is *koine* Greek, meaning "the common dialect" of the Greek language in the 1st century (pronounced *KOY-nay*).

Angels are described as "*ministering* spirits," which means they are given to serve. Whom do they serve? Their Creator first and foremost, but the verse specifies that they are "sent [by God] to serve those who will inherit salvation." This means people because we're the ones who are to receive salvation. As such, **angels are serving spirits who serve the LORD and are commissioned to minister to people**, whether by conveying news and instructions or helping us in some other manner, like provision in time of need (1 Kings 19:5-7), ministry when we physically expire (Luke 16:22), fighting demonic spirits on our behalf (Daniel 10:12-13) and protection.

A good example of the latter can be observed here:

> [11] **For he** [God] **will command his angels**
> **concerning you**
> **to guard you in all your ways;**
> [12] **they will lift you up in their hands,**
> **so that you will not strike your foot**
> **against a stone.**
> [13] **You will tread on the lion and the cobra;**
> **you will trample the great lion and the serpent.**
> **Psalm 91:11-13**

What Are Fallen Angels?

The fact that angels are ministering spirits sent to serve people shows why satan & his fallen angels do **the precise opposite**—they constantly try to hinder or oppress people, especially God's people. One of their main objectives, of course, is to keep those who are lost from eternal salvation.

The rebellion and fall from Heaven of satan & his filthy angels occurred sometime *after* the creation of the Universe and human beings, yet *before* the devil's temptation of Eve, which means sometime between Genesis 1:31 and Genesis 3:1 (according to the young Earth perspective). This time period could involve many years, plenty of time for satan's harebrained coup attempt and their subsequent ousting from Heaven (Luke 10:18).

The bottom line is: **There are angels who work for you and fallen angels—demons—who work against you.** Evil spirits are not ministering for you; they're ministering *against* you.

What Is the Diff Between the Holy Spirit and Angels?

The Holy Spirit is God who *indwells* the spiritually reborn believer. This makes every genuine Christian a "temple" of God (1 Corinthians 6:19). The Spirit's function is to help, counsel, teach, comfort and lead believers (John 14:26 & 16:13). Angels, by contrast, do not dwell in you or lead you. They are here to *minister* for you in one capacity or another.

It is the Holy Spirit's job to "guide you into all truth" (John 16:13), which is why Romans 8:14 says "those who are led by the Spirit of God are the children of God." Notice that it does *not* say "those who are led by angels are the children of God." Why? Because angels aren't here to lead us, the Holy Spirit is. Angels are here to *serve* us.

Their services include conveying Divine messages, which is why angels are also called "messengers." However, angels do not *teach* us spiritual truth (reality) as the Holy Spirit does. It's the Holy Spirit—*God*—who provides revelation knowledge.

You could say that the Holy Spirit ministers *to* believers whereas angels minister *for* us. If I lay hands on you and pray, I'm ministering *to* you whereas if I catch you when you fall, I'm ministering *for* you. Just the same, when the Holy Spirit gives you a revelation, the Spirit is ministering to you whereas when angels help you escape a trap they're ministering for you, like when an angel helped Peter escape from prison (Acts 12:5-10).

A pastor gave a testimony of how the LORD saved him from certain death while serving as a missionary. He was about to put his luggage on a plane at a small airport in the bush when he discerned a voice telling him not to do it. He obeyed and the plane crashed on takeoff. In his testimony he wrongly attributed this voice to "his guardian angel." No, it was the Holy Spirit, who indwelt him and guided him. *If* he had entered the plane and was miraculously saved when it crashed then that could be attributed to guardian angels. Do you see the difference?

Who Created Angels? Are They "Watchers"?

Angels were created by Christ:

> **The Son is the image of the invisible God, the firstborn over all creation. [16] For by him all things were created: things in heaven and on earth, visible and invisible, whether thrones or powers or rulers or authorities; all things have been created through him and for him.**
> **Colossians 1:15-16**

Angels were present when God created the Heavens and the Earth, which can be observed in Job 38:3-7 wherein the LORD refers to them as "morning stars," who sang together and shouted for joy at God's awesome creation. The point is that angels *already existed* at the time.

Angels not only observed the formation of the physical Universe and all things in it, they've been watching events on Earth ever since; at least some of them. This is akin to sports fans at a big game or spectators in an ancient Roman arena. Paul put it like this: "For it seems to me that God has put us apostles on display at the end of the procession, like those condemned to die in the arena. We have been made a spectacle to the whole universe, to angels as well as to human beings" (1 Corinthians 4:9).

Our cats like to gaze out our windows and so Carol & I dub the windows "cat TV." You could say that the Earth is "angel TV." Angels are watching us and seem to be fascinated by us; Christ pointed out that they celebrate when someone turns from sin to God (Luke 15:7,10).

The fact that at least some angels are watchers can be observed in Daniel 4 where the Chaldean Aramaic *iyr (eer)* is used to describe them, which means "a watcher; i.e. an angel as guardian" (verses 13, 17 & 23). This doesn't mean watcher in a merely passive sense, as *iyr* stems from an action-oriented Hebrew word that means "on the watch." One of their jobs is likely to record events, including our words. A minister testified that she was able to see in the spiritual realm on one occasion and saw an angel nearby chronicling the conversations. Why would an angel chronicle words? Because Christ said we'll be acquitted or condemned by them (Matthew 12:37) and this can't happen if they're not somehow recorded.

Both Cherubim and "living creatures" are described as being "covered with eyes" (Ezekiel 10:12 & Revelation 4:6-9). This is likely a figurative statement perhaps suggesting that watcher angels are of the cherub and living creature variety.

While watcher angels observe and document what's unfolding on Earth and take action to the degree that we allow them, they're not God and therefore don't know everything that's going to happen; for instance, they don't know the day or hour of Christ's return (Matthew 24:35-36).

How Do Angels "Take Action as We Allow Them"?

Angels are ministering spirits sent to serve the people **they're assigned to** (Matthew 18:10 & Psalm 91:11), but what is it they respond to? Observe:

> **Praise the Lord, you his angels,**
> **you mighty ones who do his bidding,**
> **who obey his word.**
>
> **Psalm 103:20**

Angels don't just obey the bidding of the LORD, they obey His word period. Here's a more literal translation of the verse:

> **Bless the LORD, you His angels,**
> **Mighty in strength, who perform His word,**
> **Obeying <u>the voice</u> of His word!**
>
> **Psalm 103:20** (NASB)

The purpose of angels is to **perform God's Word**. You could say that their occupation is obeying the voice of God's Word. The Hebrew word for 'voice' is *qol (kohl)*, which means "sound, voice." That's what angels obey—the *sound* or *voice* of the Word of God. But does your Bible make any sounds of itself? Does any passage make a sound when you read it or study it? No, it only makes sound *if* you **speak it**! That's why it's so important that you get the power of your tongue into play and start speaking the Word of God in faith (Proverbs 18:21), particularly the promises of God that apply to the New Testament believer. And, remember, **all the promises of God are "yes" in Christ** (2 Corinthians 1:20). This means that, if you're in covenant with God through Christ—i.e. you are "*in* Christ"—you can claim by faith any general promise of God you find in the Scriptures that strikes a chord in your spirit!

Take the promises of Divine protection from Psalm 34. When facing some type of human attack, you can claim by faith verses 7, 17, 19-20 & 22, all of which promise God's deliverance when suffering severe persecution.

Why is it that speaking God's Word in faith is so powerful, unleashing angels to perform it? Simple: **people are the only beings created in God's likeness and called to be co-heirs with Christ**:

> **So God created mankind <u>in his own image</u>,**
> **<u>in the image of God</u> he created them;**
> **male and female he created them.**
>
> **Genesis 1:27**

The LORD created the Heavens and the Earth simply by speaking them into existence (Genesis 1). People are created in God's image and thus have this power as well. Of course, our words only have power corresponding to our faith, as Christ pointed out:

> **"Have faith in God," Jesus answered. [23] "Truly I tell you, if anyone says to this mountain, 'Go, throw yourself into the sea,' and <u>does not doubt in their heart but believes that what they say will happen</u>, <u>it will be done for them</u>."** **Mark 11:22-23**

The Douay-Rheims Bible translates it as "Have the faith of God." We need to walk in faith as the LORD walks in faith. We are God's duplicates on Earth, created in our Creator's likeness…

> **Therefore, be <u>imitators of God</u>, as dearly loved children.**
>
> **Ephesians 5:1**

You are called to **imitate God**! And you can do it because you're a *child* of God, born of God's seed; just learn how to live out of your new nature.

In Mark 11 above, Yeshua goes on to say: "Truly I tell you, <u>if anyone says</u> to this mountain, 'Go, throw yourself into the sea,' and does not doubt in their heart but believes that what they say will happen, it will be done for them" (verse 23). He says "if *anyone* says." He doesn't even specify that the person has to be a Christian. This applies to *anyone* created in God's likeness, how much more so those born-anew of the seed of Christ?

He continues: "if anyone says to *this* mountain." There was a mountain nearby and the Lord used it to illustrate His point. "If anyone *says* to this mountain, 'Go, throw yourself into the sea,' and does not doubt in their heart but believes that what they *say* will happen, it will be done for them." This is an example of hyperbole, which is exaggeration for effect. The "mountain" is figurative, not literal. If there is, say, an obstacle in your way you can utilize the power of words spoken in faith and remove that obstacle. But—and this is an important "but"—you have to *believe* that what you *say* will happen and not doubt in your heart.

The Messiah doesn't go into the mechanics of how this works, just that it does. But, in view of the other passages we've examined, it's safe to say that the angels appointed to you respond to your words spoken in faith because **1.** they are assigned to you, **2.** it's their very purpose to serve you, and **3.** you are created in the likeness of God and are a co-heir with Christ. Thus they are released to help you in your situation… or they're released to *not* help you in the event that you speak words of unbelief and act accordingly.

Are Fallen Angels Also Evil Spirits and Demons?

Yes, disgraced angels that fell from Heaven after their failed coup are one-and-the-same as evil spirits, which are demons, as witnessed here:

> **...Jesus traveled about from one town and village to another, proclaiming the good news of the kingdom of God. The Twelve were with him, [2] and also some women who had been cured of evil spirits and diseases: Mary (called Magdalene) from whom seven demons had come out;**
>
> **Luke 8:1-2**

As you can see, fallen angels are described as **evil spirits**. The Greek word for "evil" is *ponéros (pon-ay-ROSS)*, meaning "bad, wicked, malicious." This shows that evil spirits are the opposite of heavenly angels, which are good spirits. The latter function in submission to the LORD and therefore serve people (Hebrews 1:14) whereas evil spirits are "bad" and so do the precise opposite—they seek to hurt people one way or another. This is in line with their leader's mandate "to kill, steal and destroy" (John 10:10).

Speaking of their leader, satan is the "father of lies" (John 8:44) and so his wicked minions constantly try to *deceive* people. Take 'ghosts,' which are supposedly the disembodied souls of the dead stuck on this plane and haunting a particular locale. Isn't it possible or even likely that this type of paranormal phenomena is the deceptive activity of demons?

Why Are Demons Described as Unclean or Filthy?

Evil spirits are also referred to as *unclean* or *impure* spirits:

> **Jesus called his twelve disciples to him and gave them authority to drive out impure spirits and to heal every disease and sickness.**
>
> **Matthew 10:1**

The Greek word for "impure" is *akathartos (ak-ATH-ar-tos)*, which simply means unclean or impure. It reveals that evil spirits are filthy. This makes sense in light of the fact that 'holy' refers to absolute purity, the natural result of being separated unto God. The LORD is absolutely pure—holy—and so anyone consecrated to God must be pure. Hence, anyone who rejects the Almighty and is cast from His presence becomes the opposite—*un*holy, *im*pure. Since you can't get further from God than the irredeemable angels, they're utterly unholy—unclean, impure, filthy.

Being filthy, there's a stench to unclean spirits in the spirit realm. This explains why one spiritually-sensitive minister said he could always recognize someone who was walking in sexual perversion, like homosexuality, when they came up for prayer at his meetings. He said there was a foul odor in the spirit.

One of my relatives married a witch and she wasted no time in getting her new husband to totally separate from his family. My nephew met her when he was a child and he kept curiously asking "What's that smell? Something stinks!" He was just a little kid at the time and said the odor smelled like vomit. No one present knew what he was talking about, so he was obviously picking something up in the spirit. Children are more sensitive to the spiritual realm and are therefore apt to pick up things that hardened adults can no longer perceive. Consider the typical scenario where kids think there's a "monster" under the bed or in the closet. Is it simply their imagination or are they picking up an evil spirit in the vicinity?

This explains why the Bible instructs us:

> **Therefore, <u>get rid of all moral filth and the evil that is so prevalent</u> and humbly accept the word planted in you, which can save you.**
>
> **James 1:21**

While believers are *born* holy in their spirits when they receive spiritual regeneration (Titus 3:5), **practical** holiness only occurs as you learn to put off your flesh—the "old self"—and live according to your new righteous nature—the "new self"—with the help of the Holy Spirit (Ephesians 4:22-

24). This is what theologians refer to as the process of sanctification—*purification.* And part of this process includes doing what James instructed: "get rid of all moral filth and the evil that is so prevalent."

Why is this important? Simple: Impure spirits are naturally attracted to that which is morally impure. Just as flies are attracted to doo-doo and rats are drawn to garbage, so filthy spirits are attracted to that which is morally filthy. So, get rid of all moral filth and you'll stop attracting filthy spirits! It's just common sense. Also get rid of fear and worry (Philippians 4:6-7).

Where Does the Bible Detail satan's Fall?

The Lord said he "saw satan fall like lightning from heaven" (Luke 10:18). This monumental event is chronicled in the Old Testament using the kings of Babylon and Tyre as types (Isaiah 14:12 & Ezekiel 28:12-17). Ezekiel shows that satan was once a "**cherub**," an **angel** (28:14,16).

The New Testament offers a flashback to satan's fall from Heaven:

> **Then another sign appeared in heaven: an enormous red dragon with seven heads and ten horns and seven crowns on its heads. [4] Its tail swept a third of the stars out of the sky and flung them to the earth…**
> **[7] Then war broke out in heaven. Michael and his angels fought against the dragon, and the dragon and his angels fought back. [8] But he was not strong enough, and they lost their place in heaven. [9] The great dragon was hurled down—that ancient serpent called the devil, or satan, who leads the whole world astray. He was hurled to the earth, and his angels with him.**
>
> **Revelation 12:3-4,7-9**

This prophecy is likely a double reference and therefore has two applications: It refers to the devil's last gasp attempt to conquer Heaven during the mid-point of the future Tribulation (Revelation 6-19), but it's also a flashback to his original fall. Verse 4 figuratively indicates that **a**

third of the angels fell with the devil—the "red dragon"—to the Earth. "Stars" are a metaphorical reference to angels (Job 38:7).

The idea that this passage is a "double reference" is in line with **the law of double reference**, which is the tendency of biblical prophecies to have two applications—one relevant to the general time of the prophecy and another far-flung, whether the distant future or past.

By the way, the fact that the devil & his filthy spirits *again* attempt to conquer Heaven shows that they're hopelessly incorrigible. They never learn from their mistakes. It's reminiscent of the saying: "Insanity is doing the same thing over & over again expecting different results." If this is so, satan & his underlings are decidedly insane.

So, satan is described as a cherub who was kicked out of Heaven, along with a third of the subordinate angels who rebelled with him.

Where Do the Devil & His Filthy Angels Dwell?

The Lord said that the lake of fire was "prepared for the devil **and his angels**" (Matthew 25:41) as their eternal prison, yet they currently roam the Earth, not in the physical realm, but the spiritual:

> **For our struggle is not against flesh and blood, but against the rulers, against the authorities, against the powers of this dark world and against <u>the spiritual forces of evil in the heavenly realms</u>.**
>
> **Ephesians 6:12**

The "spiritual forces of evil" dwell in "the heavenly realms." This refers to the **Underworld**, which is the dark spiritual dimension that underpins the Earth & Universe (Philippians 2:9-11 & Revelation 5:2-3). This is where the devil & his fallen angels operate. They don't dwell in hell because the lake of fire is hell and no one has been cast there yet.[9] They

---

[9] Hades (Sheol) is merely a "pit" in the Underworld, as detailed in chapter **15**.

inhabit the dark realm of the Underworld and operate from this plane—"roaming the earth, going back and forth in it," as satan put it (Job 1:7 & 2:2). This explains something Peter said:

> **Be alert and of sober mind. Your enemy the devil prowls around like a roaring lion looking for someone to devour.**
>
> **1 Peter 5:8**

It was pointed out in chapter 3 that the Underworld resulted *when* satan & his minions were kicked out of Heaven. The *dark* heavenlies did not exist prior to that point.

Once the devil & his filthy underlings set up shop in this dark realm—the Underworld—it naturally hindered the activity of the faithful angels on Earth. They had to descend and ascend via "Jacob's ladder" to carry out God's will in response to faith and prayer (Genesis 28:12).

Are There Hierarchies and Territories of Evil Spirits?

Yes. We know there are hierarchies of *heavenly* angels since there are 'archangels,' a term simply meaning *ruling* angel. Michael is the top one, which can be observed in his leading the fight against satan's coup (Revelation 12:7). Meanwhile Gabriel is the archangel of annunciation in light of his vital messages to Daniel, Zechariah and Mary in the Scriptures.

As for fallen angels, notice what this text says:

> **For our struggle is not against flesh and blood, but against the rulers, against the authorities, against the powers of this dark world and against the spiritual forces of evil in the heavenly realms.**
>
> **Ephesians 6:12**

The "spiritual forces of evil" are comprised of three different categories—"rulers," "authorities" and "powers." This reveals a hierarchy in the spiritual realm with the devil as the wicked despot of his dark kingdom with ranks of filthy minions under his command.

These foul spirits are assigned regions on Earth in which they negatively influence political authorities and the corresponding populace. For instance, in Daniel we observe "the prince of Persia" and "the prince of Greece," both demonic authorities consigned to these areas (Daniel 10:13,20). Additional evidence can be observed when a conglomerate of demons named "Legion" begged the Mighty Christ not to send them out of the region (Mark 5:10). Why? Obviously because it was their assigned territory, their 'home.' Also, the glorified Lord said Pergamum was where satan's throne was located (Revelation 2:13).

This data corresponds to the fact that the devil is "the god of this world" and thus "the whole world is under the control" of the kingdom of darkness to one degree or another (2 Corinthians 4:4 & 1 John 5:19). Some places, like Pergamum in the 1st century, are subject to greater satanic control than others. San Francisco, Hollywood, New York City, DC, New Orleans and Key West are prime examples in modern America.

Why Do Demons Desire to Possess People?

Evil spirits seek to possess men & women in order to operate more concretely in the physical realm. Being spiritual in nature, they're limited to the spiritual plane and only operate in the physical realm in an indirect manner, unless they can take total possession of a person, which they can only do with the person's consent, conscious or subconscious.

Mark 5:12-13 shows that demons sometimes even seek to possess animals, but this requires authorization from the Sovereign LORD. Why do they need Christ's permission? Obviously because animals lack the ability to grant or reject consent.

That said, Genesis 6:1-4 shows that demons have the power to operate in the physical realm in a more direct manner. On this occasion fallen angels—the "sons of God"—copulated with women, which gave birth to people with demonically tainted DNA. God considered this a great transgression and so imprisoned these evil spirits in *tartaroó* to be held for judgment (2 Peter 2:4 & Jude 1:6). This of course deterred the rest of the fallen angels from sinning in this manner and so the height of their manifestation in the physical realm is via possession of a person or animal.

Why Do Evil Spirits Hate People So Much?

Because:

1. People are created in the image of God.
2. Angels lack the privilege and position granted redeemed people; that is, being co-heirs with Christ and thus seated with Him at the right hand of the Father in a positional sense (Romans 8:17, Hebrews 1:13 & Ephesians 2:6).
3. Unlike demons, people are redeemable. Fallen angels are *ir*redeemable because they had full knowledge of the consequences of their rebellion whereas Adam & Eve did not. This is covered in chapter **3**.
4. Angels are commissioned to serve people, and since arrogant angels didn't want to do this, they rebelled, which resulted in their ouster from Heaven.

What Is the Prime Directive of Foul Spirits?

To answer, consider Christ's encounter with a man in the Decapolis:

> **They went across the lake to the region of the**
> **Gerasenes. 2 When Jesus got out of the boat, a man**
> **with an impure spirit came from the tombs to meet**
> **him. 3 This man lived in the tombs, and no one could**
> **bind him anymore, not even with a chain. 4 For he had**
> **often been chained hand and foot, but he tore the**
> **chains apart and broke the irons on his feet. No one**
> **was strong enough to subdue him. 5 Night and day**

among the tombs and in the hills he would cry out and cut himself with stones.
6 When he saw Jesus from a distance, he ran and fell on his knees in front of him. 7 He shouted at the top of his voice, "What do you want with me, Jesus, Son of the Most High God? In God's name don't torture me!"
8 For Jesus had said to him, "Come out of this man, you impure spirit!"
9 Then Jesus asked him, "What is your name?"
"My name is Legion," he replied, "for we are many."
10 And he begged Jesus again and again not to send them out of the area.

Mark 5:1-10

This demon-possessed man[10] had great strength and so no one could subdue him. People in the area were understandably scared of him. Yet notice that the spirits who possessed him were *terrified* of Christ.

The man's inordinate strength can be attributed to the numerous wicked spirits that possessed him. They interestingly referred to themselves in a composite sense as "Legion," which is a Latin word for a division of the Roman army, 5120 infantry, with additional cavalry at the time of Christ. In general terms, the word refers to a very large number and so we can assume that there were hundreds or even thousands of demons in this man. Think of it in regards to a snake pit in which hundreds of snakes writhe together. The name of this group of demons—"Legion"—is akin to the names delinquent gangs adopt, like The Bloods or The Mecca Knights.

Notice what these wicked spirits compelled the man to do—he wandered amongst the tombs and hills crying out in torment day & night, regularly cutting himself with stones. Today we call this type of behavior self-harm or self-injury. People who do this are being harassed by demons. They

---

[10] Luke's account also records only one demon-possessed man (Luke 8:26-39) whereas Matthew's rendition cites two possessed men (Matthew 8:28-34). How do we explain this seeming discrepancy? Obviously one of the demoniacs was much more prominent, likely due to the myriad demons possessing him, and so Mark & Luke simply disregarded the secondary man in their accounts.

may not necessarily be possessed, but they're definitely being oppressed to the point of harming themselves. Anytime you come across people bent on self-destruction you can be sure that evil spirits are involved.

A good example of this is this Swedish band that promotes suicide and self-harm in whatever form. The vocalist nonchalantly informed that there have been several cases of fans committing suicide or, at least, *trying* to commit suicide upon consuming the group's music. He testified to his own struggles with depression & torment, including frequent stays at mental health facilities. Needless to say, evil spirits are attracted to this band like snakes to a snake pit; and they use this man & his music to spread mental illness and self-destruction to anyone attracted to the group.

Richard Speck, who slew 8 nursing students at a Chicago dorm in July, 1966, tried to commit suicide in his hotel room two days later. His senseless murder spree was obviously spurred by the kingdom of darkness. You see, wicked spirits *use* people to carry out their directive to destroy life and then *lose* them, inspiring them to destroy their very selves.

Demons revel in the destruction of people because they hate us for the four reasons cited earlier. They're gravely envious and mad as hell, literally, because fallen people are redeemable whereas they're *ir*redeemable. Thus demons do the very opposite of heavenly angels. Angels *serve* people (Hebrews 1:14) whereas evil spirits harass and destroy.

Actually, demons are hell-bent on destroying life period. This can be seen in the three Hebrew letters of satan's name—shin/tet/nun—which define his prime directive: the destruction of anything that contains life.

The fact that filthy spirits are obsessed with destroying life can be observed by this conglomerate of demons—"Legion"—who begged Christ to allow them to possess a herd of pigs nearby, which he allowed. The spirits thus left the man and went into the roughly 2000 swine wherein the herd promptly rushed down the steep bank and into the lake where they drowned (Mark 5:11-13). Why would they drive the pigs to do this? Because demons are hell-bent on the destruction of life.

How Do You Prevent Demonic Oppression?

How did this man from the Gerasenes get possessed by so many demons? Was he just innocently walking along one day and an evil spirit suddenly possessed him and proceeded to invite his buddies to join in? No. As noted earlier, demons are *impure* or *filthy* spirits and so they're naturally attracted to that which is morally filthy. If a person yields to fleshly thoughts and starts to dwell on them to the point of obsession and the corresponding evil behavior it'll attract demonic spirits, which can lead to oppression or, worse, possession. Once a person is possessed, additional demons are attracted to the wicked "party."

This is one of the reasons why James 1:21 instructs us to "get rid of all moral filth and the evil that is so prevalent" and, instead, feed on the Word of God (Matthew 4:4). It's why Paul encouraged believers to get in the habit of meditating on what is true, noble, right, pure, admirable, excellent and praiseworthy; he even stressed that this attracts the peace of God (Philippians 4:6-9). Do you want the peace of God in your life or the torment of wicked spirits? Obviously the former. Then "**be careful what you think, because your thoughts run your life**" (Proverbs 4:23 NCV).

This is what the Bible calls **renewing the mind** (Romans 12:2 & Ephesians 4:22-24). It's simply changing your thought life from the bad and destructive to the good and productive. If we truly knew the power and life that is available to us through using our imagination for the positive, we'd be jumping up & down with enthusiasm!

All this is linked to what theologians call **the process of sanctification**. This simply refers to **purification**, which starts with spiritual rebirth (James 1:18) and continues throughout the believer's life as you're "transformed by the renewing of your mind." This not only saves believers from flawed ideologies and poisonous mindsets, it protects us from demonic oppression or, worse, possession. Poisonous mindsets, by the way, are *noémas (noh-AY-mahs)*, which are mental strongholds that develop over time and by-and-large determine a person's actions. There are whole ideologies that are demonic in nature, like communism.

As important as it is to "get rid of all moral filth and the evil that is so prevalent" and feed on God's Word (James 1:21), it's just as vital to **cultivate a relationship with the LORD** by drawing near:

> **Submit yourselves, then, to God. Resist the devil, and he will flee from you. [8] Come near to God and he will come near to you. Wash your hands, you sinners, and purify your hearts, you double-minded. [9] Grieve, mourn and wail. Change your laughter to mourning and your joy to gloom. [10] Humble yourselves before the Lord, and he will lift you up.**
>
> **James 4:7-10**

Verse 7 says to "resist **the devil** and **he** will flee from you." This is not solely referring to satan himself, but rather to the kingdom of darkness in general and specifically the evils spirits that are attacking the believer. How do I know? Because James was addressing multitudes of believers scattered amongst many nations, which includes us today (James 1:1), and the devil's *not* omnipresent, like the Almighty (everywhere at the same time). As such, satan can only attack one believer or a group of believers at a point in time, like he did with his temptation of Christ in the desert (Matthew 4:1-11). To attack numerous believers across the globe he *has* to use the network of demonic powers under him. Think about it in terms of one nation attacking another. We say, for instance, that "Bush invaded Iraq" when, in fact, Bush was half a planet away. It's the same thing in the kingdom of darkness. The devil may be assaulting you, but it's not satan himself, but rather foul spirits working under his perverse command.

With this understanding, notice what this passage says about deflecting the kingdom of darkness: The key is to simply **draw near to God**, which results in God drawing near to you. Coming near to the LORD includes repenting of immorality and feeding on the Word of truth, but it's also a matter of fostering a close *relationship*. This sends evil spirits fleeing!

That said, spirits of infirmities are a different issue. These types of evil spirits induce a mental or physical malady in those they assault, such as muteness/deafness (Mark 9:17-29) or a crippling condition (Luke 13:10-

16). The victims of these spirits are not necessarily involved in moral filth, but rather are people who are spiritually feeble and ignorant, particularly in regards to spiritual warfare. In other words, **spirits of infirmities take advantage of *ignorance*** (Hosea 4:6). Thankfully, knowledge and wisdom empower people and will protect you from such spirits (Proverbs 24:5).

Why Are Evil Spirits Attracted to "Dry Places"?

Christ taught that impure spirits naturally seek "arid places," which means dry, waterless areas (Matthew 12:43). This isn't referring to places that are *physically* dry, like deserts, but rather spaces that are *spiritually* dry; that is, **places where God is absent**. You see, the LORD is likened to Living Water in the Bible—God is ***The* Fountain of Life** who gushes forth life (Psalm 36:9). This parallels what Christ said about Himself and the Spirit:

> **...Jesus stood and said in a loud voice, "Let anyone who is thirsty come to me and drink. 38 Whoever believes in me, as Scripture has said, rivers of living water will flow from within them." 39 By this he meant the Spirit, whom those who believed in him were later to receive.**
>
> **John 7:37-39**

The Lord encourages those who are spiritually thirsty—spiritually dry—to come to Him and drink. He then points out that those who receive the Holy Spirit will have "rivers of living water" flowing within them.

The key to repelling demonic spirits is to stay well-watered by cultivating a relationship with the LORD. Saturate yourself with the things of God: prayer, simple communion, Scripture reading & meditation, praise & worship, fellowship with genuine believers, mutual submission (Ephesians 5:21), etc. As you do this, you automatically stave off wicked spirits. How so? Because **demons seek places absent of God's presence**.

This reveals the danger in becoming spiritually dry. When a pastor & his assembly become spiritually arid it attracts evil spirits, who'll start "whispering in their ears." Spiritually-dry people are naturally susceptible to "doctrines of demons," which gets them off track if embraced (1 Timothy 4:1). "Doctrines" refers to teachings or instructions; so "doctrines of demons" simply means *teachings* or *instructions* of demons. Take, for example, white or black fellowships that embrace racist ideologies: Members of the KKK typically profess to be Christians, with some members even being church leaders; then there's Jeremiah Wright's hateful, crackpot false gospel. How can people of God—even fulltime ministers—go so far astray? Because they allowed themselves to become spiritually dry, which attracted evil spirits; and out of desperation they gave ear to doctrines of demons.

What Is the "Put Off" / "Put On" Principle?

Let's read the full passage where Yeshua said demonic spirits seek dry places:

> **"When an impure spirit comes out of a person, it goes through arid places seeking rest and does not find it. 44Then it says, 'I will return to the house I left.' When it arrives, it finds the house unoccupied, swept clean and put in order. 45 Then it goes and takes with it seven other spirits more wicked than itself, and they go in and live there. And the final condition of that person is worse than the first."**
>
> **Matthew 12:43-45**

When a filthy spirit leaves a person, it seeks rest in arid places—spaces absent of God and the living waters thereof. The presence of God torments wicked spirits and so they seek succor in dry places. If the demon can't find such a place it will simply go back to the "house" it left—*if* it can.

But why wouldn't a demon be able to find a waterless place—a space lacking God and the things of God? We can only conjecture based on the scriptural evidence. We know that evil spirits are territorial; that is, they're assigned specific areas (Daniel 10:13,20). We also know that they're lazy.

In Jesus' hypothetical example, the demon couldn't find anywhere in its immediate territory for rest so it lazily goes back to the person it left and finds him "swept clean and put in order" yet "unoccupied." This reveals that the person had enough discipline to get his life in order and "cleaned up his act," but he wasn't occupied with God and the corresponding things of God. It was an outward change lacking inward reality. So, the demon acquires seven other spirits more malevolent than itself and returns to the unoccupied "house." The end state of the man is thus worse than before.

This is a spur to seek more than mere superficial change based on self-discipline. You can't just "quit a habit" or "break a habit" without filling the vacuum with something positive. And God—who is *The* Fountain of Life—is the most positive 'thing' with which you can fill yourself. That's why the Bible teaches the principle of "putting off" ***and*** "putting on" (Ephesians 4:22-24). Right patterns must replace wrong ones. Good behaviors must replace sinful activities. Productive thoughts must displace destructive ones.

On a side note, this passage shows that some demons are more malevolent than others.

How Do Evil Spirits Get Attached to Kids?

Demons can get attached to kids or youths if they're regularly in an unhealthy environment where there's significant demonic activity. For instance, if a child grows up in a household where there's substantial immoral activity (including pharisaical legalism) or one of the parents is demon-possessed or if they get involved with libertine gangs or groups.

The reason demons are able to attach themselves to children or youths in such situations is because—being young and influence-able—they're vulnerable. Parents and guardians have a responsibility to protect kids under their authority, not just physically, but spiritually. Why do you think the Messiah took the time to bless the children (Matthew 19:13)? Yet, even in these cases, evil spirits *have* to have the permission of the individual—conscious or subconscious—to increasingly oppress them and ultimately possess them.

9

Questions About Human Government

What Does the Bible Say About Government?

The righteous laws of human governments and enforcement of those laws are God-ordained for the purpose of punishing criminals, which includes the right to execute when appropriate (Romans 13:1-6). In short, the LORD uses flawed governments in general as an instrument to bring order to societies in our fallen world since they protect innocent citizens from thugs. This is addressed further in chapter **12**.

Unfortunately, governments can become corrupt wherein they do more harm than good for its citizens; and potentially other nations. How can noble citizens prevent their government from becoming corrupt? Obviously, they *have* to be involved in the political process on one level or another otherwise evil people will take the reins.

What Is the Most Prominent Form of Government

The most "popular" or reoccurring form of government in human history is the kingship or dictatorship where what the ruler says goes. Different societies use different names for such an authoritarian ruler—king, queen, pharaoh, lord, caesar, sultan, kaizer, emperor, maharaji, khan, führer, general secretary, dictator, etc.—but **they all come down to one person calling the shots for a country of people** with the corresponding nepotism. Even tribes have their chiefs.

The best-case scenario in an authoritarian-type government is, of course, to have a good ruler. The problem with this is that the ruler will eventually perish and someone else will take over, often a family member. What happens when the new person lacks the nobility of the former? A good example from the Bible is the righteous kings of Judah, such as Jehoshaphat, Jotham, Hezekiah and Josiah. The nation was blessed under the noble leadership of these kings but, unfortunately, all of their sons were ignoble, destructive authorities and the people suffered accordingly.

Even if you have a good ruler, what if he or she goes bad, as was the case with Saul, Solomon, Joash, Amaziah and Uzziah in the Bible?

In any case, this authoritarian model is the default setting for government throughout human history. The top-down hierarchy consists of: Ruler, officials (including religious ones), militarists, scribes, merchants, artisans, farmers/ranchers and prisoners/slaves.

What Is God's Preferred Form of Government?

Originally, it wasn't God's will for Israel to be a *human* kingship. The LORD had in mind a bottom-up model with a *spiritual* kingship.

Israel was the first huge nation to have no king in history. I'm referring to the Hebrews after they escaped slavery. For 400 years they had no king. Instead, the LORD was their spiritual King and they had noble human representatives, like Moses, Joshua or Deborah, with priests teaching the Law and the people being accountable to God based on conscience.

While technically a theocracy, it was a republic from a natural perspective. This was the start of the concept of equality on a national scale with the

Law supporting the notion of no respecter of person, rich or poor. Ideally, everyone was to be treated the same and by the same standard.

This Hebrew republic was God's original plan for the Israelites, but eventually the people wanted to be like all the nations around them (1 Samuel 8:19-20), so the LORD reluctantly gave them their first king, which was Saul, who started out good, but became corrupt.

Why Does God Favor a Republic Form of Government?

While a king rules absolute in a kingship, the people rule in a **democracy** (the Greek word *demos* means 'the people' and *kratia* means 'rule'). The Athenian democracy in 508–507 BC was the first large-scale democracy.

In a **republic** the people rule as well, except that they appoint *representatives* to do the political work, which frees-up the people to raise families and conduct the business of their livelihoods (the Latin *res* refers to an 'entity concerning' and *publicus* means 'the public').

Countries today that are called 'democracies' are actually republics since the people of the various regions elect representatives to go to the capital cities and carry out the political duties. America is a good example.

Our LORD naturally prefers a form of government that provides the most freedom for citizens because **liberty is core to God's very nature**:

> **Now the Lord is the Spirit, and where the Spirit of the Lord is, there is freedom.**
>
> **2 Corinthians 3:17**

Thus you'll find several statements like this in the Scriptures:

> **Our God is in heaven; he does whatever pleases him.**
>
> **Psalm 115:3**

The Lord does whatever pleases him,
in the heavens and on the earth,
in the seas and all their depths.

Psalm 135:6

As you can see, **God functions in a state of total freedom and therefore does whatever he wants**. Guess what? People—male and female—are created in God's image & likeness and so **have this same desire**. We intrinsically *hate* captivity and the restraints thereof. We want freedom!

The problem of course is that humans have a flesh or sinful nature which corrupts their desires. Thankfully, the LORD has provided a way for us to "escape the corruption in the world **caused by evil desires**" (2 Peter 1:4); it's called "participating in the divine nature" otherwise known as walking in the spirit (Galatians 5:16). When you learn to "put on the new self" you'll be spirit-controlled rather than flesh-ruled (Ephesians 4:22-24) and, hence, your desires will be *righteous* rather than corrupt (Proverbs 11:23).

Think about it, **if** believers "escape the corruption in the world caused by evil desires" via walking in the spirit, the community in question will have virtue—a spirit of goodness—which is the opposite of lawlessness. This is one of the reasons the American settlements were so successful in the 1600s, attracting throngs of freedom-seeking people in the 1700s, the vast majority of them being believers and, often, pastors & their congregations.

While all forms of government in a fallen world are imperfect, the republic model—often called 'democratic'—is the best for individual liberty and opportunity. People tend to flourish in republics whereas they languish in the restraints of communist countries or dictatorships, which explains why folks naturally try to escape communist states and dictatorships in preference for the freedom-loving republics and not vice versa.

For instance, have you *ever* heard of anyone trying to go through the Iron Curtain to a communist nation in order to escape freedom in the West?

In republics, the Word of God is freely spread and believers gather & worship at liberty whereas in communistic states, or corrupt dictatorships/kingships, believers have to meet secretly and—if they're caught—are fined, imprisoned or worse.

What Is the Capacity for Freedom in Each Govt?

I've heard it explained in the following manner, with my additions. Say you're a citizen who owns two cows under each form of government...

- COMMUNISM: The government takes both cows, milks 'em, and provides you a pint of milk per day. They also intern or murder millions of your fellow citizens for "crimes against the State."
- SOCIALISM: The government takes both cows, milks one and provides you a quart while giving the other cow to some folks who don't want to work. They also persecute your fellow citizens for "crimes against the State," but are more secretive about it.
- LIE-BERALISM: Your neighbor has no cows, so you vote for politicians who tax your two cows and you have to sell one to pay the tax. The politicians take the money, launder most of it, but give a pint of milk per day to your neighbors and you feel virtuous.
- BIG GOVERNMENT BUREAUCRACY: The government takes both cows, milks 'em, and pours it on the ground.
- CAPITALISM: You milk your cows, sell the product, buy a bull and build a herd while paying reasonable taxes for government services, like representation, protection, education, and so on. (Capitalism is what naturally occurs when the government leaves citizens alone beyond fulfilling the duties they're paid to perform).

These comparisons are amusing, sure, but they're pretty close to the truth.

What Are the Three Basic Options for Government?

The two extremes are **no government** and **total government**.

- With no government there's **anarchy** wherein the person or gang that is the strongest reigns. The "strongest" typically have the most physical prowess, manpower or superior weapons.
- With total government you have a leader who reigns supreme, which is a **kingship** or **dictatorship**. Forms of **Marxism** also fit this category because the State becomes the supreme leader; instead of one person calling the shots, a ruling class of people do so. Of course, some 'rulers' are merely puppets controlled by a group of elites behind-the-scenes.
- The middle ground is the **people-ruling republic**.

In both anarchy and authoritarian-type governments, the leaders rule by fear: Do what they say or they'll imprison you or execute you. In essence, the State becomes "god" because it is through the State that the citizens get their rights and they are accountable to the State. The saying "power corrupts and absolute power corrupts absolutely" is relevant.

The best option of the three is the "middle ground," the people-ruling republic. In this form of government, the individual gets his/her rights from the Creator and is accountable to their Maker. The citizens' political leaders are merely representatives and ideally have term limits.

Can Republics Become Corrupt?

Yes, because we live in a fallen world. So, a republic can become corrupt if the people don't maintain a modicum of virtue; that is, a communal sense of nobility or honor. When the people of a community have virtue there's little need for police. However, if the people become depraved, lawlessness results and they'll choose fools as representatives, which naturally results in a corrupt or ineffectual government.

Consider how America was challenged by two flooding disasters in 2005—flooding in five Midwestern states, which caused the governors of Ohio and Indiana to declare states of emergency, and the flooding of New Orleans due to Hurricane Katrina. In the Midwest the people came together and helped each other through the crisis while in The Big Easy a dog-eat-dog scenario emerged marked by heinous criminal acts.

What can explain the diametrically opposed responses to the *same* kind of natural calamity in the *same* nation? Simple: In the Midwest the communities had a spirit of virtue and goodwill whereas inner city New Orleans had developed a dangerous, depraved spirit. I'm not saying there weren't any good people there (even Sodom had a handful of noble souls), just that the widespread atrocious acts speak for themselves.

The Hebrew republic of the first 400 years after escaping slavery in Egypt didn't always work but, when it did, it was because the community had virtue, which was fueled by the Mosaic Law advocated by a noble national representative, like Moses or Deborah, as well as the service of the priests. In such a scenario 'virtue' is based on **1.** the Almighty seeing everything, **2.** God insisting on honesty, fairness and repentance-when-applicable, and **3.** everyone ultimately being accountable to their Creator.

If a populace embraces this perspective, it naturally creates societal order because the people are policed by their God-fearing conscience above law officers. This explains why the Pilgrims based their government on the Hebrew republic and the USA was originally "one nation under God."

Unfortunately, during the time of the "judges," Israel fell into periods of anarchy in which "everyone did as they saw fit" (Judges 17:6 & 21:25).

This illustrates why fallen people desperately need new spiritual 'software' and the corresponding redemption *if* any republic is to be successful in the long term. This is what the message of Christ and resulting spiritual regeneration is all about (2 Timothy 1:10 & Titus 3:5).

Why Were the American Colonies So Successful

After the Pilgrims set up their New England colony in 1620, towns started springing up across the landscape, all Judeo-Christian republics. A group with their pastor would find a location in which a building would service both spiritual gatherings *and* political meetings, aka the townhouse.

One good example is Puritan ministers Thomas Hooker and Samuel Stone who led a group of about 100 people in 1636 to establish the settlement of Hartford, Connecticut. Hooker also founded Windsor and is unsurprisingly considered to be the "founding father" of Connecticut. Meanwhile theologian Roger Williams founded Providence, Rhode Island, wherein he established the first Baptist assembly in America.

These ministers & their people were naturally involved in the politics of their settlements. The word 'politics' comes from the Greek *polis*, which means "city." In short, politics is the business of the city. On a national level, it's the business of the nation. It's as simple as that.

These communities in the New World were very successful and naturally attracted increasing people from Europe who understandably grew weary with governmental tyranny and the corresponding religious oppression. Of course, they also desired land to farm or ranch. Whole congregations migrated to the colonies with their pastors and pioneered settlements.

In the 1700s up to the Revolutionary War, a wave of 450,000 immigrants arrived mostly from Germany, Ireland, and Scotland, including throngs of Pietist Lutherans from Deutschland. Thus the population of the American colonies skyrocketed and the independent nation of the USA was born in 1776 with the Declaration of Independence.

The Puritan immigrants of the 1600s were very involved in the governance (politics) of their communities in America in which practically everyone was a believer. Hooker, for instance, delivered his most famous sermon on governmental power in Hartford, 1638, wherein he declared "The foundation of authority is laid firstly in the free consent of the people."

This was revolutionary in the 17th century when Europe was controlled by monarchs or oligarchs and the common people had precious little say on the running of their governments. Is it any wonder that Hooker was dubbed "the father of American democracy"?

Harvard University, incidentally, was established in 1636 by the Massachusetts Bay Colony and named after its first benefactor, a minister. What would America's wise ancestors think of the Leftist propaganda & perversion that is spewed out of this once-great institution today?

What Was Notable About the Pilgrims' Government?

The Pilgrims were members of the Puritan sect of the Church of England, known as Separatists because they considered their congregations separate from the English State church (as opposed to the non-separatist Puritans). They fled tyranny in Europe on the Mayflower and used the Hebrew republic as a model for government when they arrived in 1620 at Provincetown Harbor & Plymouth, Massachusetts (they were actually heading for the Colony of Virginia, but a storm blew them off course).

- The Pilgrims in America focused on the model of pre-King Saul Israel, which was the Hebrew republic.
- Back in England, King James I, preferred the Israel of King Saul-onward.

James naturally favored the Saul-onward model due to the notion of "the divine right of kings" in which Kings have subjects who are subject to the monarch's will. This is in contrast to a democracy or republic that the Pilgrims had in mind based on the pre-Saul Hebrew republic.

Is it any wonder that the American colonies were so successful and attracted so many people?

Is Being Involved in Politics "Unholy"?

The Fundamental Orders of Connecticut, 1639, is considered the first written constitution in history and thus Connecticut was nicknamed "the Constitution State." Unlike the Mayflower Compact, this agreement made no mention of the British monarch and it became the blueprint for the American colonies and the U.S. Constitution. The document is profoundly

Christian-oriented with the eleven orders prefaced by the statement "to maintain and preserve the liberty and purity of the Gospel of our Lord Jesus which we now profess, as also, the discipline of the Churches."

This is in contrast to the Pietist Lutheran immigrants of the 1700s, who felt that believers should focus on God's Kingdom, the Church, and not be involved with "man's kingdom" because it was somehow unholy. The obvious problem with this outlook, of course, is that it discourages believers from being active in the governance of their communities and encourages the less devout to take the reins of politics, i.e. power.

This is a recipe for disaster since—if every believer did this—it would guarantee a society governed by *un*believers or, at best, nominal "believers." In other words, it takes control away from noble believers to determine how they should be governed. Imagine, today, giving all governmental power over to loony Leftwingers who ludicrously believe there are hundreds of genders, that homosexuality is natural & healthy, that mentally ill males should be legally permitted to use the women's restroom, and that practicing the truths of the Bible is bigoted and hateful.

You've no doubt noticed that this is increasingly happening in America and other Western nations with the radical Left gaining more and more power through propaganda in schools, universities, media and art, as well as voting fraud that enables them to take control of key political positions.

This leaves two possibilities for believers:

1. Government can get dirty so don't get involved because you'll get dirty (and, after all, God wants you to be holy).
2. Government can indeed get dirty so make sure you're involved to help clean it up and keep it clean.

The latter option is just common sense, particularly if you want to leave your children—physical children or spiritual children—a nation that's noble and free; a nation where the Word of God is freely spread without hinderance, including truths that (supposedly tolerant) **LIE**berals don't like and desperately want to suppress.

10

Questions About Spiritual Development

Are There Stages of Spiritual Growth?

Yes, the Bible speaks of going "from glory to glory" (2 Corinthians 3:18) and "strength to strength" (Psalm 84:7). The four basic stages of spiritual growth are detailed in this passage by John:

> **Anyone who claims to be in the light but hates a brother or sister is still in the darkness. [10]Anyone who loves their brother and sister lives in the light, and there is nothing in them to make them stumble. [11] But anyone who hates a brother or sister is in the darkness and walks around in the darkness. They do not know where they are going, because the darkness has blinded them.**
>
> **[12] I am writing to you, dear children,**
> **because your sins have been forgiven on**
> **account of his name.**
> **[13] I am writing to you, fathers,**
> **because you know him who is from the beginning.**

I am writing to you, young men,
because you have overcome the evil one.
14 I write to you, dear children,
because you know the Father.
I write to you, fathers,
because you know him who is from the beginning.
I write to you, young men,
because you are strong,
and the word of God lives in you,
and you have overcome the evil one.

1 John 2:9-14

John wasn't being literal with his references to "children," "young men" and "fathers," but rather figurative.

The Four Stages can be summed up as follows:

1. "In the darkness" refers to the **spiritual darkness** of STAGE ONE where an unbeliever is separate from the light of God because his or her spirit is dead to the LORD.
2. "Children" is a reference to the **boot camp fundamentalism** of STAGE TWO in which the believer establishes a foundation. Unfortunately, too many Christians get stuck in this stage and never grow beyond it. They live and die as spiritual children.
3. "Young men" refers to the **growing individualism and sense of freedom and adulthood** of STAGE THREE.
4. "Fathers" is a reference to the **maturity and independence** of STAGE FOUR wherein believers naturally propagate.

Since there's neither male nor female in Christ (Galatians 3:28) we can broaden the terms for STAGE TWO, THREE and FOUR as such: children, young people and parents or, better yet, **childhood**, **youth** and **maturity**:

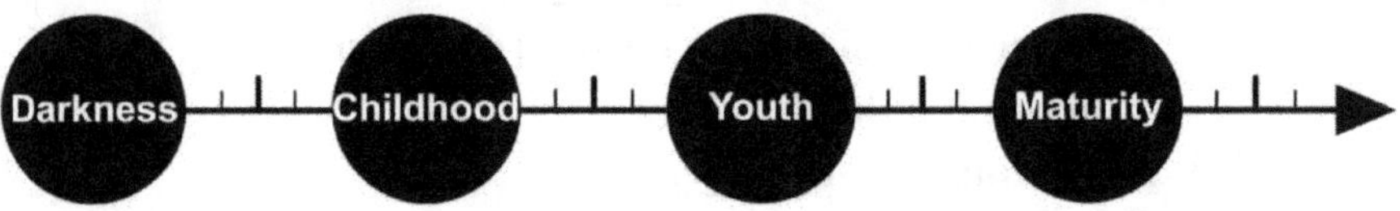

Can You Provide Details on Each Stage?

Yes…

STAGE ONE Is Separation from God / Chaos

This is the classic 'sinner' stage where the individual is separate from God and therefore in spiritual darkness. At this stage people are in bondage to the flesh—the sinful nature—to one degree or another. Being that they are separate from God and in spiritual darkness, you could also describe this stage as moral chaos, which is glaring in modern times with lost souls so confused they have trouble figuring out their gender.

I'm not saying, by the way, that people in this stage don't have a spirit, as every human being has a spirit, but rather that their spirit is dead to God and therefore in need of regeneration.[11]

STAGE TWO cannot occur until the individual is enlightened to his/her needy spiritual condition and turns to God via the good news of the gospel, which is called "the message of *reconciliation*" in Scripture (2 Corinthians 5:18-20). This salvation comes through ***repentance*** and ***faith*** (Acts 20:21).

STAGE TWO Is Institutional / Fundamental

After reconciliation with God, the new believer will naturally join an assembly/ministry/sect. The group's oversight and instruction provide the necessary structure for him or her and (hopefully) the Bible as well. The **chaos** of STAGE ONE transforms into **order** as the organization provides protection & accountability for the convert along with opportunities to learn, participate, serve, grow and eventually lead in some capacity.

STAGE TWO can be described as "fundamental" because those at this level become attached to the doctrines and rules that their organization advocates, which the elders decree to be fundamental to their faith. Not

---

[11] See chapter **5** for details.

surprisingly, STAGE TWO believers become discombobulated when these fundamentals are threatened, regardless of whether these doctrines and rules are true, false or somewhere in between. As such, those in this stage are "fundamentalists."

STAGE TWO is essentially **Christian boot camp**. It's a stage of spiritual immaturity where the believer is learning and growing. It's an immature stage in the sense that the believer is typically *dependent* upon the group to maintain their spiritual status. Just as recruits in boot camp need their drill instructors and the military institution or they'll revert back to their civilian ways, new Christians are dependent on their assemblies/sects and elders without which they'll likely fall back into STAGE ONE.

Ideally, the new believer will be in STAGE TWO while simultaneously budding in STAGE THREE and STAGE FOUR, as shown here:

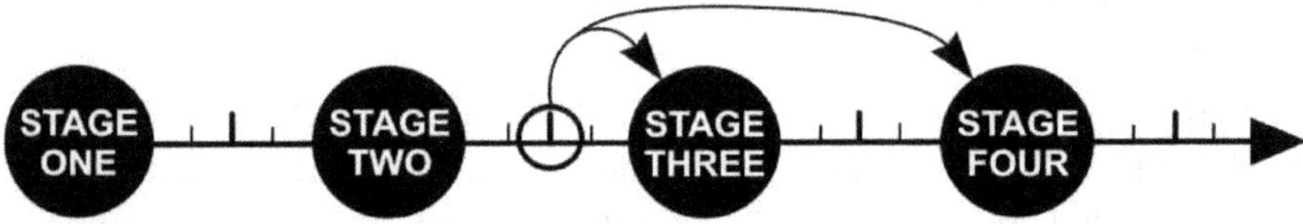

Whilst believers in STAGE TWO should be concurrently growing in the next two stages, it unfortunately doesn't always happen. Sometimes they get stuck in STAGE TWO, usually because the assembly or sect they hook up with is infected by legalism, which is sterile (counterfeit) Christianity and characterized by rigid sectarianism.

When this occurs, the organization fosters a spirit of dependency in the believer rather than independence, bondage rather than freedom, and weakness rather than strength. It's actually spiritual *abuse* and it harms or limits the believer's growth. Abuse, by the way, is the misuse of power.

STAGE THREE Is Individual / Seeker

Healthy believers will grow as **individuals** and develop an identity separate from their group. They'll start to question doctrines or practices that don't really gel with the Scriptures or make sense. They'll seek truth—

reality—beyond the limitations of their sect and elders, that is, *if* they sense they're in error in one area or another. This is good because error cannot set people free, even if it's disguised as "truth" by one's church or pastor. Only the truth sets free, as Christ taught (John 8:31-32).

Also, as believers develop in STAGE THREE, they will cultivate discernment to spiritual abuse and not tolerate it, which explains why **weak "pastors" try to keep individuals in STAGE TWO**. I put "pastors" in quotes here because *real* pastors passionately desire for believers to grow spiritually.

Now, just because believers in STAGE THREE discover error or abuse in their group it doesn't mean they'll automatically leave. They'll likely stay and do their part to help correct any problems, but this depends on many factors, like: How deeply involved are they in the group? What about their families and close friends? How severe is the error or abuse? What do they discern the Holy Spirit leading them to do? How long have they been trying to help without any appreciable change?

In STAGE THREE believers will find themselves questioning beliefs—possibly even their faith. Because of this, it's a risky and unstable stage.

I've known people in STAGE TWO who were believers for years, but as they seemed to transfer to STAGE THREE, they totally fall away from God and faith. Usually, the signs will be there that this is the way they're heading. Such people failed to "guard their heart as the wellspring of life" (Proverbs 4:23) and allowed things to enter in that took their hearts away from pure devotion to the LORD. Guarding your heart is a matter of wisdom and believers make a big mistake when they allow negative things to take root that rob them of their "first love" (Mark 4:18-19).

Thankfully, STAGE THREE doesn't end this way for those who *genuinely* seek God and persist rather than use STAGE THREE as an excuse to backtrack to STAGE ONE, as illustrated here:

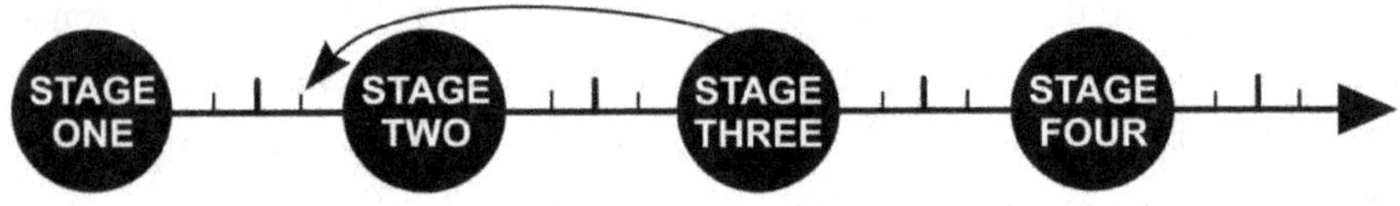

This is an extreme form of what the Bible calls backsliding.

STAGE THREE can be difficult due to its inherent growth pangs just like the teenage years and early 20s can be in the natural, but it's a necessary stage of progress in the spiritual journey. It develops one's sense of individuality apart from the group and motivates them to seek out the truth for more accuracy, not to mention this stage clarifies their objectives.

Without STAGE THREE believers will be stuck in STAGE TWO and they cannot move on to STAGE FOUR.

STAGE FOUR Is Knowing God and Propagating

STAGE FOUR is the stage where believers develop a living *relationship* with God rather than just knowing *about* God or being known *by* God (Galatians 4:9). This is the goal of Christianity and explains why the gospel of Christ is called the "message of reconciliation."

STAGE FOUR is **enlightenment**, **independence** and **strength**, as follows:

It is **enlightenment** because the believer is in direct communion with God. This communion becomes a 24/7 thing where one is in constant connection with their Creator. This is what Paul was referring to when he mentioned "praying without ceasing" (1 Thessalonians 5:17). Enlightenment in this manner includes the constant awareness of God's presence via the Holy Spirit and also the awesomeness, beauty and mystery of actually knowing the LORD.

Those stuck in STAGE TWO, by contrast, only have an inkling of this and basically view God as a big cop in the sky. This is an *outward* perspective of God and it's frankly an Old Testament mentality. The New Testament emphasizes the believer's spiritual regeneration and the indwelling empowerment of the Holy Spirit—God is *within us!* See 1 Corinthians 3:16, 6:19 and Ephesians 1:19.

STAGE FOUR is **independence** from bondage to the error and corruption that often comes with the institution of STAGE TWO. This isn't to say that the assembly/sect/pastors that believers are hooked up with in STAGE TWO are *always* bad or that they're all bad—not at all—they're usually good and definitely necessary, but error and abuse come with the territory of people and groups, even Christian churches and sects.

Furthermore, STAGE FOUR is **independence** from the uncertainty of STAGE THREE. How so? In STAGE FOUR the believer knows God personally. They've "tasted and seen that the LORD is good" (Psalm 34:8). As such, it's impossible for someone to convince them that God doesn't exist because they personally walk with the LORD.

This isn't to say, of course, that those in STAGE FOUR are exempt from falling from faith, only that it's much harder for them than those in STAGE TWO or THREE. Why? Because they're actually walking with God 24/7.

This combination of enlightenment and independence makes for **strong** believers. They're spiritually mature. These are people who know God and increasingly know their calling. They don't just sacrifice 10% of their finances as a tithe since their whole lives are "living sacrifices" when they wake up in the morning (Romans 12:1). Because they discern and fulfill God's will on both minor and major levels they become a threat to the enemy's kingdom, which naturally draws attack. This includes opposition from people at lower stages of spiritual growth, including quasi-believers and religious legalists, like the Pharisees of the 1st century.

Furthermore, those in STAGE FOUR become increasingly **independent** of the need of others in order to stay tight with God and fulfill their call. What I'm saying is that believers in STAGE TWO and even THREE will fall back into STAGE ONE without the service and support of fellow believers, particularly in the context of church services, but those firmly walking in STAGE FOUR don't need others to walk free of the pitfalls of the flesh and legalism. They don't need others to motivate them to spiritual disciplines, like prayer, study, praise, worship, fasting, service, etc.

Don't get me wrong here, Paul was encouraged and blessed by other believers, as every Christian should be, but Paul performed spiritual disciplines and fulfilled his calling without people over him compelling him to do so. It goes without saying that every believer should aspire to this level of spirituality. The ones who don't are not spiritually mature.

I'm not saying, of course, that believers in STAGE FOUR shouldn't attend assembly services. Going to healthy church gatherings as led of the Spirit is always good, regardless of where you are spiritually. But those in STAGE FOUR will often lead their own ministries within other ministries or start their own, whether within an existing camp or otherwise. (It depends on if they're an "official" minister or an independent one).

In light of all this, STAGE FOUR is a stage of **strength**. But there is a downside: "Higher levels bigger devils." Thankfully, those in STAGE FOUR can handle the increased attacks and their intensity because, again, they're tight with the LORD.

A good scriptural example is Paul who endured great persecutions while he traveled the eastern Mediterranean area starting numerous churches and overseeing them. He was trailblazing; and trailblazers are usually very independent, spiritually speaking. Check out Paul's list of persecutions in 2 Corinthians 11:23-28; it's incredible. Someone in STAGE TWO or STAGE THREE could never endure such hardships without falling away, but those in the higher levels of STAGE FOUR can, as Paul did.

Are Some Believers Stuck in STAGE TWO?

As already noted, believers in STAGE TWO should simultaneously be budding in STAGE THREE and FOUR. In other words, as believers grow in the realm of **Christian community** (STAGE TWO), they should also be growing as an **individual** (STAGE THREE) and in their **relationship with God** (STAGE FOUR). Healthy believers always have a finger, hand or foot in the next stage (or the next level of the stage they're in). The Bible refers to this maturation from one level to the next as going "from strength to strength" or "glory to glory" (Psalm 84:5,7 & 2 Corinthians 3:18).

But what of those who get stuck in STAGE TWO? These are people who fail to develop spiritually as individuals and in relationship with their Creator. Instead, the institution they are involved with replaces both. This isn't good because, in essence, the institution itself takes the place of God. They become "sheeple"—mindless automatons dedicated to perpetuating the machine of the institution, their "god."

This explains why those stuck in STAGE TWO typically become rigid sectarians who eye outsiders suspiciously and get irate when someone merely questions the legitimacy of a rule or doctrine of their group. Why? Because the institution has taken the place of the LORD. You see this with cults like the Jehovah's Witnesses. It's really a form of idolatry.

There are awesome pastors out there, praise the Lord, but some are weak—or even counterfeits—in that they encourage the pastoral *dependency* of STAGE TWO ("children") and are threatened by those trying to move into the next two stages. Instead of thinking in terms of apprehending new disciples—converts—they think in terms of "holding on" to their current fold by keeping them in the dependent phase of STAGE TWO.

They don't want to 'lose' them, not realizing that 'losing them' is the best thing for them because they would grow up spiritually, becoming "young men" (STAGE THREE) and "fathers" (STAGE FOUR).

Are There Non-Christian Substitutions to the Stages?

There are obvious secular *substitutions* to STAGE TWO. Prison is a good example. Individuals in the lower/mid levels of STAGE ONE inevitably break the law because of their darkened spiritual condition, which predictably lands them in jail or prison. Their new environment provides the parameters and order they need to escape the chaos of STAGE ONE, but as soon as they're released back into the public, they revert back to

STAGE ONE because they can't handle the freedom. They're ***dependent* on the institution** to keep them from iniquity, at least outwardly.

Religious and non-religious institutions are also substitutes, like Sciencefictionology, Mormonism, TM, rehabs, psych wards, 12-step programs, martial arts groups and a gazillion others. They're not all bad, of course, at least as far as helping the individual escape the darkness and chaos of STAGE ONE, but all such disciplines pale in comparison to the effectiveness of genuine Christianity (as opposed to sterile, religious "Christianity") because true Christianity solves humanity's root problem—the condition of spiritual death and separation from God.

The family can also be a substitute (and in the believer's life it plays an accessory role). For instance, individuals who grow up in strong families that have a lot of love, order and discipline essentially grow up without experiencing the darkness and chaos of STAGE ONE. They were, in essence, born into STAGE TWO.

This is normally a good thing and those with healthy families like this should be praising the Lord that they largely skipped STAGE ONE. It only becomes a problem if the individual becomes arrogant (spoiled) due to his or her good fortune, which is a sure slide into STAGE ONE, keeping in mind that arrogance—a superiority complex—is sin *numero uno* in God's eyes. This brings up an important question…

Are Those in STAGE FOUR Arrogant?

Since STAGE FOUR believers are at the highest stage of spiritual growth (although not necessarily the highest *level*, as there are levels within each stage), it's easy to assume that they'd be arrogant, but this isn't the case at all. People who genuinely know the LORD are extremely humble because "God resists the proud, but gives his favor to the humble" (James 4:6 & 1 Peter 5:5). As such, only the humble can get close to God. The LORD only knows arrogant people "from afar" (Psalm 138:6).

If you know domineering Christians who love to bloviate and abuse, they're not in STAGE FOUR. They're in STAGE TWO or THREE with their big heads in STAGE ONE.

Does the Bible Offer a Plan to Spiritual Maturity?

Yes, Peter provides seven keys that *guarantee* spiritual growth here:

> **Grace and peace be yours in abundance through the**
> **knowledge** ***(epignosis)*** **of God and of Jesus our Lord.**
> **3 His divine power has given us everything we need for**
> **life and godliness through our knowledge** ***(epignosis)***
> **of Him who called us by his own glory and goodness.**
> **4 Through these he has given us his very great and**
> **precious promises, so that through them you may**
> **participate in the divine nature and escape the**
> **corruption in the world caused by evil desires.**
> **5 For this very reason, make every effort to add to your**
> **faith goodness; and to goodness, knowledge** ***(gnosis)*****;**
> **6 and to knowledge, self-control; and to self-control,**
> **perseverance; and to perseverance, godliness; 7 and to**
> **godliness, mutual affection; and to mutual affection,**
> **love. 8 For if you possess these qualities in increasing**
> **measure, they will keep you from being ineffective and**
> **unproductive in your knowledge** ***(epignosis)*** **of our**
> **Lord Jesus Christ. 9 But whoever does not have them**
> **is nearsighted and blind, forgetting that they have**
> **been cleansed from their past sins.**
> **10 Therefore, my brothers and sisters, make every**
> **effort to confirm your calling and election. For if you**
> **do these things, you will never stumble, 11 and you will**
> **receive a rich welcome into the eternal kingdom of our**
> **Lord and Savior Jesus Christ.**
>
> **2 Peter 1:2-11**

The opening verses reveal that grace (favor) and peace in abundance can be yours *through* the knowledge of God. Actually, everything we need for life and godliness can be attained *through* the knowledge of God. Observe how 'knowledge' in these verses is translated from the Greek word *epignosis (EP-ee-NOH-sis)*, which is simply *gnosis* with the prefix *epi.* This isn't just textual knowledge or doctrinal knowledge; it's *experiential* knowledge. One lexicon defines it as "contact knowledge" or "experiential knowing" and hence "knowledge gained through first-hand relationship."

How do you attain experiential knowledge of God? Verses 5-7 provide the seven-point plan, which is to add to your faith goodness, knowledge, self-control, perseverance, godliness, mutual affection and love. Let's consider some insights on what each of these virtues mean in this context:

Goodness

Verse 5 instructs us to "make every effort to add to your faith **goodness**; and to goodness, **knowledge** *(gnosis)*." Every believer has a "measure of faith" otherwise they wouldn't be a believer (Romans 12:3). And this faith can grow by adding these seven virtues. But why add goodness *before* knowledge? Because the heart is likened to soil in the Bible (Luke 8:15) and goodness prepares the soil of your heart for the seed of knowledge.

To explain, "goodness" is translated from the Greek word *arête (ar-ET-ay)*, which means "moral excellence," "uprightness" or "good quality." So "adding goodness" to your faith ensures that the soil of your heart is **good quality** and will produce good fruit once the Word of God is planted in it.

This involves "guarding your heart as the wellspring of life" (Proverbs 4:23) from negative things that will grow up in your heart and choke the Word (knowledge) from producing fruit in your life. These bad things can be likened to weeds or thorns, which fit into three categories: **the anxieties of this life**, **the deceitfulness of wealth** and **the desires for other things** (Mark 4:19). In short, **worries**, **riches** and **pleasures** (Luke 8:14).

The negative things that you guard your heart against and purge from your life don't necessarily have to be sinful in-and-of-themselves. For instance, watching sports is a neutral activity but, if you do it too much, it will limit your time for more productive things. Working is good, but overworking is not good if it ruins your health or you lose your marriage & family.

Hebrews 12:1 says to "throw off **everything that hinders** and **the sin that so easily entangles**." The "thing that hinders" is not a sin in-and-of-itself; it's something that weighs you down because you're doing it too much. Of course, the "sin that so easily entangles" refer to a sin and, more particularly, the sin your flesh developed a taste for in your past. To add goodness to your faith in preparation for the seed of the Word involves keeping these things from spoiling the soil of your heart. *Throw them off!*

Knowledge

Adding knowledge to goodness (verse 5) simply means exposing yourself to the revelation of God. "Knowledge" is *gnosis* in the Greek and refers to textual knowledge of the Holy Scriptures in this context. You add knowledge by reading or hearing the Scriptures yourself through regular exposure to the Bible (1 John 2:27) or reading/hearing teachings from sound, *fruit-bearing* and *anointed* ministers of God.

Now, some might say that they don't have much passion for God's Word or they find most sermons or Bible studies boring. The good news is that the LORD has made the human heart in such a way that it'll develop a passion for pretty much anything you decide to give your heart over to—good, bad or otherwise. How much more so the very Word of God?

Exposing yourself to the "word of truth" (2 Timothy 2:15) is important because Jesus said: "Man does not live on bread alone, but on every word that comes from the mouth of God" (Matthew 4:4). Just as your material being needs physical sustenance to live *physically*, so your immaterial being needs spiritual sustenance to live *spiritually*.

As for finding most sermons or Bible studies boring, the remedy is to disconnect from ministers or environments that don't manifest a spirit of freedom, life, joy, power and **love**. For instance, if the ministers you're receiving from are cantankerous, condemning grumps or deadly dull religious zombies, that pretty much tells you everything you need to know. Jesus said, "By **their fruit** you will recognize them" (Matthew 7:16,20). Leave them and seek out ministers and ministries (assemblies, Bible studies, books, websites, radio programs or videos) that have a spirit of life and truly inspire you. This explains why Christ instructed believers in regards to fruitless teachers/preachers: "***Leave them***; they are blind guides. If a blind man leads a blind man, both will fall into a pit" (Matthew 15:14).

Yet keep in mind that **those who transfer knowledge are also able to transfer error**. Just because a minister is strong in certain areas of knowledge doesn't mean he or she is strong in every area. This applies to anyone, anywhere, any sect, small or great. Cultivating the "Berean spirit" will help you discern error and discard it, no matter where it comes from (Acts 17:10-11). The Bible instructs us to "Test everything. Hold on to the good" (1 Thessalonians 5:21), which in modern vernacular means **eat the meat and spit out the bones**.

Self-Control

Verse 6 of our text (2 Peter 1) says we're to add self-control to knowledge. 'Self-control' in the Greek is *egkrateia (eng-KRAT-ee-ah)*, which means self-mastery, self-restraint or dominion within. Since we're to add self-control *to* knowledge it contextually means we're to **control ourselves according to the knowledge we received**. In other words, we're to **put into practice God's Word after we receive it**. That's all it means.

The reason for adding this quality is obvious: What good is knowing the word of truth if you don't actually practice it?

The Lord pointed out in Matthew 7:24-27 how there are two kinds of people who hear the Word of God. One is wise because he puts it into practice whereas the other is foolish because he *doesn't* put it into practice. In both cases Yeshua says the "rain came down, the streams rose, and the winds blew." This refers to attacks from the kingdom of darkness "for the Word's sake" (KJV). You see, those who receive God's Word will undergo a "time of testing" (Luke 8:13). Mark's account puts it like this: "trouble or persecution *come* **because of the word**" (Mark 4:17).

Whenever someone receives a truth from the Word the enemy will come and try to steal it via some manner of attack. The wise person who puts into practice the word of truth will withstand the attack whereas the foolish person who fails to put it into practice will not. The latter person is apt to conclude that "God's Word doesn't work" when it has nothing to do with the truthfulness of the Word of God or the faithfulness of the Lord.

So "build your house on the rock" by simply putting into practice God's Word. If it says "husbands love your wives," then love your wife if you're a husband (Ephesians 5:25). If it says "slander no one," then be sure to slander no one, which includes gossip since gossip typically involves slander (Titus 3:2). Whatever the Word of God instructs you to do—as long as it's relevant to the New Testament believer[12]—put it into practice. In short, DO IT. If your life is messed up due to the flesh or adhering to false beliefs, practicing the word of truth is the remedy; it'll turn your ship around, so to speak, just give it time.

This doesn't just apply to practical truths, but revelational and positional truths as well. A revelational truth isn't practical, but it reveals something important; and so changing your beliefs accordingly will benefit you, such as the nature of eternal life (see chapter **16**). Meanwhile a positional truth reveals your *position* in covenant with God thru Christ, such as being holy in God's sight (Colossians 1:22) and dead to sin (Romans 6:11,14,18).

Adding self-control to the knowledge you receive includes controlling your tongue. Remember, "the tongue has the power of life and death" (Proverbs 18:21). The Bible likens it to the small rudder of a large ship that steers the vessel wherever the pilot wants it to go (James 3:2-6). In other words, the very course of your life is linked to the words you speak.

So, speak constructive words of life and faith, not destructive words that cancel out faith. Amen?

---

[12] In other words, don't practice anything that's *strictly* applicable to someone else of a different era and covenant, like the Israelites under Old Testament Law who offered animal sacrifices to cover their sins; Jesus took care of all that in the new covenant so believers don't have to concern themselves with it.

Perseverance

Verse 6 of our text (2 Peter 1) says to add perseverance to self-control. 'Perseverance' in the Greek is *hupomoné (hoop-om-on-AY)*, which means endurance, stead-fastness or to wait patiently. This means that, after preparing the soil of your heart to ensure that it's good soil and then adding the Word and putting it into practice, **it's *then* necessary to add perseverance for the Word to produce fruit in your life**.

The Bible emphasizes that it's through faith *and* patience that we inherit what is promised, not just faith:

> **We do not want you to become lazy, but to imitate those who <u>through faith and patience</u> inherit what has been promised.**
>
> **Hebrews 6:12**

I needed knee surgery in 2013 wherein it was difficult to simply walk across the room. Carol & I decided to handle the situation through prayer & faith. The healing manifested after three months and I've been fine ever since, but what if I gave up after 11.5 weeks? The healing wouldn't have manifested. This shows that you have to persevere when you practice the Word in order for it to produce lasting fruit.

It's also necessary to add perseverance to your pursuit of truth, i.e. acquiring knowledge, understanding and wisdom. Notice what Christ said:

> **"If you <u>continue</u> in my word, you are truly my disciples; and you will know the truth, and the truth will make you free"**
>
> **John 8:31-32** (NRSV)

Only those who *continue* in His Word—persevere in it—will know the truth, not those who give up after a season of seeking and studying. Notice He didn't say that those who conveniently and lazily embrace the official doctrines of this or that sect will know the truth. No, only those who *continue* in God's Word will know the truth; and the more you continue—

honestly seek and study—the more knowledge, understanding and insight you'll have. Needless to say, *persevere* in God's Word and don't give up!

Practicing the First Four Keys Will Produce Fruit

Applying the first four keys to your faith—goodness, knowledge, self-control and perseverance—*will* result in fruit in your life. In other words, these four keys guarantee the fruitfulness of God's Word. They concern the planting, cultivation and fruit-bearing of the word of truth.

The last three keys, by contrast, involve **walking in love** in your **relationships**, starting with the LORD ("godliness"), then fellow believers ("mutual affection") and, lastly, people in the world ("love"). The reason this is important is revealed here:

> **For in Christ Jesus neither circumcision nor uncircumcision means anything, but faith working through love.**
>
> **Galatians 5:6** (NASB)

Our covenant with God is a covenant of faith and therefore it works through faith; and faith ***works*** *through* **love**, including tough love when necessary (e.g. Mark 11:15-18 & Acts 13:8-12). If you cancel out love, you cancel out faith, and your covenant won't 'work' as it should.

Godliness

The Greek for "godliness" in the Bible is not the same as the Greek for "religion." The former is *eusebeia (yoo-SEB-ee-ah)* whereas the latter is *thréskeia (thrays-KIH-ah)*. E.W. Bullinger distinguishes the two:

> *Eusebeia* [godliness] relates to a real, true, vital, and spiritual relation with God while *thréskeia* [religion] relates to the outward acts of religious observances or ceremonies, which can be done in the flesh. Our English word "religion" was never used in the sense

> of true godliness. It always meant the outward forms of worship (335).

So, **godliness refers to genuine spiritual relationship with the LORD** as opposed to religion, which applies to outward religious acts. Godliness *cannot* be performed by the flesh whereas religion can.

Godliness could simply be translated as "like-God-ness." In other words, it's behaving and speaking as the Lord would behave and speak. You could say it's *imitating* God, which we are plainly instructed to do in the Bible (Ephesians 5:1 & 1 Peter 4:11). There are two ways to do this. One is to find out what the Word of God instructs and simply put it into practice. Since this is *already covered* in verses 5-6 of our main text—i.e. adding self-control to knowledge—this is not what the end of verse 6 is talking about when it says we're to add godliness. No, godliness in this context refers to loving God in a different way than obeying His Word (1 John 5:3); it's referring to loving the Creator in a *relational* sense.

How would this make a person godly, that is, *like*-God? Simple: The more time you spend with a person—particularly someone you respect—the closer you'll become and the more *like* him/her you'll naturally be. It's the same with your relationship with God. The more time you spend together, the closer you'll become and the more *like* God you'll be. The LORD will "rub off" on you and you'll thus be increasingly *like*-God, aka godly.

With the understanding of what godliness is, we are encouraged to *pursue* it in the Bible (1 Timothy 6:11), to *train* ourselves to be godly (1 Timothy 4:7-8). This shows that godliness won't automatically happen; it must be pursued and you have to "train yourself" to habitually walk in it. This is understandable when you consider that **all good relationships take time, energy, attention and discipline**. It's no different with your relationship with God.

Adding Mutual (Christian) Affection and Love (for the Lost)

Again, the last three virtues we're instructed to add to our faith in 2 Peter 1:5-7 have to do with **walking in love in our relationships**. "Godliness" has to do with loving God whereas "mutual affection" and "love" have to do with loving **1.** fellow believers and **2.** people in the world.

These last two qualities stem from two well-known Greek words for love. The Greek for "Mutual affection" is often translated as "brotherly kindness" in other English versions. The revised NIV obviously changed it to "mutual affection" to make it more applicable to all believers, whether male or female (Galatians 3:28). The Greek word for "mutual affection" or "brotherly kindness" is *philadelphia*, which is where the name of the American city was derived, "The City of Brotherly Love."

Adding *philadelphia* love to your faith simply means walking in love toward your brothers and sisters in the Lord with the emphasis on growing in affection, meaning warm feelings. By contrast, the Greek word for the seventh virtue — "love" — is *agape (uh-GAHP-ay)*, which doesn't primarily refer to affection, but rather *practical* love.

To differentiate these two kinds of love, consider **the four types of love**:

1. ***Storge*** **love** is familial love, which refers to the bond, affection and loyalty that develops between family members. Although the word itself, *storge (STOR-gay),* is not found in the Bible we see numerous examples of it, like Martha & Mary's love for their brother Lazarus in John 11.

2. ***Phileo*** **love** is friendship love or brotherly love like the platonic affection of David and Jonathan (2 Samuel 1:25-26). You could say that *phileo (fil-LAY-oh)* love is *storge* love applied to non-family members or that *storge* love is *phileo* love applied to family members. In either case, there's an element of "tender affection" or a bond, respect. Jesus' love for Lazarus is a good example of *phileo* love (John 11:35-36).[13]

3. ***Eros*** **love** is *phileo* love between members of the opposite sex and includes a romantic element, but it doesn't refer to shallow sexual lust. While the word *eros (eer-ROSS)* doesn't appear in the original

---

[13] The word *phileo* can be found 25 times in the original Greek text of the New Testament whereas the noun form, *philia (fil-EE-ah)*, appears much less often.

manuscripts there are many examples of this type of love in Scripture, such as in the amazing Song of Songs (e.g. 2:14).

4. *Agape* love is simply practical love or love-in-action and is therefore not dependent on affection or respect. This can be observed in the scriptural definition of *agape (uh-GAHP-ay)* love found in 1 Corinthians 13:4-7, which says that *agape* love is patient, kind, does not envy, does not boast, is not proud, is not rude or selfish or easily angered, etc.

The word 'love' in the most popular passage of the Bible is *agape:*

> **For God so <u>loved</u> the world that he gave his one and only Son, that whoever believes in him shall not perish but have eternal life.**
>
> **John 3:16**

The Creator was walking in love toward all humanity when the Father allowed the Son to die in our place as our substitutionary death. This was *agape* love—practical love—and not *phileo* love.

The LORD ***is*** *agape* love and so God loves the world in the *agape* sense, just as John 3:16 states. What this means is that God is extending practical love to all human beings even though unbelievers are un-regenerated "objects of wrath" (Ephesians 2:1-5). For instance, I was only saved and "made alive with Christ" because of God's great *agape* love!

But God doesn't *phileo* love everyone, that is, have tender affection or respect for them. He doesn't have a close bond with everyone. For instance, do you think God is up there observing pedophiles and saying, "Oh, I just have so much warm affection for these sick perverts?" Do you think the LORD was close buddies with tyrannical mass murderers, like Stalin, Mao or Pol Pot?

This info should help you better understand the last two virtues…

Mutual Affection

Adding "mutual affection" to your faith in 2 Peter 1:7 refers to loving your brethren & sistren in the Lord since the Greek word for "mutual affection" is *philadelphia* and corresponds to *phileo* love. In short, the Bible encourages us to *phileo* love—*philadelphia* love—our Christian brothers and sisters. Romans 12:10 is a good example of this, as is this verse:

> **Now about your love** *(philadelphia)* **for one another we do not need to write to you, for you yourselves have been taught by God to love** *(agapaó)* **each other.**
>
> **1 Thessalonians 4:9**

Believers are to *phileo* love one another by cultivating tender affection in our relationships. If every believer did this it would be revolutionary!

Notice how the second time "love" appears in this verse it's the Greek word *agapaó (uh-gahp-AH-o)*, which is the verb form of *agape*. Why? Because it's much easier to *agape* love someone when you have *phileo* love for them, which is the way it *should* be with all genuine believers. If you find it difficult to muster *phileo* love for someone who *says* they're a Christian, but who is typically obnoxious due to arrogance and other fleshly traits it's likely that you're dealing with a wolf in sheep's clothing.

> **Now that you have purified yourselves by obeying the truth so that you have sincere love** *(philadelphia)* **for each other, love** *(agapaó)* **one another deeply, from the heart.**
>
> **1 Peter 1:22**

In other words, now that you're a spiritually regenerated believer and therefore have genuine affection—*phileo* love—for your fellow believers, be sure to *agape* love them—walk in practical love toward them—and let it stem from the heart, that is, the warm affection of *phileo* love.

Elsewhere, Hebrews 10:24 instructs us to "spur one another on toward love and good deeds." This should be done in accordance with your particular grace gifts, as detailed in Romans 12:6-8. What are *your* grace gifts?

Love

Adding "love" in the context of 2 Peter 1:7 refers to walking in love toward those who are lost & dying in the world. The Greek word for 'love' here is *agape*, which, again, refers to *practical* love as shown in this passage:

> **Love is patient, love is kind. It does not envy, it does not boast, it is not proud. [5] It does not dishonor others, it is not self-seeking, it is not easily angered, it keeps no record of wrongs. [6] Love does not delight in evil but rejoices with the truth. [7] It always protects, always trusts, always hopes, always perseveres.**
>
> **1 Corinthians 13:4-7**

Since *agape* love is practical love, it doesn't require *phileo* love to walk in it (or *storge* love or *eros* love). You don't have to have any affection or respect whatsoever toward a person to *agape* love him/her, which explains Jesus and Paul's instructions to love your enemies. You don't need warm feelings or respect for your enemies in order to *agape* love them because the **biblical definition of *agape* love** shows that it's practical in nature.

Nor does *agape* loving someone mean being constantly sugary-sweet. Yes, *agape* love is kind, but sometimes the kindest thing you can do for a person is boldly tell them the truth (Proverbs 27:5). This is because it's only the truth that will set them free. Christians aren't mandated to be nice; we're mandated to be good. And sometimes doing the good thing isn't the nice thing; but it is the right thing, as long as you're led of the Holy Spirit. Of course, you should only take the tough love route if it's absolutely necessary and more gentle measures have proven ineffective.

The Bible encourages us to add *agape* love to our faith because it's easy to get saved, hook up with a fellowship/sect and not have much to do with unsaved people. It's so easy to get preoccupied with activities within Christian circles that we forget about the multitudes who are captive and hurting in this lost world. There are believers who pretty much refuse to have anything to do with unbelievers, not unlike the Israelites during Jesus' era who shunned Samaritans. Let's not be like that! Yeshua wasn't. He went out of His way to talk with the outcast Samaritan woman and ministered to her (John 4:4-26). He *agape* loved her. Also, even though Christ was called specifically to "the lost sheep of Israel," He ministered to a Canaanite woman and, indirectly, her daughter (Matthew 15:21-28).

What are some ways that you can *agape* love unbelievers? Pray for them regularly, bless them in some manner, do a good deed, share the message of Christ, and "turn the cheek" when necessary. Also, be sure *not* to be a Pharisaical hypocrite.

Here's a relevant passage:

> **But in your hearts revere Christ as Lord. Always be prepared to give an answer to everyone who asks you to give the reason for the hope that you have. But do this with gentleness and respect,**
>
> **1 Peter 3:15**

The important thing is that you don't forget the lost on your Christian pilgrimage. *Agape* loving them will undoubtedly get their attention and could be the very thing to turn them to the LORD!

You probably noticed that there are *seven* virtues to add to your faith. This is fitting since the number 7 is identified with something being finished or complete in the Bible. Thus, if you are diligent to add these seven qualities to your walk, ***you*** will be complete as a man or woman of God.

The closing verses of our main text point out: "*if* you do these things, you will never stumble, and you will receive a rich welcome into the eternal kingdom of our Lord and Savior Jesus Christ" (2 Peter 1:10-11). Do you want to come to a place where you never stumble spiritually? Do you want to hear "Well done, good and faithful servant" when you stand before the Lord? Of course you do. Regularly adding these seven virtues to your faith ensures both.

How Can I Obtain My (Righteous) Desires?

The secret to building and maintaining constant momentum in your life is to discern, pursue and obtain your desires. As Christ said, "My **food** is to do the will of him who sent me and to finish his work" (John 4:34).

Of course, there's a difference between righteous desires and unrighteous ones. The desire to steal is obviously unrighteous, but "**The desire of the righteous is only good**" (Proverbs 11:23 NASB/KJV). 'Desire' here is the Hebrew word *ta'avah (tah-âv-AW)*, which means "that which you earnestly ***long*** for." It's a desire that **stays with you** and is good! Religion has told us that all desire is bad. No, only evil desires are bad. **Christianity is not the death of desire—it's the death of selfish and ungodly desire**.

You must get a hold of the fact that God has strategic purposes for every believer, including YOU. How does the LORD reveal these purposes? **As you make God first priority, He puts burning desires in your heart—*ta'avahs*—to motivate you to go in the direction He wants you to go**.

Every believer is "God's handiwork, created in Christ Jesus **to do good works**" (Ephesians 2:10). A good example of this is Paul: God had plans for him to be an apostle even from his mother's womb (Galatians 1:15). Here's a 3-point plan to fulfill any righteous desire you have, big or small:

1. Acknowledge God in your life and He will *direct* your paths (Proverbs 3:5-6 & Psalm 32:8-9). The Bible doesn't teach to seek God only, but rather to seek God first (Matthew 6:33). We're to make our Creator first priority—sell out to the LORD—yet not get out of balance.

How exactly does God "direct your path" when you acknowledge Him? By dropping desires in your heart to motivate you. You can't obtain your desires until you know what they are; so, get close to the LORD, look deep within, and **draw them out**: "The purposes of a person's heart are deep waters, but one who has insight draws them out" (Proverbs 20:5).

You'll have thoughts, ideas or desires concerning a certain area of your life. You may want a house in the country or there may be a certain person you're interested in or perhaps you feel called to be a physician or a minister. Whatever the case, share it with the LORD in prayer and "**He will cause your thoughts to become agreeable to His will**, and so shall your plans be established and succeed" (Proverbs 16:3 Amplified).

Once you have an earnest desire, keep praying about it to ensure that it's of God. If it is, it will grow stronger; if not, it'll die out.

2. Plan your way to meet your righteous objective. God has given you a course—an objective—now you need to *plan* your way for the LORD to direct your steps. The Bible puts it like this: "The mind of a person plans their way, but the LORD directs their steps" (Proverbs 16:9 NASB).

Your mind is an awesome gift and should be utilized for good. Use it to **plan your way**. Say you're seeking the LORD and you discern a persistent desire to be a nurse. This is your course. Now **plan your way** to meet that objective. Start by asking the most obvious questions: What schools are available for you? How are you going to apprehend funds? Where are you going to live? This is planning your way to fulfill your **course** utilizing the resources at your disposal. The plan you come up with is your **path** or **way**. Remember: No one plans to fail, but failures fail to plan.

3. Start moving toward your goal led of the Holy Spirit. Once you have a plan **it's time for action**. Move toward your goal via the plan you devised. The LORD will "direct your steps" by the Spirit (Proverbs 16:9).

It's important to discern the difference between **course**, **path** and **steps**:

- Your **course** is your goal, which is based on the longstanding desire—the *ta'avah*—the LORD gave you as you sought Him.
- Your **path** is the way you planned with your mind to fulfill your course; that is, obtain your objective.
- Your **steps** are you walking down that path day by day utilizing God's direction by the Holy Spirit.

Be alert for "golden opportunities" and "golden connections" and "Let the **peace** of Christ rule in your heart" (Colossians 3:15) in any decision.

11

Questions About Sex, Romance and Marriage

Is It Okay to Be Promiscuous?

Over and over in the Bible's Song of Songs, the Shulammite maiden advises "Do not arouse or awaken love until it so desires" (2:7, 3:5 & 8:4). The Berean Study Bible phrases this as "Do not arouse or awaken love **until the time is right**." In other words, don't be so quick to jump into an intimate romantic relationship. Patiently wait until you're mature enough to discern the worthy soul your heart truly loves and can be committed to for life. Solomon elsewhere wrote "There is a time for everything, and a season for every activity under the heavens" (Ecclesiastes 3:1). The time for a man and woman to enjoy sexual union is marriage, which occurs *after* they've found the worthy one who has genuinely stirred their love.

In short, love must wait for the right soulmate to come along. Don't rush getting married for the sake of getting married. Don't be more enchanted with the *idea* of a wedding and marriage than the person you're marrying. Anyone who does so is setting themselves up for great heartbreak.

This truth is especially apropos in our modern **LIE**beral-influenced culture where teens are pressured to have sex as early as possible and as often as possible (and, even worse, as perverse as possible), which—it goes without saying—is a recipe for all kinds of unnecessary troubles.

Is There Such a Thing as Love-at-First-Sight?

Yes, but it would more accurately be described as wholesale-attraction-at-first-sight, which can ideally develop into deep love and a life-lasting relationship. This is illustrated in the Song of Songs with the Shepherd's observation about the Shulammite maiden:

> **You have stolen my heart, my sister, my bride;**
> **you have stolen my heart**
> **with one glance of your eyes**
> **with one jewel of your necklace**
>
> **Song of Songs 4:9**

This isn't to say that *all* marriages begin with love-at-first-sight. For instance, my mother said she found my dad "egotistical" when she first met him and naturally wasn't attracted to him. My father, however, said he was crazy about Mom the second he laid eyes on her. He eventually won her over and they were together till death did they part.

The love-at-first sight phenomenon was obviously one-sided in this case, but it was still key to bringing the two together, without which I wouldn't be writing this. I wouldn't even exist.

Is Sex Evil?

There's this false idea that God is anti-sex, but the LORD created both the sex organs and the pleasure of sexual intimacy, not to mention romantic attraction. Romance and eventual consummation are God's gift to be enjoyed within the context of a committed relationship. The devil didn't create any of this, he just perverts it as "the god of this world" (1 Corinthians 4:4). God is pro-sex, but anti-sexual immorality.

What Is Marriage?

Marriage was defined by our Creator at the very beginning of the human race as a man leaving his father and mother and being united with his wife in which they become "one flesh" (Genesis 2:24). This was corroborated by Christ during his earthly ministry (Matthew 19:4-6) and confirmed by Paul (Ephesians 5:31).

So, **marriage is a lifelong-committed relationship between a biological man and a biological woman, which makes them "one flesh" in God's eyes**. It's a *covenant* between a man and a woman—a vital and enduring social contract (Proverbs 2:17). We observe this in the divinely-orchestrated marriage of Isaac and Rebecca:

> **Isaac brought her into the tent of his mother Sarah, and he married Rebekah. So she became his wife, and he loved her; and Isaac was comforted after his mother's death.**
>
> **Genesis 24:67**

There was no wedding ceremony in the conventional sense that we understand today; the marriage was official due to the agreement between the two families and, most importantly, Isaac and Rebecca. The financial arrangements were established beforehand. There was no minister or judge required to pronounce them husband & wife and no written document is mentioned. The couple and their families had a verbal contract, a financial agreement and Isaac & Rebecca's decisive willingness (Amos 3:3).

The bottom line is that this is what a marriage is: **A man and a woman *agreeing* to be united as man & wife—"one flesh"—as long as they live.** It's a lifelong commitment between a biological male and female (which automatically discounts the idea of same-sex marriage).

While being "one flesh" presumes sexual intercourse will occur, that is not the definition of marriage, as Joseph was married to Mary *before* consummation (Matthew 1:24-25). When older couples stop having sex, are they still married? Of course.

This biblical definition of marriage shows that a man and woman could legitimately marry in a remote location, such as if they were castaways on a deserted island or settlers in remote areas of the globe. Obviously, they'd want to make it legal if/when they returned to civilization.

Why Make Marriage "Legal"?

Because **1.** believers are to be submitted to the righteous laws of the governing authorities (Romans 13:1-6) and **2.** to avoid "all appearance of evil" (1 Thessalonians 5:22 KJV). The latter is important to being an effective 'witness' to others (2 Corinthians 8:21).

Another glaring reason to make one's marriage legal is that marriage is **the defining point** of fornication, adultery and divorce:

- **Fornication** is sex before marriage
- **Adultery** is sex outside of marriage
- **Divorce** is the dissolution of marriage

When it's not clear who is married and who is not married it leads to moral ambiguity and the corresponding lawlessness.

What Is the Purpose of Marriage?

Social chaos results from unbridled or casual pairings. So, God set up the lifetime commitment of husband & wife—the marital covenant—as the firm base for a healthy society. Show me a community where the family unit breaks down or is nonexistent due to fornication, unfaithfulness and so on and I'll show you a lawless society with many glaring problems.

The LORD instituted marriage as the means by which a man and a woman become "one flesh" in its fullest and most satisfying sense. Casual sex may have its allure, such as temporary fleshly gratification, but it results in death in one form or another (Romans 6:23). Nothing beats the ongoing joy and peace of a healthy marriage and family!

Other purposes include intimate fellowship with another soul—spiritually, mentally and physically (Matthew 19:4-6); procreation; a legit outlet for sexual activity; the corresponding pleasure; and preventing the spread of immorality and related sexual diseases (1 Corinthians 7:2).

So, Procreation Is Not the Main Purpose of Sex?

While procreation is important, it's not the main design of sex in light of the fact that it's never mentioned as the reason for the couple's physical relationship in the Song of Songs, which is the Creator's sole book on romance, marriage and sex in the God-breathed Scriptures (2 Timothy 3:16). In short, the LORD sanctioned and blessed the lovers' romance & sexual intimacy **in and of itself**.

Consider this relevant passage from the biblical book of wisdom:

> **18May your fountain be blessed,**
> **and may you rejoice in <u>the wife of your youth</u>.**
> **19A loving doe, a graceful deer**
> **may her breasts <u>satisfy you</u> always,**
> **may you ever be captivated by her love.**
> **20Why be captivated, my son, by an adulteress?**
> **Why embrace the bosom of another man's**
> **wife?**
>
> **Proverbs 5:18-20**

"Fountain" in verse 18 is figurative of a man's wife and the intimacy they share, which is intended by our Creator to bring pleasure and "satisfy."

Pleasure is only one of three God-given benefits of sex. The other two are intimacy and procreation. Pleasure is noted by Solomon in the above passage while intimacy is inferred. He stresses children in Psalm 127:3-5.

In contrast to a shallow one-night stand or foolish affair, the marital covenant provides the God-blessed context where physical delight, close fellowship, enjoyment, amusement and security are fully realized.

Does the Bible Support Arranged Marriages?

In Old Testament times arranged marriages were accepted in biblical regions, organized by the families of the bridegroom and bride in question. Sometimes they were the result of political alliances, such as Solomon's marriage to Pharaoh's daughter (1 Kings 3:1). The obvious problem with such arrangements is that the individual is not *choosing* his/her spouse and so there's a good chance that he/she won't find the person a fitting or desirable mate-for-life. This is a potential recipe for disappointment.

I'm not saying that arranged marriages *can't* work. The best-case scenario is that the two spouses in an arranged marriage *develop* love for each other. But shouldn't the beginning step for a happy marriage be that the man or woman is *attracted to* the spouse and *enjoys* spending time with her/him and vice versa? I'm not talking about mere physical attraction here, but rather all-around physical/mental/spiritual allure.

For instance, I may find a Leftist celeb *physically* attractive, but—if I were single—I wouldn't even want to go on a date with her let alone entertain the idea of marrying her. Why? Because I don't find her *inwardly* appealing and we're on different planets *ideologically*.

Another defense for arranged marriages is that fathers & mothers are the best people to choose a life-partner for their children. Yet I know (and you know) many fathers and mothers who are the *last* persons on Earth to entrust such an important decision. Personally, I wouldn't want *anyone* else choosing my wife for me, except God. Speaking of which…

Ideally, all Christian marriages should be arranged marriages in the sense that the man and woman have diligently sought their Creator on whom to marry and the Spirit leads them to their future spouse. In essence **God arranges the marriage**. A good example of this is when the LORD orchestrated the marriage of Isaac & Rebekah in Genesis 24.

However, that's not what we're talking about here. We're talking about marriages being contractually arranged by families or regional leaders wherein romantic desire isn't a factor in the negotiation (which, again, isn't to say that such feelings *can't* come later). In these kinds of marriages neither the young woman nor the man pursued each other prior to the arrangement and, often, didn't even know what the other looked like, particularly in cultures where the woman wore a veil.

Yet this is not what we observe in the Song of Songs, which is God's biblical model for romantic love and marriage. The two lovers—who would go on to wed and consummate—are clearly head-over-heels in love with each other. For instance, observe how aggressively the Shulammite woman pursues her shepherd lover in 3:1-4. Even if this sequence is a dream or daydream it reveals her great *longing* for "the one [her] heart loves." Likewise, the man describes the maiden in terms of being *intoxicated* by her all-encompassing beauty and love (4:10).

This kind of intense all-around attraction forms the basis for a lasting marriage. We call it the "honeymoon stage." Sure, this stage doesn't last forever, but it's the *foundation* upon which a lifelong marriage is set.

For anyone who argues that the relationship of the Shulammite and her shepherd was orchestrated by their families and is therefore an arranged marriage: **1.** The two initially met under an apple tree (8:5b), **2.** they became familiar with each other, **3.** they totally adored one another, and **4.** they *wanted* to spend the rest of their lives together as a couple, all of which indicates that their committed relationship wasn't an "arranged marriage" in the sense that we're talking.

What About Polygamy?

While God *permitted* Israelite men to marry several wives, polygamy is not the Creator's ideal for marriage, as plainly observed in Matthew 19:4-6. Polygamous marriages chronicled in God's Word suffered conflict with the predictable jealousy of the wives, such as Rachel and Leah in Genesis.

In the New Testament era, servant-leaders in the Church are instructed to have but one spouse (1 Timothy 3:2, 3:12 & Titus 1:6), which was to be an ***example*** to the believers in their midst (1 Timothy 4:12 & 1 Peter 5:3).

So, while the New Covenant Scriptures don't exactly prohibit polygamy, they definitely encourage the LORD's ideal as established in Genesis 2:24—one husband, one wife, till death do they part.

But why did God permit polygamy in ancient times? Here are a couple of likely reasons:

- The world at the time generally consisted of patriarchal societies where females relied on their fathers, brothers and husbands for provision & protection. Thus marriage, even if it was polygamous, protected women from a life of poverty, prostitution or slavery.
- Polygamy also facilitated God's Genesis directive to "be fruitful and multiply, and fill the earth" (Genesis 1:28, 9:1 & 9:7) seeing as how husbands could impregnate other wives while one was pregnant/giving birth. This allowed men to have several children per year, as opposed to just one, and this was conducive to the increase & spread of humanity on the planet.

What About Divorce?

The definition of marriage shows that it is meant to last until one of the spouses dies. "God hates divorce," the Bible says (Malachi 2:16). The Law only permitted divorce because of the hardness of hearts (Matthew 19:8).

That said, Christ acknowledged that unfaithfulness is grounds for divorce (Matthew 5:32, 19:9 & Luke 16:18). However, if the guilty spouse is penitent, I encourage working it out. In other words, while divorcing due to unfaithfulness is permissible, it's not mandated. At the end of the day, it's up to the offended spouse in question and the leading of the Spirit.

Further grounds for divorce would be abandonment or criminal abuse:

> **But if the unbeliever leaves, <u>let it be so</u>. The brother or the sister is not bound in such circumstances; <u>God has called us to live in peace</u>.**
>
> **1 Corinthians 7:15**

Concerning abuse, the verse stresses that “God has called us **to live in peace” in relation to the marriage covenant**. Obviously this *cannot* be accomplished if a spouse is seriously abusive and unrepentant about it.

Every individual is unique and every marital situation is distinctive. So I always encourage seeking the Lord on what to do when your spouse is unfaithful or wickedly abusive. Obviously if the offender is stubbornly impenitent the marriage will not work out. “Can two walk together, unless they are agreed?” (Amos 3:3 NKJV).

Speaking of one spouse being impenitent and this leading to the break-up of the marriage, consider the LORD’s judgment on the men of Judah:

> **“Therefore <u>I will give their wives to other men</u> and their fields to new owners. From the least to the greatest, all are greedy for gain; prophets and priests alike, all practice deceit.”**
>
> **Jeremiah 8:10**

Since the men of Judah were stubbornly unrepentant, God’s judgment was going to fall. (When God’s great mercy ends, judgment begins). This judgment would manifest partially in **the LORD giving their wives over to other men**. Chew on that.

At the end of the day, you have to be led of the Spirit (Romans 8:14) and do what you have a peace about doing (Colossians 3:15 & Philippians 4:7).

What About Remarriage?

If an individual divorces for one of the legitimate reasons noted above, s/he can remain single, which has its benefits (1 Corinthians 7:7,28,32-34), or remarry if led of the Spirit to do so. Obviously you don’t want to make rash decisions about marrying an individual.

If someone divorces for biblically *illegitimate* reasons, they’ll have to work it out with the LORD as far as staying single, remarrying their former spouse or possibly marrying someone else. It's between them and their Maker. Do what you have the faith to do (Romans 14:23 & Titus 1:15).

Divorcing for illegitimate reasons is a sin, but nowhere does Scripture say that it's an *unforgiveable* sin. As with any offense, the LORD will forgive us when we humbly confess (1 John 1:8-9) and God casts the sin into the sea of forgetfulness (Micah 7:19). Then you move on guided by the Spirit. Anyone—including Christian servant-leaders—who imply that they *never* sin is a **liar** (Proverbs 20:9, Ecclesiastes 7:20 & 1 John 1:8).

Should a Believer Marry an Unbeliever?

No. If a believer does this s/he will get the devil as a father-in-law (John 8:44 & 1 John 3:10) and they will be unequally yoked (2 Corinthians 6:14).

That said, if a believer *does* foolishly marry an unbeliever there's always hope for the situation with the LORD involved (Psalm 71:14 & 130:7). We serve a God of miracles who can do *anything* in response to simple faith! Look up Jeremiah 32:27 and Mark 9:23.

In cases where one of the spouses of a couple gets saved, the Scriptures instruct to continue in the marriage unless the unbelieving spouse decides to abandon the union (1 Corinthians 7:15). Obviously the other two legitimate grounds for divorce noted earlier apply as well.

What's the Secret of a Successful Marriage?

The Bible says that "a cord of three strands is not quickly broken" (Ecclesiastes 4:12). In a marriage the three-strand cord consists of **husband**, **wife** and the **LORD**. As the husband and wife draw nearer to the Lord (James 4:8), they naturally come nearer to each other.

Here's an illustration:

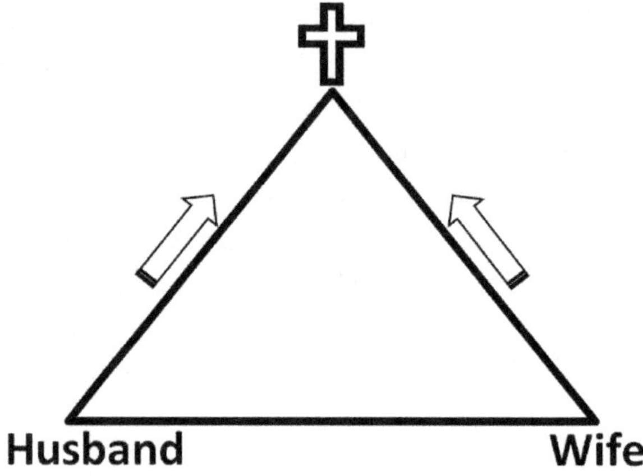

Now consider these additional biblical insights for a successful marriage:

Speak Words of Blessing/Adoration

Learn to focus on your mate's attributes and creatively praise him/her, which will enrich your marriage. This should continue as the decades pass and your spouse is no longer in his/her physical prime. Of course, there's a time & place for constructive criticism (Proverbs 9:8-9), which is a form of tough love. (Spouses should never condone godless carnality in their mates).

Like the lovers in the Song of Songs, speak grandly of your mate, as if she's the most amazing woman on Earth (4:1-5) and he can leap over mountains (5:10-16). This will have a positive effect on his/her self-image and will enhance your relationship and intimacy. Anyone who constantly puts down their spouse—whether privately or publicly—will spoil or even destroy the relationship.

Your Mate Needs You as a Best Friend, Not Just a Physical Lover

The maiden in the Song of Songs plainly speaks of her lover as her beloved *and* **her friend** (5:16). She certainly wants him for intimacy—and overtly so (7:12-14) (note the reference to mandrakes, an ancient aphrodisiac)—yet she also desires her husband to be a brother to her (8:1-4).

In other words, she wanted to be **playmates**. She feels so comfortable with her committed lover that she can be imaginative & playful, spinning tales, knowing that he will not laugh at her, but *with* her. Wives want their man to open his heart to them, to not just be a caring physical lover—as good as that may be—but a playful sibling and a communicative, imaginative, honest **best friend**.

Take heed because truer words have never been spoken.

Take Care of Your Appearance/Hygiene

The shepherd's description of his Shulammite maiden (Song of Songs 4:1-5) and her descriptions of him (5:10-16) show that they were careful to look, smell and sound their best for their partner. While this is easy to do during the honeymoon stage of a relationship—which these two were in at the time—it's important to strive to look/smell/sound your best for your partner as the decades progress.

I include "sound" because the maiden describes the mouth of her lover as "sweetness itself" (5:16). Was she describing his literal maw or the sweet, encouraging words that proceeded from it? I believe the latter.

Naturally everyone is disheveled & sweaty after doing serious yard work or what have you but, even then, a relatively solid body and a healthy attitude go a long way in keeping one attractive whatever his/her age or body type. The Shulammite says of her lover: "**His arms are rods of gold** set with topaz. **His body is like polished ivory** decorated with lapis lazuli" (5:14).

If you're a man, don't give up on the battle of the bulge. I realize it's tough to keep fit today, especially if you have a stationary job, but keep yourself looking good for your honey. Also be sure to regularly bathe, so you don't stink. Remember, God is *holy*, which means absolutely pure, and believers are called to **be holy** *in all we do* (1 Peter 1:15-16). This includes hygiene.

Don't take this as being insensitive to those struggling with weight issues. If a person or couple is okay with being heavy, what's that to me? It's none of my business. I'm just encouraging us to look (and smell) our best for our spouses, whatever body type or age. Amen?

What Is the Most Important Quality for a Mate?

I remember a couple of old movie stars, like Kirk Douglas, making statements that they didn't believe men can be monogamous. But this is a copout to commit adultery or live in fornication. It explains why the bride & groom **vow** to be faithful to one another. In other words, yes, humans—and especially males—have a predilection for successive romantic/sexual partners, but this is precisely why it's necessary for married couples to **vow** to be committed to one another till death (Proverbs 18:21).

To be faithful is to be loyal. Faithfulness is loyalty. It's a fruit of the spirit and therefore the opposite of a work of the flesh (Galatians 5:19-23).

Loyalty is underrated these days. Honor the one who wears your ring. Write loyalty on the tablet of your heart—i.e. "love and faithfulness" (Proverbs 3:3)—and your marriage will last, assuming your partner feels the same way. Proverbs 20:28 says that love & faithfulness are crucial to the security of any "throne," meaning any position of significance. This would include the husband or wife, the nucleus of any healthy family.

Proverb 19:22 says "unfailing love" is what a person most desires in another. In other words, they want loyalty, faithfulness. Yet Proverbs 20:6 notes how hard it is to find a faithful person. It's a rare trait.

So, when looking for a spouse, loyalty should be high on your list of preferences since it's one of the most priceless qualities for a happy marriage. Perhaps the worst thing a husband or wife can experience is an impenitent unfaithful spouse, which is common in this ignoble age.

Of course, loyalty or faithfulness doesn't mean there isn't a time and place for constructive criticism (Proverbs 9:8-9 & Proverbs 27:5-6), which is a form of tough love. I repeat: Spouses should never condone godless carnality in their mates. And neither should ministry associates or business partners. It's important to hold one another accountable, assuming it's in a *godly* manner as opposed to a legalistic (pharisaical) spirit.

Is Oral Sex Okay?

The Bible doesn't specifically mention oral sex, but arguably implies it in a figurative sense in the Song of Songs. This poetic book features sensuous lyrics with suggestive imagery that applauds sexuality as a normal part of marital life between a biological man and woman. (Obviously sexual activity outside of the marriage covenant is not sanctioned by the LORD).

Here are two examples:

- The woman speaking about her man in Song of Songs 2:3-6.
- The man speaking of the one his heart desires in 7:6-9.

There are Christians who find such frank romantic sensuality in the Bible surprising, which compels some religionists to interpret the passages in a strictly symbolic sense relating to God's love for Israel or Christ's love for his "bride," the Church. While I've no doubt that these verses can be interpreted on such a level, it doesn't change the fact that we must first regard them from a purely straightforward standpoint.

So, can spouses partake of oral sex with their mates or not? It's entirely up to the individual and what they believe. If the husband & wife have no qualms, it's their choice. If they do have qualms or simply don't want to do it, then obviously they shouldn't. The Bible puts it like this: "everything that does not come from faith [belief] is sin" (Romans 14:23). The Scriptures also say "**To the pure, all things are pure**, but to those who are corrupted and do not believe, nothing is pure" (Titus 1:15).

At the end of the day, it's a private issue between husbands & wives.

What About the 'M' Word (Masturbation)?

Masturbation is not directly mentioned in Scripture—and God obviously did this intentionally—so it comes down to the individual and their Creator. In other words, it's one of those "disputable" issues that should be kept between the person and their LORD as they weigh the applicable verses, their conscience, and the guidance of the Spirit (Romans 14:22). In short, it's a *private* matter.

That said, believers are instructed to control their bodies:

> **It is God's will that you should be sanctified: that you should avoid sexual immorality; [4] that each of you should learn to control your own body in a way that is holy and honorable, [5] not in passionate lust like the pagans, who do not know God; [6] and that in this matter no one should wrong or take advantage of a brother or sister. The Lord will punish all those who commit such sins, as we told you and warned you before. [7] For God did not call us to be impure, but to live a holy life.**
>
> **1 Thessalonians 4:3-7**

Verse 5 shows how the issue boils down to knowing God or not knowing God. The spiritually-regenerated believer who walks with the Lord is expected to control his/her body in a way that is holy and honorable, not in passionate lust like unbelievers who aren't walking with the Lord.

This shows that the Creator wants his children to be in a **state of control** over their bodies & thoughts/actions and not in bondage to anything. Yet verse 4 plainly says that believers have to "learn" to control their bodies; in other words, it's a *process*. There is a *progression* that goes with sanctification (1 Thessalonians 5:23).

Secondly, while the text is pretty straightforward, there's also a degree of mystery: What exactly does "control your body in a way that is holy and honorable, not in passionate lust" mean for each individual? Obviously, the indwelling Spirit is going to have to guide & help each believer in this matter. The Spirit's guidance will depend on the maturity level of the person, their unique situation and their calling.

Now let's consider the three positions on the matter:

- **The Conservative position** is that masturbation is always a sin, which they argue is supported by Christ's words, "But I tell you that anyone who looks at a woman lustfully has already committed adultery with her in his heart" (Matthew 5:28) and bolstered by Job's attitude: "I made a covenant with my eyes not to look lustfully at a young woman" (Job 31:1). These passages support the obvious connection between what goes on in the mind to potential actions, as well as the error of objectifying a woman due to her beauty. And, since it's arguably impossible to masturbate without the use of imagination, advocates of this position reason that masturbation is always a sin. The Creator has provided a natural way for a person to release bottled-up sexual energy called a "nocturnal emission," aka a 'wet dream' (Deuteronomy 23:10-11). Until the individual is married, they argue, the sexual side of life can be totally shut down through walking in the spirit (Ephesians 4:22-24). Of course, learning to live by the Spirit is a process and so the believer will have to "keep with repentance" when they miss it (Matthew 3:8 & 1 John 1:8-9).
- **The Liberal position** is that masturbation is never a sin and corresponds to the Leftie mantra: "If it feels good do it," which is the philosophy of hedonism. Those who subscribe to hedonism are libertines and embrace libertinism, aka moral lawlessness.
- **The Middle position** is that masturbation may or may not be a sin, depending on the individual and details thereof. It argues that, since masturbation is not mentioned in the Bible and there is no direct prohibition against it, whether or not it is permissible in a person's life depends on his/her unique position, their level of spiritual maturity and the leading of the Spirit within, including the conviction thereof (1 John 3:19-24). If your conscience & indwelling Spirit convict you of something, then don't do it. If there is no conviction—at least currently—then you can be certain that "to the pure all things are pure" (Titus 1:15). However, when

> the Spirit guides you to remove something from your life, you are obligated to do so since "you are not your own, you were bought at a price" (1 Corinthians 6:19-20).

Whilst the Middle Ground position respects the Conservative view and admits that believers should stick with that position if they're convinced of it, à la Romans 14:14, it objects to its black & white simplicity. For instance, both Matthew 5:28 and Job 3:1 are talking about committing *adultery* within one's heart. But what if a married man is away from home for a long period of time and releases his sexual energy by masturbating to thoughts of his wife? By doing this, he reasons, he'll be less prone to amorous temptations on the road. This obviously wouldn't be adultery and the masturbation would arguably be permissible. Similarly, if an unmarried man with a strong sex drive masturbates to an illustration of a woman, how can he be committing fornication since the image isn't an actual woman?

What are we to make of these three positions? The **LIE**beral view should be dismissed outright because it embraces the folly of libertinism. The Conservative view should be respected and works for many believers while the Middle perspective honestly explores the holes in that view and dares to tackle the ignored details. So, the truth lies somewhere between the Conservative position and the Middle one.

Being a private matter, it's up to each believer to work it out with their Maker on their spiritual journey with fear and trembling (Philippians 2:12). You can talk to a trusted mentor about it if you feel the need to do so, just be sure that he/she is actually spiritual and not a gossip (Matthew 7:15-23).

12

Questions About Offenses and Ethics

What Should I Do When Someone Sins Against Me?

Here are the Messiah's instructions for dealing with an offending believer:

> **"If your brother or sister sins against you, rebuke them; and if they repent, forgive them. [4]Even if they sin against you seven times in a day and seven times come back to you saying 'I repent,' you must forgive them."** **Luke 17:3-4**

The Lord was not talking about a serious crime here, like rape, assault, robbery or murder. If someone commits a crime like this you need to **take it to the governing authorities**, which are established by God to punish criminals and hold the power to execute when appropriate: "They are God's servants, agents of wrath to bring punishment on the wrongdoer" (Romans 13:1-6). We are instructed to *submit* to these authorities; which means we report the crime and seek justice when a serious CRIME is committed. If someone broke into your house when you weren't home and raped/killed your loved one would you just automatically dismiss the offense—that is, *forgive* the thug—or would you first contact the police and do everything in your power to apprehend justice? Obviously the latter.

Christ was talking about personal offenses, like snubbing, malicious gossip, insults, lying, minor theft and so forth. When fellow believers offend in this manner they should first be confronted and, then, forgiven ***when* they repent**. 'Forgive' means to "cancel the debt" or "dismiss the charge." When the offender is stubbornly unrepentant **you are *not* to dismiss the offense**. The Lord specified this condition in more detail here:

> **"If your brother or sister sins, go and point out their fault, just between the two of you. If they listen to you, you have won them over. [16] But if they will not listen, take one or two others along, so that 'every matter may be established by the testimony of two or three witnesses.' [17] If they still refuse to listen, tell it to the church; and if they refuse to listen even to the church, treat them as you would a pagan or a tax collector."**
>
> **Matthew 18:15-17**

When a fellow believer sins against you, you're not to go to others and gossip about it, but rather go to the offender in private and share with *them* what they did to offend you. As far as is possible, you should do this with a meek, compassionate spirit, which sometimes isn't possible because the transgression in question is so offensive. If the offender refuses to repent then you are to get one or two *spiritual* believers and confront the person again. I stress *spiritual* people because enlisting the aid of an immature or carnal Christian will not benefit the confrontation, but rather ruin it.

These additional people will naturally help make sure the charge is *authentic*. If the offender is still not penitent then you're to tell it to the church in general so that the person is socially pressured to 'fess up and make a turnaround. If the offender continues to be stubborn and impenitent *then* you're to regard him/her as a pagan or tax-collector. A pagan is an unbeliever, which means you stop treating the person as if they were a brother or sister in the Lord since his/her actions have proven otherwise.

Notice that Christ himself said that you are *not* to dismiss the offense—that is, forgive the person's transgression—when s/he is stubbornly impenitent, but rather excommunicate him/her from the fellowship. If the offender doesn't go to your assembly, which is often the case today, then you excommunicate him/her from your personal fellowship; meaning **you cut relational ties**. The offense in question is only to be dismissed—*forgiven*—**if** the offender repents. Only then should he or she be forgiven and welcomed back into the assembly or personal fellowship.

Paul taught the same thing when there was an unrepentant fornicator in the Corinth church; he instructed the believers in no uncertain terms to *expel him* from the assembly (1 Corinthians 5:1-5,12-13). Thankfully, the guy later 'fessed up and so Paul encouraged the Corinthians to forgive him and warmly welcome him back to the fellowship (2 Corinthians 2:6-11). Paul only instructed them to forgive this man **when he was willing to humbly repent**. The obvious reason for this is that it holds offenders accountable to their behavior and encourages penitence, i.e. positive change.

This is further supported by Paul when he instructed believers to "Forgive ***as*** the Lord forgave you" (Colossians 3:13) and "forgive each other, ***just as*** in Christ God forgave you" (Ephesians 4:32). We are to forgive ***just as*** the LORD forgave us, which is followed up in the very next verse with "**be imitators of God**... as dearly loved children" (Ephesians 5:1).

If we're to imitate the LORD by forgiving ***just as*** He forgives, the question is naturally raised: *When* specifically does God grant us forgiveness after we've missed it? Answer: When we humbly confess (1 John 1:8-9 & Psalm 32:5). Since confessing sin would be a useless gesture if we intended on continuing in the transgression, the phrase is synonymous with repentance. To 'repent' means to change one's mind in response to truth (Isaiah 55:7). Without humble repentance, God forgives nothing (Mark 1:15), which explains why repentance is the first basic doctrine of Christianity (Hebrews 6:1-2) and why "Repent" was the first word of John the Baptist & Jesus' debut sermons (Matthew 3:2 & 4:17).

This shows that **the most important personages of the New Testament plainly taught believers to not dismiss the offense—to *not* forgive—on**

occasions where the offending believer is stubbornly unrepentant. When this happens, we should of course intercede for the offender in the hope that they'll make a turn around and fellowship will be restored.

Unfortunately, most ministers and sects ignore these clear scriptural instructions. They wrongly teach that believers are obligated to forgive *everyone* for *everything* all the time, no conditions whatsoever, yet the New Testament teaches otherwise. This idea—that we are to constantly offer immediate and universal forgiveness, zero conditions—is a false doctrine. It is dangerous to one's spiritual health and can even cause people to reject Christianity altogether because it's so absurd and misrepresents it. This doctrine is foolish in that it fails to hold people accountable to their offenses and therefore perpetuates the negative behavior.

What About Matthew 6:14-15 and Mark 11:25?

Let's read the passages:

> **"For if you forgive others their trespasses, your heavenly Father will also forgive you, [15] but if you do not forgive others their trespasses, neither will your Father forgive your trespasses."**
>
> **Matthew 6:14-15** (ESV)

> **"And whenever you stand praying, forgive, if you have anything against anyone, so that your Father also who is in heaven may forgive you your trespasses."**
>
> **Mark 11:25** (ESV)

These are great passages with great truths, but they have to be balanced out by the above verses since they provide necessary detail that these two passages lack. This is the hermeneutical rule "Scripture interprets Scripture," which means that passages with more exposition naturally help interpret verses lacking detail. With this understanding, Matthew 6:14-15 and Mark 11:25 emphasize that it's imperative that we forgive on all occasions **where we are obligated to forgive**; that is, when an offending believer humbly repents, à la Luke 17:3-4 and 2 Corinthians 2:6-11.

It might help to understand that this is the only way the LORD forgives us when *we* miss it: He forgives us when we humbly confess, meaning repent (1 John 1:8-9). And we are instructed to imitate God in this regard:

> **[32] Be kind and compassionate to one another, forgiving each other, just as in Christ God forgave you.**
> **[1] Be imitators of God, therefore, as dearly loved children Ephesians 4:32-5:1**

There were no chapter divisions in the original epistles and, hence, verse 1 immediately follows verse 32. In light of this, we're to imitate God—that is, follow God's example—**in regards to forgiveness**. And we know that the LORD does *not* forgive apart from humble penitence. Again, this shows why repentance is the first of the chief doctrines of Christianity, as well as why "Repent" was the very first word out of John and Christ's mouths when they started publicly preaching.

When we fail to "rightly divide" Holy Scripture by examining all relevant passages on a topic we inevitably fall into error. And error doesn't set free; only the truth sets free (John 8:31-32).

Didn't Jesus Forgive His Murderers on the Cross?

Christ didn't forgive anyone when he was on the cross. Read the text:

> **When they came to the place called the Skull, they crucified him there, along with the criminals—one on his right, the other on his left. [34]Jesus said, "Father, forgive them, for they do not know what they are doing." Luke 23:33-34**

Yeshua prayed to the Father for *Him* to forgive His murderers, which means He was praying for His persecutors to come to repentance because *this is the only way God forgives sin* (Acts 20:21). God doesn't forgive the arrogant unrepentant; He only forgives the humbly penitent (Proverbs 28:13). It's an axiom. For now, during the Church Age, the Creator is patiently extending mercy to the unsaved in the hope that they'll be moved to repentance & reconciliation. Those who refuse will be judged and discarded in the lake of fire where they'll suffer the "second death," which means **they *won't* be forgiven by the LORD** (Revelation 20:11-15).

So what Christ was doing on the cross was **precisely what He instructed believers to do when we are mistreated for His name**: ***Pray for our persecutors.*** Stephen did the same when he was martyred (Acts 7:60).

What Is Casting Cares on the LORD (aka Venting)?

Those who support the idea that Christians must immediately forgive everyone for everything all the time, no conditions, claim that failing to forgive an offender will naturally result in bitterness and hate. But they're confusing *forgiving* with *venting*. To vent to God means **to cast your cares/ burdens/ offenses on to the Lord in prayer**, as observed here:

> **Cast your burden on the LORD,**
> **and he will sustain you;**
> **he will never permit**
> **the righteous to be moved.** **Psalm 55:22** (ESV)

> **casting all your anxieties on him, because he cares for you.** **1 Peter 5:7** (ESV)

> **Trust in him at all times, O people;**
> **pour out your heart before him;**
> **God is a refuge for us.** **Psalm 62:8** (ESV)

> 1 **With my voice I cry out to the LORD;**
> **with my voice I plead for mercy to the LORD.**
> 2 **I pour out my complaint before him;**
> **I tell my trouble before him.**
> 3 **When my spirit faints within me,**
> **you know my way!**
> **In the path where I walk**
> **they have hidden a trap for me.**
> **Psalm 142:1-3** (ESV)

Casting your cares like this should be done across the board, including situations where you are severely offended and the transgressor is impenitent. Discarding such emotional burdens on the Lord will keep you free of resentment and hatred. But venting to God is *not* forgiving. 'Forgive' literally means to "cancel the debt" or "dismiss the charge" and the Bible gives us precise instructions on when to do this and when not to. To forgive a person of a serious offense prematurely is folly. Yet we are instructed to cast—vent—our cares unto the LORD, which would include the hurt, violation and frustration. When you do this, God bears your burdens and you free yourself from bitterness or hatred taking root.

Why cast your cares/burdens/offenses on to the Lord? Because you lack the capacity to handle them. Just as you must eliminate physical waste from your vessel so you must remove emotional waste. Venting is as necessary to your spiritual/mental well-being as the large intestine is to your bodily health—**the waste must be removed**.

Those who contend that *not* forgiving someone of a transgression will automatically result in bitterness & hate argue that unforgiveness itself is a sin. But how can it be if both Christ and Paul gave clear instructions to *not* forgive transgressors when they're stubbornly unrepentant? Furthermore, if unforgiveness itself is a sin then the LORD is guilty of sin since **1.** God kicked satan & his foul minions out of Heaven after they rebelled—in other words, God held their transgressions against them and treated them accordingly—and **2.** millions of impenitent souls will be discarded in the lake of fire on Judgment Day to suffer the "second death."

What About Praying for Offenders?

When someone offends you it's important to cast the care/burden on to the Lord in prayer, but you also need to intercede *for* the individual:

> **"But I say to you who hear, Love your enemies, do good to those who hate you, [28] bless those who curse you, <u>pray for those who abuse you</u>."**
>
> **Luke 6:27-28** (ESV)

Why intercede for those who oppress you? Because prayer is the agent that *looses* the power of God into lives; it *releases* the LORD's will—which is done in Heaven—into the life of the person you're interceding for on Earth; it also releases the kingdom of God to reign in the situation.

To explain, when you pray for someone you "loose" God into his/her life and situation. It's important to understand that—although God is Sovereign and thus reigns supreme—satan & his filthy underlings have power on Earth as far as the kingdom of darkness goes. This reveals why the devil is called "the god/prince of this age" wherein "the whole world" is under his control to some degree and he "leads the whole world astray" (2 Corinthians 4:4, John 14:30, 1 John 5:19 & Revelation 12:9).

Observe that the Enemy only has power over those in "the world." The awesome news is that spiritually regenerated Christians have been *called out* of "the world" and, in fact, 'church' in the Greek means "called out of." In short, all spiritually regenerated members of the Church are "the called-out ones." We are not *of* this world because we are reconciled to the LORD in Christ and belong to a superior kingdom and, consequently, *believers have the right and authority to release God's will on this Earth*.

The Scriptures accurately describe this age we live in as "the present **evil age**" (Galatians 1:4). How come? Because the devil & his wicked spirits have lawful control in the kingdom of darkness and the corresponding Earth it underpins. This authority extends over all unbelievers. Thankfully, God has brilliantly made a way for His righteous will to be done on Earth *through* the intercession & service of those who've been "called out" of this world in Christ. In short, the will of God can be done on Earth through the prayers and ministry of those who are in covenant with the LORD thru Christ. If you're a spiritually-reborn Christian, this means YOU.

This is based on the truth that believers have the authority to "bind" and "loose" on Earth (Matthew 16:19 & 18:18). The Amplified Bible puts it like this: "…whatever you bind (declare to be improper and unlawful) on earth must be what is already bound in heaven; and whatever you loose (declare lawful) on earth must be what is already loosed in heaven." The Greek word for "bind" is *deo (DAY-oh)*, which means to literally bind or figuratively in the sense of prohibiting or hindering, while "loose" is *luo (LOO-oh)*, which means to unbind or release. So, the Church—the "called out ones"—have the authority to hinder or prohibit the kingdom of darkness on Earth and to release God's kingdom. The kingdom of darkness is prohibited in Heaven so we can prohibit it on Earth; the kingdom of light reigns in Heaven so we can loose it on Earth. It's that simple.

I trust you're seeing *why* praying for those who attack you is so vital. Say you have a dark room. How do get the darkness out? By turning on the lights. When you pray for people & situations, you're likewise switching on the Light. When you intercede for them, you're *loosing* the LORD's will to be done and, when the light of God is in operation, darkness naturally flees. Perhaps the ones who are mistreating you are non-Christians; by lifting them up in prayer and releasing the power of the Kingdom of Light into their lives it may open their eyes wherein they accept the message of Christ. You have to develop faith & patience because this might not happen overnight; it could take *years*. Or perhaps it's a case where carnal Christians are mistreating you; interceding for them can wake them up to their fleshliness, spur them to penitence and spiritual progress. Another possibility is that you're dealing with wolves or goats disguised as believers; prayer can inspire them to genuinely turn.

Of course, the person you're praying for *can* be obstinate and opt to spurn the Lord's grace. This will result in judgment, sooner or later, but deliverance will manifest for you in one form or another. God may even move you to be an instrument of radical righteousness, such as when Paul boldly reprimanded an antagonistic magician and declared temporary blindness on him to provoke repentance (Acts 13:8-12). This was obviously a situation that called for tough love.

Whatever form the LORD's grace might manifest in the situation, loosing the power of God into it through prayer is the first order of business whereas confronting & correcting those who mistreat you is secondary. Be encouraged! The kingdom of God will be in operation one way or another.

This can be observed in the early Church in the account of Herod Agrippa, who unjustly arrested many believers and even had James the son of

Zebedee put to death (Acts 12:1-5). The believers prayed for their persecutor, just as Christ instructed. God graciously gave Herod much time to wise up, but he remained pompous and stubborn. When Herod accepted praise that's only due the Most High during a political speech, "an angel of the Lord struck him down" (Acts 12:21-23). Herod's arrogance and murderous acts reached the limit of the LORD's tolerance because he refused to repent, so judgment fell. When God's mercy ends, judgment begins. Thus the believers were delivered from their persecutor.

This shows, by the way, that God does not reserve *all* judgment until the end of the age, as I've heard erroneously taught.

What About Joseph Forgiving His Jealous Brothers?

Joseph's attitude toward his brothers who sold him into slavery is renowned as a biblical example of the grace to forgive: "You intended to harm me, but God intended it for good" (Genesis 50:20). Yet preachers who quote this typically neglect to point out *why* Joseph so graciously forgave. He didn't just automatically forgive them; he forgave only after shrewdly breaking them wherein they displayed remorse & repentance.

After being sold into bondage, Joseph spent about 13 years as a slave and prisoner before miraculously becoming second in command of the greatest nation on Earth at the time. That's when his brothers traveled to Egypt to acquire food in order to survive the famine of the area. To break his siblings and bring them to humble penitence, Joseph…

- Didn't reveal his identity, a form of deception (Genesis 42:7).
- Accused them of being spies though he knew they weren't (42:9).
- Gave orders to fill their bags with grain to be taken back to their families in Canaan, which proved his compassion, but he also slyly ordered that the silver with which they paid for the food be put in the bags as well, which would freak them out (42:25-26).
- When the brothers returned to Egypt with Benjamin, Joseph *still* refused to reveal his true identity and continued to pretend like he didn't know who they were (43:15-16).

- He had the brothers' sacks filled with food to take back home but he also sneakily had his personal silver cup placed in the mouth of Benjamin's bag. After the siblings left to travel home, Joseph sent a detachment to catch up with them and (falsely) accuse them of stealing the governor's treasured chalice. After the cup was discovered in Benjamin's sack they returned to Egypt and threw themselves at Joseph's feet. Continuing his ruse, Joseph asked them why they stole his silver cup (Genesis 44:1-15).

As you can see, Joseph used sly tactics to humble his carnal brothers and spur them to repentance. These shrewd tactics included forms of deception, but they were justified. His actions are in line with Christ's instructions "Be shrewd as snakes, but innocent as doves" (Matthew 10:16). The fact that Joseph was a type of Christ makes his example (of not automatically forgiving until the offender humbly repents) all the more pertinent since 'Christian' literally means "follower of the Anointed One."

Does the Bible Support Pacifism?

The New Testament does not advocate absolute pacifism, which is the idea that believers should *never* resort to violence under any circumstances whatsoever. You see, there are two forms of pacifism:

1. **Absolute Pacifism** is a peaceable attitude that refuses to *ever* turn to violence in response to evil.
2. **Limited Pacifism** is a peaceable attitude that only resorts to violence when necessary. This position is 'selectivism' because the person *selects* whether it is just or not to turn to violence on the occasion. People who embrace selectivism are selectivists.

Absolute pacifism sounds nice in theory, but it does not work in a fallen world where people are sometimes a threat to the well-being of others because they choose to live according their sinful nature or they adopt intolerant, violent ideologies that threaten others. Take the example of thugs breaking into your home and threatening you & your loved ones.

Should you just kick back and let it happen in the name of strict pacifism? Obviously not (Luke 12:39).

So, the New Testament Advocates *Limited* Pacifism?

Yes, limited pacifism—selectivism—is the ***balanced*** **position** on violence and it is the position backed by the Bible. Of course, many people believe that Christianity supports the idea of absolute pacifism, but it doesn't. Christ's ministry team carried swords for protection from thugs as observed in Luke 22:49-50. At this juncture they had served with the Lord for over three years, which indicates that they had swords because **the Lord *permitted* it**. Why did He permit it? Because they traveled with a money box that contained their ministry earnings as they journeyed from town to town. The swords were obviously for protection from potential raiders, particularly in the many desolate regions they had to travel.

Furthermore, if Christ meant we should be doormats to every thug that comes down the pike why did He audaciously chase the "thieves" from the Temple *twice* during His 3.5 years of ministry, as shown in John 2:13-17 and Mark 11:15-18? **Jesus broke out a lash and drove out the greedy fools from the Temple—pushing over tables, swinging a whip and yelling.** These are plainly not the actions of an absolute pacifist. What the Messiah did was so radical it provoked fear in the legalistic religious leaders and so they conspired to murder him (Mark 11:18). Harmless ultra-pacifists don't inspire fear and provoke murder plots, generally speaking.

Moreover, Christ **refused to allow** murderers to apprehend and kill him on multiple occasions, as illustrated in Luke 4:28-30, John 7:30,44, 8:59 and 10:31,39. The only time the Messiah submitted his life to the hands of people with criminal intent was when he was arrested in Gethsemane because it was ***God's will*** that he suffer and die for the salvation of humanity. It goes without saying that we have to be balanced with Christ's teachings and his example in the Bible. We need to examine *all* the passages on a topic, not stress some and ignore others. 'Scripture interprets Scripture' is a hermeneutical rule for good reason. If we fail to do this we'll fall into error and embrace ideas Yeshua never actually taught.

The Bible teaches that the righteous laws of human governments are God-ordained for the purpose of punishing criminals, including the right to execute when appropriate (Romans 13:1-6, 1 Peter 2:13-14 and Titus 3:1).

Christians are clearly mandated by Scripture to submit to the civil authorities, which are established by the LORD to punish wrongdoers. Since this is so, it follows that we should do everything possible to see to it that lawbreakers are apprehended and disciplined by "God's servants," the governing authorities. If thugs commit crimes and we just spontaneously forgive them—dismiss the charges—we're clearly not submitting to these powers because we're not respecting their laws enough to pursue justice and hold the criminals accountable by pressing charges.

The majority of sane Christians realize that limited pacifism is the biblical position on violence. Unfortunately, there are a minority of extremists who refuse to be *balanced* with the Scriptures on this topic and insist that physical conflict, and especially armed conflict, is *never* appropriate. But the simple fact is that some people are so degenerate, so evil, that radical opposition and even execution are sometimes justified reactions. This is why the LORD ordained human governments to bear "the sword," which is the authority to **execute when justified** (Romans 13:1-6). It's why God had Herod Agrippa wiped off the face of the planet (Acts 12:1-5 & 19-23).

The error of absolute pacifism—the idea of *never* resorting to violence—would prevent believers from helping their neighbors who are threatened by wicked people. Keep in mind that loving one's neighbor is the second greatest command after loving God (Matthew 22:34-40). Take the first Nazi death camp at Dachau in southern Germany. The Poles that were there would've gone straight to the ovens within two days *if* the Americans hadn't come through the wall with weapons drawn on April 29th, 1945.

We must understand that "Love does not delight in evil" (1 Corinthians 13:4-8), which would include *not* tolerating evil people preying on innocent victims. If your neighbor is threatened by thugs, and it's within your power to help him or her, it would be a sin not to do so under the guise of "I'm a pacifist and must *never* resort to violence."

What About "Turning the Cheek"?

There's gross misunderstanding concerning Christ's teaching to "turn the cheek" (Luke 6:27-29). He was referring to a backhanded slap to the face, which was an insult in that culture. In other words, we can all save ourselves a lot of trouble in life if we learn to ignore the antagonism of various fools who would like to divert our focus and ruin our day. The Old Testament advocates this as well: "A fool shows his annoyance at once, but a prudent man overlooks an insult" (Proverbs 12:16).

So the Lord was talking about giving an antagonist a break for the sake of peace in situations of personal offense; he wasn't referring to cases of severe criminal acts. Again, the Bible maintains that governments are "God's servants" for good in the sense that they protect citizens from criminals; they "bear the sword," meaning they possess the power to punish and even execute criminals when justified (Romans 13:1-6).

In Ecclesiastes 3:1-8, one of the wisest persons who ever lived eloquently conveyed how **there are justifiable occasions for killing and war in this fallen world**, which should not be confused with murder (a criminal act).

What About "Thou Shall Not Kill"?

That is a quote from the King James Version. The more accurate rendering of the original text from Exodus 20:13 is "You shall not murder," as verified by other translations. There's a difference between murder and justified killing. Murder is always unjust whereas the latter is just. While all murder involves taking a human life, not all taking of life is murder. Capital punishment is a good example of justified killing, assuming the person is actually guilty. In fact, the very next chapter in Exodus supports capital punishment (Exodus 21:12) and the following chapter advocates justified killing in self-defense (Exodus 22:2).

Meanwhile violence in defense of the innocent is permissible and even commendable (Exodus 2:17-19 & Proverbs 28:1); and violence against an unjust aggressor is vindicated (Genesis 14). Both of these include the *possibility* of justified killing. The incident from Genesis 14, by the way, involved Abraham, "the father of all who believe" (Romans 4:11).

I realize that believers in Christ are under the superior New Covenant and thus "have been **released from the law** so that we serve in the new way of the Spirit, and not in the old way of the written code" (Romans 7:6). But I'm not talking about dietary laws or ceremonial laws here, which are now immaterial (Colossians 2:16-17), but rather *moral* laws, which are unchanging and applicable. All that changes for the believer in the New Covenant is how we fulfill those moral laws; they are fulfilled in us by *not* living according to the flesh, but rather to the spirit (Romans 8:4).

Is It Okay for Believers to Serve in the Military?

Some hardcore pacifists are so unbalanced they argue that a true Christian should never participate in the military, even in cases where the God-ordained authorities require it. The implication is that it's inherently sinful to serve in the military and be willing to kill in obedience to the civil authorities of one's country. War should ideally be resorted to only when absolutely necessary. Yet those who believe serving in the armed forces is *itself* evil have to explain John the Baptist's answer to some soldiers who asked him what they should do. Notice John's response:

> **John replied, "Don't extort money and don't accuse people falsely—be content with your pay."**
>
> **Luke 3:14**

John was preparing the way for the ministry of Jesus Christ by **calling people to repentance** (Mark 1:4). If merely being a soldier is intrinsically evil, John would have said something like, "It's wicked and sinful to be a soldier; flee from the military or you will suffer God's wrath!" You'll find no such statement anywhere in the New Testament, whether from Christ, Paul or anyone else. Simply put, governing authorities require police and military personnel to fulfill their God-ordained mandate to maintain societal order, which includes protecting the country.

This is not to say, of course, that individual Christians don't have the right to object to military service due to personal conscience or what have you. In such cases the military is better off without them since their hearts wouldn't be in it, so to speak (Deuteronomy 20:8 & Judges 7:3).

Nor am I saying that corrupt governments shouldn't be resisted or corrected, like the Nazi-led socialist government in Germany during WW2 or the Japanese "constitutional monarchy" of the same era (which was, in effect, a military junta). A good biblical example of resisting corrupt government can be observed when Nathan made a bold stand against the brazen corruption in David's monarchy (2 Samuel 12:1-10).

Is There Such a Thing as a Justifiable Lie?

Lying for selfish, evil purposes is always a sin (Leviticus 19:11 & Colossians 3:9). Christ plainly described the devil as "the father of lies" (John 8:44) and referred to his followers as "everyone who loves and practices falsehood," whose fate is damnation (Revelation 22:15). A "lying tongue" is one of the LORD's most hated things (Proverbs 6:16-19) and "all liars… will be consigned to the fiery lake of burning sulfur. This is the second death" (Revelation 21:8).

That said, justifiable lies may sometimes be necessary in a fallen world where the father of lies is the "god of this world" and his deceived people run things in one capacity or another (2 Corinthians 4:4 & 1 John 5:19). A justifiable lie is not a sin for the precise reason that it's justified and done with the greater good in mind. In other words, a justifiable lie is not evil, it's good. Therefore, those who implement a justifiable lie on a fitting occasion are not committing an evil act, but rather a righteous one.

One glaring biblical example is Exodus 1:15-21 in which the midwives *lied* to the Pharaoh because **1.** his command to murder newborns was evil and **2.** their purpose was to save innocent lives. These two factors made the lie justifiable. Their actions proved that they "feared God" and thus God blessed them! Someone could argue that, technically, God blessed them because they feared God, not because they were lying, but the *proof* of their fearing God on this occasion is that they saved innocent Hebrew babies by justifiably lying to the Egyptian king because his order was evil.

A similar situation can be found in Joshua 2:1-6 when Rahab the harlot lied to the king of Jericho to save two Hebrew spies. Rahab had become a believer in the LORD (verses 10-13) and verified her faith by hiding the Hebrews, then lying to her king about their whereabouts to save their lives. Her justifiable lying also saved her life and the lives of her family members when the Israelites subsequently sacked the city.

On top of this, she is hailed for her actions in the Hall of Faith chapter (Hebrews 11:31) and James commends her actions (James 2:25). The context of the latter verse is that faith without works is dead (2:14-26): Rahab's deed of saving the Israelite spies via hiding them and justifiably lying about their whereabouts *verified* her salvation! Nowhere is it suggested in the Bible that Rahab's lying to the Jericho authorities was evil; on the contrary, she's honored for her faith and corresponding actions, which preserved the lives of many people.

The moral is that it's acceptable to lie in order to save guiltless people. ('Guiltless' as in blameless in the situation in question, not sinless; no one is sinless except Christ). Let's say you were living in German-occupied territory during WW2 and hiding Jews in your abode. If Nazi authorities came to your door looking for hidden Jews, would you say "Yes, I cannot tell a lie; they are hiding in the attic"? Of course you wouldn't. In short, **you are not obligated to tell the truth to wicked authorities if speaking the truth will result in great evil**. Why? Because **evil people are not rightfully due data that they will use to abuse and slay**. You're only obligated to speak what the Holy Spirit leads you to say (Mark 13:11).

It helps to understand the difference between the English word 'lie' and the Hebrew word translated as "lie" or its variations, like "lying," "liar" "false," "falsehood" or "deceitful" (e.g. Exodus 20:16 & Proverbs 6:17,19). The English 'lie' means non-factual whereas the Hebrew word *sheqer (SHEH-ker)* refers to **fraudulence or deception with evil or hurtful intent**. Fraud means to cheat someone; and to cheat someone means to *not* give people what they are rightfully owed.

Since Nazis looking to apprehend Jews during WW2 had evil intent, they were not rightfully due factual information since it would result in evil, whether unjust imprisonment, abuse or murder. In such a scenario the person lying to the Nazis would indeed be guilty of giving non-factual information, but s/he would not be guilty of *sheqer*. Giving non-factual data in such a situation is a justifiable lie, but it's *not sheqer*. The Hebrew *sheqer*—to defraud someone or deceive with evil intent—is not used in any of the many examples of justifiable lying in the Bible.[14]

Is trickery inherently evil, that is, *sheqer*? Only if the intent is to con someone out of what s/he is rightfully due. If the intent of trickery is good then it's not *sheqer*. For instance, the LORD instructed David to use deceptive tactics to defeat the Philistines in 2 Samuel 5:22-25. This was justifiable because the Philistines were the enemies of Israel—God's nation—and the noble goal was to defeat them. How about the use of trickery in games, like football? When a quarterback fakes a handoff to a running back it's trickery, but it's not *sheqer*. Why? Because the context of the trickery is a contest and the goal is to win, not to be transparently honest with the opponent which, needless to say, would be asinine.

Another Hebrew word translated as "lie" is *kazab (kaw-ZAB)*, which is used in this passage: "God is not human, that he should <u>lie</u> *(kazab)*, nor a human being, that he should change his mind. Does he speak and then not act? Does he promise and not fulfill?" (Numbers 23:19). *Kazab* literally means "Vain words spoken **to deceive, cause failure or disappoint; that which does not function within its intended capacity**" (Benner). This explains the use of *kazab* in this passage:

> **"You will be like a well-watered garden, like a spring whose waters never <u>fail</u> *(kazab)*."**
>
> **Isaiah 58:11**

---

[14] Other examples include 1 Samuel 20:27-31, 21:1-4, 2 Samuel 17:20, Jeremiah 38:24-27, Judges 4:17-24, 1 Samuel 11:1-11, 1 Samuel 27:1-12, 1 Samuel 29:7-9, 2 Kings 10:18-30 and Joseph deceiving his brothers to break them (Genesis 42-44).

A spring whose waters **fail** is *lying* spring because it's not functioning according to its intent. When the Bible says "God is not human, that he should lie" it means that God is not going to speak vain words that deceive in the sense of failing or disappointing the person rightfully due. When Christ—God in the flesh—lied to His brothers about going to the festival in Jerusalem it was a justifiable lie since He was following His Father's instructions to go to the feast **in secret** (John 7:1-10). It was technically a lie—giving non-factual information—but it wasn't *sheqer* or *kazab.*

Something else to consider: A person can be guilty of *sheqer* or *kazab* even if what they say is factual and they're not technically lying. Say a man is selling a naïve lady a house: Everything he says is true, but he shadily leaves out vital data that would dissuade her from purchasing because he's only interested in getting a big commission. This would fall within the definition of *sheqer* or *kazab.* He didn't technically lie, but his actions where fraudulent; he *failed* to walk in a spirit of love toward his neighbor.

A genuine "white lie" wouldn't be *sheqer* or *kazab* either if it's done because you love the person and don't want to *unnecessarily* hurt them. Say a wife shows off her short haircut to her hubby and he doesn't like it, but says it looks good because he doesn't want to hurt her and, besides, telling the truth would do little good since it would take months for her hair to grow back. Once it does, of course, he can tell her the truth.

This is *not* an excuse to be a bullcrapper. Nor is it a justification to cover up your own sin because you don't want to hurt the person, like covering up adultery. I'm talking about rare occasions where telling a person how you feel would *unnecessarily* hurt them and you don't want to do that **out of love**. Nor am I talking about situations where someone asks you for your honest opinion concerning a work, like an item that's going to be sold publicly. For instance, if someone gives me their song, artwork or book for my evaluation I'm going to be explicitly honest, albeit tactfully.

These kinds of white lies may technically be lies, but they're not *sheqer* or *kazab*. When David declared "I hate and detest <u>falsehood</u> *(sheqer)*" (Psalm 119:163) he was referring specifically to *sheqer,* not justifiable lies.

13

Questions About Various Interesting Topics

What Is the "Unpardonable Sin"?

Let's read the two most informative accounts on this topic:

> **And the teachers of the law who came down from Jerusalem said, "He is possessed by Beelzebul! By the prince of demons he is driving out demons."**
> **[23]So Jesus called them over to him and began to speak to them in parables: "How can Satan drive out Satan? [24] If a kingdom is divided against itself, that kingdom cannot stand. [25] If a house is divided against itself, that house cannot stand. [26] And if Satan opposes himself and is divided, he cannot stand; his end has come. [27] In fact, no one can enter a strong man's house without first tying him up. Then he can plunder the strong man's house. [28] Truly I tell you, people can be forgiven all their sins and every slander they utter, [29] but whoever blasphemes against the Holy Spirit will never be forgiven; they are guilty of an eternal sin."**

[30] He said this because they were saying, "He has an impure spirit."

Mark 3:22–30

Then they brought him a demon-possessed man who was blind and mute, and Jesus healed him, so that he could both talk and see. [23] All the people were astonished and said, "Could this be the Son of David?"
[24] But when the Pharisees heard this, they said, "It is only by Beelzebul, the prince of demons, that this fellow drives out demons."
[25] Jesus knew their thoughts and said to them, "Every kingdom divided against itself will be ruined, and every city or household divided against itself will not stand. [26] If Satan drives out Satan, he is divided against himself. How then can his kingdom stand? [27]And if I drive out demons by Beelzebul, by whom do your people drive them out? So then, they will be your judges. [28] But if it is by the Spirit of God that I drive out demons, then the kingdom of God has come upon you.
[29] "Or again, how can anyone enter a strong man's house and carry off his possessions unless he first ties up the strong man? Then he can plunder his house.
[30] "Whoever is not with me is against me, and whoever does not gather with me scatters. [31] And so I tell you, every kind of sin and slander can be forgiven, but blasphemy against the Spirit will not be forgiven.
[32]Anyone who speaks a word against the Son of Man will be forgiven, but anyone who speaks against the Holy Spirit will not be forgiven, either in this age or in the age to come.

Matthew 12:22-32

Whether or not these accounts are discussing the same episode or two different-yet-similar episodes is irrelevant. In both cases Christ was talking to religious leaders who weren't actually in touch with God and were, in reality, children of the devil, as revealed elsewhere (John 8:44). They saw evidence of Yeshua driving out demons from afflicted people and attributed it to the power of the prince of demons, Beelzebul.[15] He then explains the illogic of such reasoning—the absurdity that satan's power could be overthrown by satan's aid—but adds that anyone who speaks against the Holy Ghost will not be forgiven, whether in this age or the eternal age to come. "They are guilty of **an eternal sin**" (Mark 3:29).

We know that Christ was "full of the Spirit" (Luke 4:1) and this empowered him to exorcize demons and execute other miracles. So, when the Teachers of the Law and Pharisees said he was driving out evil spirits by the prince of demons they were, in essence, calling the Holy Spirit an evil, unclean spirit, which is slander. This was speaking *against* the Holy Spirit, aka blasphemy against the Holy Spirit, a transgression that is unpardonable and therefore an eternal sin. Why? Because these people's hearts were so hardened with unbelief that they attributed something clearly done by the power of God to satan! How spiritually blind and dull could they be? These are the same people who, a little earlier, objected to the Messiah's amazing healing of a man with a shriveled hand on the Sabbath and thus plotted to murder Him (Mark 3:1-6).

So, the unpardonable sin is unbelief so gross that the person attributes an obvious work of the Holy Spirit—aka God—to the devil or demons. Their eyes have become so tightly closed to the light that it has become darkness; and good has become evil. This is such imbedded unbelief that the person is incorrigible. In other words, someone who commits the unpardonable sin isn't someone who is *concerned* that they committed it.

Anyone who is concerned that they committed the unpardonable sin did not commit it. The very fact of their concern is proof they didn't. Any person who wants to make things right with his/her Creator did not commit the unpardonable sin. "The blood of Jesus… purifies us from *all* sin" for anyone who's penitent (1 John 1:7-9). Those who commit the

[15] Beelzebul (or Beelzebub) had once been the name of a Canaanite idol, "the lord of the high place," but by the time of Christ it was used by Hebrews in reference to the "lord of dung," the ruler of the Underworld, satan, the devil.

unpardonable sin, by contrast, want *nothing* to do with the truth—reality—which includes the LORD, the Almighty Creator (John 14:6).

We need to be careful: Just because someone puts on the airs that they're radically against God and truth, it doesn't automatically mean they've committed the unpardonable sin and cannot be reached. For instance, Paul was formerly a Pharisee named Saul who fiendishly opposed Christians in the 1st century to the point of apprehending believers for imprisonment or execution (Acts 8:1-3) and even tried to get them to blaspheme (Acts 26:11). Despite being a "blasphemer and a persecutor," Saul was shown mercy because "he acted in ignorance and unbelief" (1 Timothy 1:13) and thus the Lord was able to reach him on the Road to Damascus and he became the most strategic vessel for Christianity (Acts 9:1-30).

The only way Paul would've committed the unpardonable sin is if, **when he saw the (literal) light on the Road to Damascus**—experiencing clear evidence of the truth—he willfully closed his eyes & ears to it and continued on with his gross persecution of the Church. In such an event, he wouldn't have even recognized his actions as sin and therefore wouldn't seek forgiveness, but would've gone on stubbornly thinking he was doing the work of God with an undisturbed conscience. You see, people who commit the unpardonable sin no longer have a functioning conscience because it has been seared as with a hot iron and their hearts are thus hopelessly hardened (1 Timothy 4:2).

A good modern example would be Blackie Lawless of the shock rock/metal band W.A.S.P. Few others would seem as far away from God as Blackie, but one day he decided to read the Bible with the intention of disproving it once and for all. Growing up in the Church, he understood that the Bible contained 66 books written by approximately 40 different authors spread out over 1530 years in three continents, most of whom didn't know each other. His goal was to prove it wasn't true from an attitude of extreme prejudice. The more he read, however, the more he realized that the writers weren't just answering each other's questions, they were finishing each other's sentences! In short, Blackie recognized he was looking at something supernaturally conceived—the Living Word of the Living God. It was impossible that man could have written it.

Conversions of radically anti-Christian individuals like Saul and Blackie show that we have to be very careful about assuming someone has committed the unpardonable sin. Christ obviously discerned by the Spirit that these religious Hebrews, the ones who said he was driving out demons by satan, were so hardened by their unbelief that they were hopeless.

Now consider what the Messiah said in Luke's account:

> **"I tell you, whoever publicly acknowledges me before others, the Son of Man will also acknowledge before the angels of God. 9 But whoever disowns me before others will be disowned before the angels of God. 10 And everyone who speaks a word against the Son of Man will be forgiven, but anyone who blasphemes against the Holy Spirit will not be forgiven."**
>
> **Luke 12:8-10**

The Lord says here that those who disown Him to people on Earth will be disowned by the Son in Heaven (cf. Matthew 10:33). These are individuals who deny the truth, which is Christ (John 1:1-4 & 14:6). He immediately follows this up with the sin of blasphemy against the Holy Spirit. These two sins are technically different and yet they both result in the Lord holding the sin against the individual and not forgiving him/her. This reveals a connection: Both offenses have to do with **gross unbelief that stubbornly rejects the truth despite glaring evidence to the contrary**.

With that in mind, you could say that *every soul* rejected by God on Judgment Day and discarded in the lake of fire to suffer the second death will have committed the unpardonable sin (Revelation 20:11-15, Hebrews 10:26-27 & Matthew 10:28). Every such person had been exposed to the truth one way or another in their lives, but rejected it in preference to their pet sin or godless ideology. Thus, they are thrown away in the lake of fire where they reap the wages of their sin (Romans 6:23).

How do we explain the Lord's statement in verse 10: "And everyone who speaks a word against the Son of Man will be forgiven, but anyone who blasphemes against the Holy Spirit will not be forgiven"? Answer: People in Israel were understandably uncertain about the carpenter's son, Yeshua, being the prophesied Messiah (Deuteronomy 18:15,18) and His identity would gradually dawn on many of them. You could say that the true nature of "the Son of Man" was veiled in His humanity & humility and thus people could've easily failed to grasp His identity. The same goes for other people up to this day. As such, a person's statements against Christ based on false, fragmentary or conflicting information would be understandable and forgiven, assuming s/he is penitent.

It is true that Peter denied knowing Jesus out of fear for his life (Matthew 26:69-75) but—while his lips turned traitor—his heart did not apostatize, not to mention he was repentant (Luke 22:31-32), which paved the way for the Spirit's healing favor and thus Peter became a mighty apostle for the Lord. The saying "You've got to lose to know how to win" applies.

The Holy Spirit, however, is the invisible Divine Power on Earth strategic to human redemption, as detailed in chapter **6**. Hence people with hardened hearts of unbelief who badmouth the glaring work of the Spirit of God have committed an eternal sin and are thus irredeemable.

Let's end with four further points relating to the unpardonable sin:

- The difference between the unpardonable sin and the "sin that leads to death" (1 John 5:16 & Hebrews 6:4-6) is that the unpardonable sin applies to spiritually un-regenerated people (keeping in mind that the Judaic religious leaders weren't spiritually reborn) whereas the "sin that leads to death" applies to seasoned born-again believers who willfully turn away from the LORD; that is, they commit apostasy. Of course, those who commit the "sin that leads to death" are also arguably committing blasphemy of the Holy Spirit since they foolishly chose to reject the Spirit who had been indwelling/guiding them.
- In addition to gross unbelief, the unpardonable sin is **slandering God** since it slanders the Holy Spirit as the devil (or *a* devil). Keep in mind that 'devil' literally means "slanderer" and so one of the key marks of a person who follows the devil is being a slanderer.

- The fact that there is an unforgiveable sin disproves the doctrine of Universalism, which argues that *everyone* will eventually be forgiven and redeemed.
- People who are guilty of committing the unpardonable sin always do so due to their embracing the flesh and false beliefs. For instance, the religious leaders of Israel slandered Christ as being possessed by the prince of demons because they were *envious* of His great works and *jealous* of His increasing following (Matthew 27:18). Today a lot of people blaspheme the Holy Spirit because of their unrepentant commitment to satanic ideologies, e.g. the secular religion of **LIE**beralism.

So, the unpardonable sin is deliberately closing one's eye to the light and absurdly calling good evil despite glaring evidence to the contrary. It's wantonly ascribing the activity of the Spirit to a demonic agency. The person who does so is incorrigibly lost by his/her own stubborn volition. Any person *concerned* about committing the eternal sin did not commit it because their very concern is proof to the contrary. ***Anyone*** **open/willing to make things right with God can** (Proverbs 28:13 & Isaiah 1:18).

What Is the "Sin That Leads to Death" in 1 John 5:16?

Let's read the passage:

> **If you see any brother or sister commit a sin that does not lead to death, you should pray and God will give them life. I refer to those whose sin does not lead to death. There is a sin that leads to death. I am not saying that you should pray about that.**
>
> **1 John 5:16**

The topic here is a fellow believer seen committing a sin and the reader being encouraged to pray for him/her, which is encouraged elsewhere in Scripture as well (James 5:15 & Galatians 6:1). Then John adds that he's only talking about a believer whose sin does not lead to death followed by the fact that there is a sin that leads to death and it's useless to pray for that person. Notice that he doesn't say you *can't* pray for this individual, he just implies it's useless to do so.

John was not referring to physical death even though there is evidence in the New Testament of genuine believers receiving the judgment of premature death due to their sinful actions (1 Corinthians 11:28-32 & Acts 5:1-10). This does not mean they're not saved, but they'll have to answer for their sin at the Judgment Seat of Christ (2 Corinthians 5:10). How do we know for sure John wasn't referring to physical death?

1. 'Context is king' is a hermeneutical rule and physical death does not fit the context. For instance, the antithesis of death is life and the seven times that John uses 'life' in chapter 5 all refer to either eternal life or spiritual life and not solely physical life. Verses 11-12 are a good example. Moreover, in the very verse in question—John 5:16—John refers to 'life' and it's clear that he's talking about spiritual life (in the sense of fellowship with God) since the person in question is already physically alive.
2. The only other time John refers to death in this entire epistle is twice in 1 John 3:14 where he's clearly referring to spiritual death and the corresponding eternal death.
3. The idea of physical death wouldn't 'work' in regards to John's instructions in the verse. To explain, John implies that we *shouldn't* pray for the believer who has committed the sin that leads to death. If John was referring to Divine discipline in the form of physical death, how would we know if a brother or sister has committed a sin that has incurred the judgment of physical decease? For instance, in the case of 1 Corinthians 11:28-32 some believers were getting sick and some dying because, as Paul put it, they "eat and drink judgment on themselves." The answer is that we wouldn't know and thus we *would* apply the aforementioned verses on praying for those who have sinned and are sick (i.e. James 5:15 & Galatians 6:1). The exception of course would be if the Holy Spirit informed you specifically not to pray for a certain believer who has sinned because it has incurred the judgment of premature death. But, let's be honest, how many believers then or now are able to discern the Spirit's leading with

> accuracy concerning something which would compel the person to disregard the clear teaching of Scripture in such matters (that is, praying for those who have sinned and are now sick)?

So, John was talking about a sin that a believer can commit that leads to spiritual death & the corresponding eternal death. What sin is that?

> **It is impossible for those who have once been enlightened, who have tasted the heavenly gift, who have shared in the Holy Spirit, [5] who have tasted the goodness of the word of God and the powers of the coming age [6] and who have fallen away, to be brought back to repentance. To their loss they are crucifying the Son of God all over again and subjecting him to public disgrace.**
>
> **Hebrews 6:4-6**

The topic of these verses is believers who have "fallen away" even though they had once been enlightened to the truth of the message of Christ, tasted of the heavenly gift (Titus 3:5), were filled with the Holy Spirit, had fed well upon the Word of God and, evidently, had experience with the gifts of the Spirit. If a believer experiences all of this, they obviously have some degree of spiritual maturity. In other words, we're not talking about a Christian relapsing into sin or struggling with sin (1 John 1:8-9 & Isaiah 1:18), but rather someone who knows the truth and has walked with the Lord as a mature believer to some measure, but has willfully chosen to ***turn away*** **from the faith in outright denial and rebellion**.

This is the sin of apostasy, which means the abandonment or renunciation of one's faith. It's why the sin is referred to as "fallen away" and not merely falling down. Believers who fall down can get back up and continue moving forward (Proverbs 24:16) whereas those who willfully fall away have abandoned the road of Christian faith altogether and have set a new course that doesn't include the LORD or the Holy Scriptures.

This is what John was talking about in 1 John 5:16—**apostates**—since he earlier addressed those who had left the worldwide Church (which is different from leaving a particular assembly) and denied that Christ is the Messiah (1 John 2:19 & 2:22). Don't pray for apostates like this because it's useless seeing as how **it is impossible for them to be brought back to repentance** (Hebrews 6:4-6). Again, John was talking specifically about those who were reasonably mature in the Lord, not young believers struggling with a sin problem, like many of us have done with relapses.

Here's a modern example. A dozen years ago Carol & I were part of a fellowship in which a new family joined the assembly and the husband (who was in his late 30s) was an experienced praise & worship leader. He became one of three such leaders and he would effectively lead the congregation in praise & worship. A year and a half later the Lord called Carol & me out of that fellowship to serve elsewhere, but I reunited with the man a few years later. We would have friendly chats now and then, mostly on Christian doctrine and current issues; sometimes debates.

Everything was great until he started becoming increasingly contentious, arguing for the sake of arguing, which I found curious (and reveals a lack of the peace of God). Then one day he dropped a bomb by saying that the Holy Scriptures were written by the devil. It was a bunch of gobbledygook, but he was serious. I couldn't believe it. This was once a formidable man of God who led people in praise & worship. Now he's outrageously contentious and blathering about God's Word being of the devil.

I bring up this sad story because the man is a modern example of an apostate—someone who has left the Christian faith altogether and is actively preaching gross error. It's useless to pray for him since he was a relatively mature believer in a leadership position who had chosen to turn away from the faith. This is the sin that leads to death, as John put it.

Is Art Cited as an Industry in the Bible?

Yes, the first mention of art as a human work, and even an industry, can be found in the first book of the Bible. (By 'industry' I mean the production of goods or services for people in the community to utilize):

> **Adah gave birth to Jabal; he was the father of those who live in tents and raise livestock. [21] His brother's name was Jubal; he was the father of all who play stringed instruments and pipes. [22]Zillah also had a son, Tubal-Cain, who forged all kinds of tools out of bronze and iron.**
>
> **Genesis 4:20-22**

Three major industries are noted:

- **Livestock**, which relates to human sustenance.
- **Music**, which relates to art as a craft and the corresponding human appreciation or entertainment (in the positive sense).
- **Tool manufacturing**, which relates to technology and human convenience or advancement.

The point is, art is cited in the same breath as two other vital industries.

Furthermore, tool manufacturing and the corresponding technology includes an element of art since various tools and the items created from them are typically made with aesthetics in mind; and are themselves art in a sense. For instance, chairs, tables, desks, shelves, utensils and weapons, like swords. (For anyone who doubts that a chair or table relates to technology, technology is defined as the application of scientific knowledge for practical purposes, so designing and building a wooden chair or table would be an application of technology).

Consider vehicles in the modern era, which are a tool to travel from point A to point B: They *can* be created solely with utilitarian concerns in mind, but that's usually not the case. Manufacturers are also concerned with aesthetics, which explains the existence of car shows.

All three of these industries were birthed at the same time in history. Obviously, people are not meant to just eat and use tools, they can also create and appreciate art, whether music or otherwise.

What Forms of Art Are Noted in the Bible

Several art forms can be observed in Holy Scripture:

- Music, as noted in the Psalms and Song of Songs. These songs feature a wide range of expression from praise & worship and historical commentary to emotional venting and romantic expression.
- Poetry, such as the book of Job, Ecclesiastes and the poetry used throughout the prophetic books.
- Fictional stories, like Christ's parables and Jotham's fantastical tale (Judges 9:8-15).
- Visual arts, including graphics, sculpture, crafts, décor and architecture (1 Kings 6). This would include the aesthetics of the Ark of the Covenant and the Tent Tabernacle (Exodus 25-26).
- The artistic element in tools, weapons, armor and so on would fall within the parameters of visual art.
- Performance art, as observed with Isaiah walking around partially nude and barefoot for three years (Isaiah 20), Jeremiah creating and wearing a yoke, which was destroyed by another prophet to symbolize the breaking of the yoke of the king of Babylon (Jeremiah 27-28) and Ezekiel "sieging Jerusalem," lying on his side for long periods of time, etc. (Ezekiel 4-5). This shows that art can be used as a tool to minister truth to others.
- Since the Song of Songs contains multiple speaking parts, including choruses of people, it's likely that it was acted out as a musical, perhaps during the week-long wedding celebration. Poetry, songs and stories were entertainment in ancient times, just as concerts, films and TV programs are to us today.
- Dance would be a form of performance art. Ecclesiastes 3:4 says there is "a time to weep and a time to laugh, a time to mourn and **a time to dance**." Meanwhile the Psalms encourage us to praise the LORD with dancing and music (Psalm 149:3 & 150:4). David danced before the LORD with all his heart, which some took in the wrong spirit (2 Samuel 6:14-23). Aren't there always those who take offense to an artist despite perfectly noble intentions?

All of these art forms separate human beings from animals. Beasts do not create or perform with aesthetics in mind, even if what they create for practical purposes can be deemed artistic, such as a spider's web.

Can a Style of Art Be Evil? What About R-Rated Films?

Let's first define art: **Art is creative expression to entertain or share a message.** While it's usually centered around aesthetic pleasure, this isn't always the case; sometimes the artist focuses on ugliness/offensiveness to shock or create a mood and convey a message, assuming there is one. Forms of art include paintings, illustration, sculpture, music, photography, films, poetry, crafts and storytelling. Styles of art refer to the differing *types* of art in any form. Even the works of architects, engineers and landscapers—buildings, bridges, etc.—could be considered artistic works to some degree, combining the practical with the aesthetical.

Where does the desire to create originate? The answer can be found in the very first verse of the Bible: "In the beginning God **created**..." Human beings are created in God's likeness (Genesis 1:26-27) and the Scriptures show that it's *spiritual* to **imitate** our Creator (Ephesians 5:1). In other words, we create because our Maker is a creator.

No art form or its particular style is intrinsically evil. As Paul put it by the Holy Spirit: "I am convinced, being fully persuaded in the Lord Jesus, that **nothing is unclean in itself** " (Romans 14:14). Art is simply a tool for people to use. It's neutral. Only the message it conveys can be evil. But evil shouldn't be confused with heavy, brooding, shocking or ugly. While these things aren't light, fun, pleasant or beautiful, they're relevant to the human experience in a fallen world. Hence, the God-breathed Scriptures are full of heavy, shocking and ugly material.

Furthermore, just because an individual might be an unbeliever it doesn't automatically make his/her art evil. For instance, an atheist who hates Christianity could paint an outstanding picture of a beautiful landscape. Would this make the painting evil? No, the piece simply conveys the inspiring beauty of the Earth; the spiritual condition of the artist is irrelevant. So, a Christian could hang this work in his/her home and enjoy it for what it is. You could say that believers are free to enjoy works of art that aren't stamped "safe" by their local Christian store (or pastor/sect).

Conversely, just because a Christian creates a painting or writes a song, it doesn't automatically elevate it to "sacred art." They could be derivative, shallow or mediocre art; the fact that the artist is a believer is immaterial. Believing in God, by the way, shouldn't be an excuse to produce bad art.

Of course, art is a matter of taste and so not everyone likes the same kinds of art or styles of the art in question. But just because someone doesn't personally *like* a particular form/style of art doesn't make it evil or worthless. It just means they don't like it; and that's *their* prerogative.

To illustrate, I don't like movies that are musicals in which people suddenly break out in song & dance while doing mundane activities, but that doesn't negate these kinds of musicals as a form of art. Nor do I look down on those who appreciate these films. My mother loved 'em. (Just so there's no confusion, I don't mind musicals where the singing/dancing is intrinsic to the story, like the excellent 1952 version of *Moulin Rouge*).

I also don't favor country music or rap, generally speaking (although I like Western music), but that doesn't make those styles of music evil or worthless. Nor do I negatively judge those who listen to these styles. It's a matter of a person's subculture and personal preference.

Every style of music is art; and art is not inherently evil. But it can *become* evil if the creators use it to convey a wicked message, like encouraging sin and glorifying evil, whether satanism, the occult or what have you.

Also, you don't have to approve of the 'look' that a particular artist cops. Christian musicians look/dress a certain way because, in many cases, they came *out of* a particular subculture and therefore minister to that demographic, which is a biblical principle (1 Corinthians 7:20-24 & 9:22). So we have to be careful about hastily denouncing artists as "worldly" because their style of dress or hairstyle might strike us as different and aren't akin to what we would likely see at a conventional church service. Read the Bible's actual definition of worldliness in 1 John 2:16-17.

As far as the claim that metal music is inherently evil goes, it *has* been called "the devil's music" and there have been several bands with a satanic message, although often it's just a shtick to draw attention and sell albums/tickets. Nevertheless, the idea that metal music is *innately* "of the devil" is a stereotypical myth. Again, all art forms are a neutral tool for what the artist wants to convey, whatever his/her ideology.

This style of music has been slandered by sincere-but-sincerely-wrong people as evil when that's obviously not the case. It's a lie; and the devil is the "father of lies" (John 8:44). You may not like (or understand) it—and that's okay—but please don't slander the good examples of this music or the genuine children of God who like it, write it and perform it. Anyone who does so—and is stubbornly impenitent—will have to answer for it when they come face-to-face with Christ at the Judgment Seat.

Praise & Worship is indeed spiritual, but it isn't the only God-approved music out there. Praise & worship is its own genre and is made *specifically for* Christian devotion. Praise ushers in God's presence and worship (adoration) is the response to being in the Lord's presence. This explains why I spend more time listening to praise & worship than any other style of music. It facilitates a *spiritual* atmosphere. Need I say more? But let's not be stupid and suggest that this is the only kind of musical style that Christians *can* listen to or the only genre that's approved of God.

Consider the songs we observe in the Bible, like the Psalms, which consist of the lyrics to actual songs. These songs, as well as poetry in the Bible, don't only feature praise & worship. They also include brutally honest venting, historical accounts, prophecy, evangelism, romance and more.

Let's face it, praise & worship is limited in its topical scope. It's all about praising & worshiping the LORD, which means this style of music ***omits* a lot of important truths chronicled in the Bible**. For instance, generally speaking, praise & worship doesn't detail the sobering prophecies chronicled in Revelation & elsewhere or the importance of spiritual warfare or the horrors of Divine judgment or the historical truths of our spiritual forefathers & foremothers (that is, the good, the bad and the ugly of their lives). Christian metal, by contrast, addresses all of these things and much more; and is often very frank about it.

So, let's drop this notion that praise & worship is the only God-approved music. It isn't. For instance, Solomon's 'hit' song was about true romance and doesn't even mention God; I'm talking about the Song of Songs, which happens to be a whole book of the Bible. The LORD's not one-dimensional and it's healthy for us to imitate that quality (Ephesians 5:1).

Keep in mind that **everything we do**—including the music we listen to—must be done with moderation lest it become a hindrance in our lives (Hebrews 12:1-2). That includes collecting & listening to various forms of music and keeping up with the myriad artists, including praise & worship.

Some will argue that horror movies and R-rated movies in general are evil. They can be. But, again, it depends on the message that's delivered. If the message is good then that makes the film good in at least one sense. And, if the message is neutral, that means it can be viewed as a piece of art & entertainment, depending on the tastes of the viewer. Some Christians don't like horror movies—or movies period—and that's their prerogative.

I heard one preacher make a blanket statement denouncing all horror flicks because they're theoretically created for the purpose of creeping people out one way or another, which—he argued—creates a spirit of fear. But what if the purpose of scaring/shocking people has a worthwhile moral, like good people can overcome evil if they rise to the challenge?

Speaking of which, what about all the horrific or shocking accounts **chronicled in God's very Word**? Here are some glaring examples:

- Lot's daughters' incestuous actions (Genesis 19:30-38);
- Judah unknowingly having sex with his daughter-in-law who was posing as a prostitute (Genesis 38);
- Phinehas, a priest, driving a spear through both a brazenly rebellious Israelite & his Midianite woman (Numbers 25:8);

- whole cities put to the sword, including women and children (Joshua 11:11-23);
- Jael (a woman) hammering a tent peg through snoozing Sisera's temple into the ground (Judges 4:17-21);
- the witch of Endor (1 Samuel 28:3–25);
- David chopping off Goliath's head and parading it around as a trophy (1 Samuel 17:50-57);
- David's lust for the nude Bathsheba and his subsequent adultery and murder of Uriah (2 Samuel 11);
- the mass slaughter of infants (Matthew 2:16-18);
- the naked demoniac (Luke 8:26-39);
- the shocking global bloodshed in Revelation (chapters 6-19);
- the monstrous "locusts" of the Tribulation (Revelation 9:7-11);
- the overt eroticism of the Song of Songs.

The reason I added the Song of Songs to this list is because—while it's certainly not horrific—it can be shocking the first time or two you read it. For instance, I initially read it when I was 20 and my jaw dropped at the express sexual descriptions within the figurative language. Yet this poetic book is a blessing to God's people because it shows that sex is a beautiful thing in the context for which the Creator intended. Only outside of this context does it become dirty and destructive.

The bottom line is that horror movies are art and art is good, bad or neutral depending on the content and message, as well as the leading of the Spirit in the life of the potential viewer in question.

Examples of quality horror flicks include *Jaws*, *The Exorcism of Emily Rose*, *Stigmata* and even the *Jurassic Park* films, which include seriously horrific moments. You may not like some of these movies, but I appreciate most of them for their artistic merit, entertainment value and, in some cases, their ultimate message, which doesn't mean I think they're flawless.

Speaking of the *Jurrasic Park* films, the characters are not fleshed-out enough in my opinion, although they're certainly flesh-eaten.[16]

---

[16] That's a joke.

Which brings us to gore. Is the presence of overt gore in a movie automatically evil? No, God created blood and the insides of human bodies. When a surgeon operates on a patient to save life & limb it's good, not negative. Similarly, *The Thin Red Line* has gory battle scenes, but they illustrate the horrors of warfare and point to something deeper. Even some slasher flicks have a good message about the reality of evil people, the immorality of promiscuity, boldly confronting evil and triumphing.

To conclude, Solomon said about life:

> **So I commend the enjoyment of life, because there is nothing better for a person under the sun than to eat and drink and be glad. Then joy will accompany them in their toil all the days of the life God has given them under the sun.**
>
> **Ecclesiastes 8:15**

"Enjoyment of life" is relevant to our earthly sojourn, which would include **the appreciation of art**. But, as with anything, we need to keep wisdom in view and be careful to "guard [our] hearts as the wellspring of life."

Are Dinosaurs Mentioned in the Bible?

The term 'dinosaur'—meaning powerful reptile—wasn't coined until 1841 by Britain's leading paleontologist, Richard Owen. Yet dinosaurs are noted in the Bible using other terminology, such as the behemoth and leviathan conveyed in Job 40-41, as well as references to literal "sea monsters" and "dragons" elsewhere. The latter are translated from the Hebrew word *tannin (tan-NEEN)*. Psalm 74:13 and 148:7 are good examples of possible references to dinosaurs.

The herbivorous "behemoth" described by God in Job 40:15-24 has been speculated to be a hippopotamus or elephant, but these animals have thin tails and nothing akin to a cedar tree, as detailed in verse 17. By contrast, dinosaurs like the *Brachiosaurus*, *Diplodocus* and *Apatosaurus* (*Brontosaurus*) had huge tails that fit the description.

The "leviathan" that the LORD boasts of in Job 41 smacks of a fire-breathing dragon. Before writing this off as fantasy, large animals would have breath containing gases, which could theoretically be ignited in some manner when blown out, like by the clicking of teeth, similar to the way a flintlock rifle works. It has been surmised that the leviathan refers to a member of the *Plesiosaur* family in light of the reference to the beast stirring up the sea and leaving a glistening wake behind it (verses 31-32).

However, a creature akin to the *Spinosaurus* or *Tyrannosaurus rex* are more likely in light of verses 33-34, which point out, "Nothing on earth is its equal—a creature without fear… it is king over all that are proud." Just because leviathan "leaves a glistening wake" doesn't mean that it *has* to be an animal that *solely* dwells in the water, like the *Plesiosaur*. Actually, the *Spinosaurus* spent more time in the water than land. Meanwhile the *T. rex* could go anywhere it wanted any time it wanted, including any body of water outside of the deep parts of lakes, seas and oceans.

How Old Is the Earth?

The Bible does not say what the age of the Earth is and so people draw conclusions based on various data. It's a non-essential issue and believers can hold to one position or another without it affecting their relationship with God or their Christian service. The more important an issue is, the more directly and fully the Bible addresses it. For instance, our moral responsibilities and the means to eternal salvation are clearly addressed at length, but less critical topics are not, such as the age of the Earth. When it comes to God's Word "The main things are the plain things."

That said, let's consider the young Earth view, commonly held by Evangelicals, as well as the old Earth perspective and, more specifically, the gap theory, which isn't as widely accepted.

Young Earth advocates maintain that the Earth is only about 6000 years old, a figure they get from adding up the life spans of biblical figures from the time of Adam. How do we reconcile this with the evidence of geologists, who say the Earth is about 4.5 billion years old (and the

Universe 13.8 billion years old)? Supporters of young Earth creationism argue that, if God creates something in a mature state, like a human being, it would have the *appearance* of age and thus it is with the Earth.

How old was Adam one minute after God created him? One minute, but how old did Adam *look?* About 25-30 years old, certainly not like a newborn baby. The same principle can be applied to plants, trees, mammals, birds, fish, mountains, Earth, planets, stars and the Universe.

If doctors studied Adam's body—his skeletal development, the size of his organs, his mental capacity, etc.—they'd conclude that he was an adult male of about 25-30 years of age. God's creation of Adam in a mature state (in which his growth was perhaps accelerated to a brief period) is included in the creation account of Genesis 1-2 wherein God's creation of the Heavens and Earth is also chronicled. If the LORD created Adam in a mature state—with the obvious *appearance* of age—is it not possible, even likely, that God did the same with the Earth & Universe?

Notice how the LORD refers to the creation of the Heavens and Earth:

> **" 'The Israelites are to observe the Sabbath, celebrating it for the generations to come as a lasting covenant. [17] It will be a sign between me and the Israelites forever, <u>for in six days the LORD made the heavens and the earth, and on the seventh day he rested and was refreshed</u>.' "**
>
> **Exodus 31:16-17**

We know from authentic science that the Earth & Universe *appear* to be ancient—billions of years old—but we see here that the LORD created them in six days **as a testimony to the Israelites**. The physical creation *is* incredibly old, but God evidently condensed the aging process of each phase of creation into six days. Since the LORD was addressing Moses & the Israelites in the above passage, and they understood the "six days" to be six literal days, it stands to reason that God meant six literal days.

Think about it like this: If you had a huge project that would take 50 years to accomplish, yet you had the power to condense the time into 5 minutes, would you do it? Of course you would. How much more so if your purpose for doing this was to **illustrate a point to people**? It's the same principle with God's creation of the Earth & Universe.

Consider those science videos where a plant is filmed over the course of a year or so and then this growth is condensed to seconds for viewers. If filmmakers can do this via cinematic wizardry, would **the Almighty** have a problem doing something similar with the *initial* creation of people, animals, plants, trees, mountains, canyons, planets, stars and galaxies? There's even a blatant example in Scripture of God supernaturally **condensing the growth-time** of something in Jonah 4:6. So why wouldn't the LORD do the same thing when creating the Earth & Universe?

Where do dinosaurs fit in this young Earth scenario? In the post-flood years, they largely died out due to changing climate, lack of food or disease. Much as threatening animals like lions, tigers, bears, crocogators and pachyderms have been killed or driven out of populated areas by humans, so the last vestige of land-dwelling dinosaurs were slain or driven out. This would explain the "slay the dragon" myth in so many cultures, as well as the ancient art testifying to humans and dinosaurs coexisting.

As for the old Earth perspective, the top view is **the gap theory**, which speculates that there were billions of years between the first verse of Genesis 1 and the second verse. As such, Genesis 1:2 describes the Earth *after* some great cataclysm, which made the Earth "formless and empty":

> **In the beginning God created the heavens** [the Universe] **and the earth. 2 Now the earth was formless and empty, darkness was over the surface of the deep, and the Spirit of God was hovering over the waters.**
>
> **Genesis 1:1-2**

The mystery of this passage is the obvious contrast between verses 1 and 2: The first verse says that God created the Universe and the Earth, but then verse 2 states that the Earth was formless, empty and dark. Since when does God create something that's "formless and empty"?

Gap theorists argue that Isaiah 45:18 lends support: "He is God who formed the earth and made it, He established it and did not create it to be a waste place, but formed it to be inhabited" (NASB). The words "waste place" are one word in the Hebrew, *tohu (TOH-hu)*, and this is the same word translated as "formless" in Genesis 1:2. This word means "formless," "desolation," "waste place," "chaos" and "emptiness." The hermeneutical principle that "Scripture interprets Scripture" applies: Isaiah 45:18 plainly states that God did not create the Earth to be *tohu*—formless, empty, chaotic, desolate, a waste place—yet Genesis 1:2 shows that the Earth was *tohu* sometime after the LORD created it.

Lending further support to this theory, they say, is the statement in Genesis 1:2: "Now the earth *was* formless and empty." If you look at the footnote in the New International Version of the Bible it shows that the word 'was' could possibly be translated as "became" because the Hebrew verb *hayah (haw-yaw)* is often translated as such. As a matter of fact, it's translated as "became" 59 times and "become" 164 times in the New International Version. However, it's translated as "was" 305 times.

Further evidence can be observed in Hebrews 11:3, which states: "By faith we understand that the universe was **formed** at God's command, so that what is seen was not made out of what was visible." The word 'formed' in the Greek is *katartizó (kat-ar-TID-zoh)*, which means "to complete," "to perfect," "make complete," "**mend**," "**restore**" and "**bring into its proper condition** (whether for the first time, or after a lapse)." While this doesn't negate the young Earth theory, it's friendly toward the gap theory.

Supporters of the gap theory argue that Jeremiah 4:23-26 lends additional support for their position as it gives us a picture of cataclysmic global judgment whereupon no living thing survives, which they say only fits the pre-Adamic context between Genesis 1:1 and 1:2. The prophet says in verse 23: "I looked at the earth and it was **formless and empty**; and at the heavens and their light was gone." This is the exact same description as Genesis 1:2. 'Formless' is the same Hebrew word *tohu* and 'empty' (or 'void' in some translations) is the same Hebrew word *bohu (BOH-hu).* **These Hebrew words appear *together* in Scripture only these two times and, in the case of Jeremiah 4:23, it's clearly an occasion of global-spanning judgment.**

Verse 25 goes on to say that the prophet couldn't see any people on the planet, at least from the perspective of his vision, nor could he see any birds. We know there will be people and animals on the Earth after the Tribulation judgments noted in the book of Revelation because, after all, Christ will judge the living nations upon His return, which is The Sheep and Goat Judgment, aka The Judgment of Living Nations (Matthew 25:31-46). As such, adherents of the gap theory argue that Jeremiah 4:23-26 more likely refers to the Earth after a pre-Adamic cataclysm or judgment that took place between Genesis 1:1 and Genesis 1:2.

This cataclysm would explain the extinction of the dinosaurs, they argue.

Gap theorists also maintain that God's command to the survivors of the Noahic flood to "Be fruitful and increase in number and <u>fill</u> the earth" (Genesis 9:1) meant to *replenish* the Earth, which is how the Hebrew word for 'fill,' *male (maw-LAY)*, is translated in the KJV. This is the same word used in the similar command to Adam in Genesis 1:28, which suggests that it could also mean replenish in that context, particularly since it's the *same command* from God given to two different sets of people.

If you're interested, check out the responses from youth Earth advocates to these gap theory arguments; then look up the rebuttals by gap theorists. It's healthy to consider opposing views and the support for each before drawing an informed conclusion or, at least, a hypothesis.

While I suppose I lean toward the young Earth position, I confess agnosticism on the topic. I wasn't present when the LORD created the Universe and neither were you. The best we can do is make an educated guess based on biblical and scientific data, keeping in mind that, however old the Earth is, it has no bearing on one's spiritual growth and service. Also keep in mind that this is decidedly a side issue. As it is said: ***In essentials unity, in non-essentials liberty, in all things charity.***

14

Question About Human Damnation

Human damnation isn't a cheery subject; it's a dreadful reality in Christian thought. Unfortunately, false teachings abound on the topic, typically due to blind adherence to flawed religious tradition or superficiality and bias in biblical studies. So, what does the Bible *really* teach about human damnation? You might be surprised.

What Is Hell?

The English word 'hell' is not found in the Greek or Hebrew Scriptures, but the term is often used in English translations to interpret three different biblical words that refer to different things: *gehenna*, *hades* (or *sheol* in Hebrew) and *tartaroo*. Let's look at each:

1. ***Gehenna*** *(geh-HEN-nah)* literally means "Valley of Hinnom" *(HIN-im)*. This valley was a ravine located outside the walls of SW Jerusalem that had an infamous past of idol worship and child sacrifice (2 Kings 16:3, 21:6 & 23:10). At the time of Christ, Gehenna was a trash dump and incinerator for the city.

Jesus used Gehenna as an *example* of the lake of fire because it was something all his hearers readily understood; observe:

> **"Do not be afraid of those who kill the body but cannot kill the soul. Rather, be afraid of the One** [God] **who can destroy both soul and body in hell** *(Gehenna)*.**"**
>
> **Matthew 10:28**

Trash was discarded in Gehenna for the purpose of **disposal and eradication**, as were the corpses of animals and despised criminals. Just the same, on Judgment Day those people who choose sin over reconciliation and eternal life through Christ will be discarded and destroyed in the lake of fire (Revelation 20:11-15).

2. ***Hades*** **or** ***Sheol*** *(Sheh-OHL)* are two other biblical words often translated as "hell" in English Bibles but, unlike Gehenna, Hades/Sheol **does not refer to the lake of fire**, but rather to the *intermediate state* of the unredeemed between physical death and their resurrection on Judgment Day. This topic is addressed in the next chapter.

3. ***Tartaroo*** *(tar-tar-OH)* only appears once in the Bible (2 Peter 2:4) and refers to the nether region where certain demons are held captive. It has nothing to do with human damnation.

Which One of These Words Refers to the True Hell?

Gehenna, because the Valley of Hinnom was an *illustration* of **the lake of fire**, which is where the unrepentant wicked will be cast:

> **The sea gave up the dead that were in it, and death and Hades gave up the dead that were in them, and each person was judged according to what they had done. [14] Then death and Hades were thrown into the lake of fire. The lake of fire is the second death. [15] Anyone whose name was not found written in the book of life was thrown into the lake of fire.**
>
> **Revelation 20:13-15**

So, only *Gehenna*—the lake of fire—refers to the true hell (since it applies to the damnation of the unredeemed). In light of this, it's not a good practice to translate *hades (sheol)* and *tartaroo* as "hell" since they *don't* refer to the lake of fire. Doing so just confuses the issue and this explains why some modern English translations do not translate these terms as "hell," like the NASB and NRSV.

Why Must People Be Damned?

Because God is just and therefore must punish transgression against divine law, i.e. sin. But **the good news is that no person has to be damned to the lake of fire** to suffer the "second death." That's what the gospel of Christ is all about—redeeming people from eternal damnation and reconciling them to their Creator, not to mention giving them eternal life!

Notice what the most popular passage of the Bible says: "For God so loved the world that he gave his one and only Son, that whoever believes in him shall **not perish** but **have eternal life**" (John 3:16).

What Is the Penalty for Sin?

Death. As the Bible plainly declares: "The wages of sin is **death**, but the gift of God is **eternal life** in Christ Jesus, our Lord" (Romans 6:23). Could it be stated any plainer? The wages for sin is revealed to be death; and eternal life is a gift from God, not something people already have.

Doesn't Damnation Consist of Eternal Torture?

Not for human beings. Jesus clearly said that the lake of fire was originally *prepared for* the rebellious angels (Matthew 25:41,46). However, the lake of fire is defined for human beings as the "second death" (Revelation 20:13-14). This is where God will "**destroy** both soul and body," as the Lord declared (Matthew 10:28). Paul described it as "everlasting

destruction" (2 Thessalonians 1:9)—destruction that lasts forever. The lake of fire is the LORD's chosen instrument to execute the second death.

Christ and others in the Bible backed-up this notion of literal everlasting destruction with numerous easy-to-understand ***examples***. For instance, the Messiah said "***Just as*** the weeds are pulled up and **burned** in the fire ***so it will be*** at the end of this age" (Matthew 13:40). Jesus was talking about human damnation here—the "second death"—and He likened people to weeds that will be pulled up and discarded in fire. What happens to literal weeds when they're thrown into fire? Why, they burn for a little bit and then BURN UP. The Lord said *"**just as**"* this happens with literal weeds *"**so it will be**"* with unredeemed people at the end of this age. Was the Lord giving an inappropriate illustration or did He mean what He said?

There are many other unmistakable examples of literal destruction in the Bible, like Luke 19:11-27, which ends with this statement by the king in the parable (representative of God on Judgment Day): "But those enemies of mine who did not want me to be king over them—bring them here and **kill them** in front of me."

What About "Eternal Punishment"?

There's a difference between eternal punishment and eternal punish***ing***.

The Greek word for "punishment" is *kolasis (KOL-as-is)*, which refers to a "penal infliction" and is therefore a judicial sentence. Yeshua does not say in Matthew 25 what the penal infliction will be, only that it will take place in the lake of fire ("the eternal fire") and that this infliction will last forever. Since Christ doesn't specify what exactly the penal sentence is, we must turn to the rest of Scripture for answers. "Scripture interprets Scripture" is an interpretational rule. And we see above that Christ plainly said God would "destroy both soul and body" in the lake of fire.

So, the ultimate wage of sin is **death**—death that lasts forever; in other words, everlasting destruction. This eternal punishment takes place on the

Day of Judgment when those who chose sin over reconciliation and eternal life will be cast into the lake of fire.

The Bible uses the word "eternal" to describe the results of an act even when it is clear that the act itself is not of endless duration. For instance, Hebrews 9:12 speaks of the "eternal redemption" that Christ obtained for us; yet no one absurdly supposes that this redemption will be an endless process that goes on through all eternity "because by one sacrifice he has made perfect forever those who are being made holy" (Hebrews 10:14).

Also, Hebrews 6:2 speaks of "eternal judgment," yet no one ludicrously claims that the work of judging goes on forever and ever without end. In the same way, the act of punishment need not go on endlessly for the punishment to be eternal. Like eternal redemption and eternal judgment, eternal punishment is eternal in the sense that **its results are eternal**.

How Can 'Immortal Souls' Be Destroyed?

Because the Bible plainly declares that **immortality and eternal life are only available through the gospel of Christ** (2 Timothy 1:10). Immortality is something we're called to seek and not something we intrinsically possess **apart from Christ**, as shown in Romans 2:7.

Furthermore, **nowhere does the Bible state that the human soul, once created, is immortal and can never die**. The Hebrew word for "soul," *nephesh,* appears over 750 times in the Old Testament and the Greek word for "soul," *psychē,* appears over 100 times in the New Testament. These over 850 references should tell us all we need to know about the soul, yet none say anything about it being immortal by nature. If the immortal soul doctrine is true, why did God inspire hundreds of references to the soul without mentioning anything about it being inherently immortal?

On the contrary, God plainly informed Adam, who was a "living soul," that he would "**surely die**" if he sinned (Genesis 2:7,17). He also pointed out in Ezekiel 18:4,20 that "the soul *(nephesh)* who sins… will **die**." And, as we've already observed, the Lord plainly declared that God would "**destroy** both soul *(psuche)* and body in hell" (Matthew 10:28). A usual knee-jerk, but hollow, response is to argue that these Scriptures "are taken out of context." I would like to use this same argument and point out that biblical references to the immortal soul apart from Christ are taken out of context, but I can't *because no such passages exist.*

Where Did the Idea of the 'Immortal Soul' Originate?

From the devil, the "father of lies," as Yeshua called him (John 8:44). Remember what God said to Adam and Eve would be the consequence of disobedience? He warned them that they would "surely die" (Genesis 2:17). In other words, the LORD made it perfectly clear way back in the beginning that going the wrong way—the way of selfishness and rebellion—would lead to **death**. This is in harmony with the biblical fact that "the wages of sin is **death**" (Romans 6:23).

When "the father of lies" tempted Eve to sin in Genesis 3:4, he contradicted what God said by saying that she would "*not* surely die" if she sinned. This is the very first lie recorded in the Bible. The devil was saying in essence, "What God said is a lie, you will not surely die—you have an immortal soul." Unfortunately, people have been believing this lie about the so-called immortal soul ever since; this false doctrine infiltrated Christianity early on and has gone on to become the "orthodox" view even though the Bible does not teach it, which reveals the power of religious tradition and sectarian allegiance.

This long-lasting mass deception explains why I refer to the doctrine of the immortal soul (apart from Christ) as **The Great Lie**.

After the fall of Adam and Eve, notice what the LORD said to Himself:

> **And the LORD God said, "The man has now become like one of us, knowing good and evil. He must not be allowed to reach out his hand and take also from the tree of life and eat, <u>and live forever</u>."**
>
> **Genesis 3:22**

God would not have said this if Adam *already* possessed an immortal soul (that is, unconditional immortality). Secondly, this statement makes it clear that human beings can obtain unconditional immortality ***if*** they eat of the tree of life. The obvious reason God did not want Adam to eat of the tree of life is because he was unredeemed. If Adam ate of the tree of life in his unredeemed condition, he would have attained unconditional immortality and thus would have condemned himself & his descendants to live forever in a fallen, ungodly state (like the devil and his angels).

The LORD is just, righteous and merciful and didn't want such a horrible tragedy to befall humanity, so he immediately banished Adam & Eve from the garden and was sure to guard the way to the tree of life (verses 23-24). Our Creator would have to redeem humankind before allowing us to eat "from the tree of life and live forever."

That's what the gospel of Christ is all about. And this explains Jesus' statement in Revelation 2:7: "To him who overcomes I will give the right to eat from the tree of life, which is in the paradise of God." Notice clearly that only those who are born of God and overcome the world by faith (1 John 5:4) have the right to eat of the tree of life and live forever. That's because **eternal life and immortality are only available through the gospel** (2 Timothy 1:10).

So, People Will Be Destroyed in the Lake of Fire?

Yes, this is explicitly stated throughout the Bible. Notice for yourself:

> **"Enter through the narrow gate, for wide is the gate and broad the road that leads to destruction and many enter through it. But small is the gate and narrow the road that leads to life, and only a few find it."**
>
> **Matthew 7:13-14**

> **"For God so loved the world that he gave his one and only Son, that whoever believes in him shall not perish but have eternal life."** **John 3:16**

> **For if you live according to the sinful nature, you will die; but if by the spirit you put to death the misdeeds of the body, you will live.**
>
> **Romans 8:13**

> **The one who sows to please the sinful nature from that nature will reap destruction; the one who sows to please the spirit, from the spirit will reap eternal life.**
>
> **Galatians 6:8**

As you can see, the two possible destinies for people are life or death, not eternal life in heavenly bliss and eternal life in roasting torment. **Life** and **death** are the two polar opposites.

Do People *Choose* Hell?

No, people choose sin over reconciliation with God; and the wages of sin is **death**. The LORD will execute this death sentence in the lake of fire, which is why it's called the "second **death**."

So, People Will Be Destroyed Forever in Hell?

Yes, remember Christ plainly said to fear God "who is able to destroy both soul and body in hell" (Matthew 10:28). This shows that the LORD is going to do one of two things with people based on their decisions: save those who repent & believe (Mark 1:15)—blessing them with eternal life—or condemn them to the lake of fire where they'll suffer "everlasting destruction." James put it like this: "There is only one lawgiver and judge, the One [God] who is able to **save** and **destroy**" (James 4:12).

Many don't realize this, but we are actually saved from God's wrath—yes, **we are saved from *God Himself*.** Notice how the gospel of John puts it:

> **"Whoever believes in the Son has eternal life, but whoever rejects the Son will not see life, for God's wrath remains on them."**
>
> **John 3:36**

Observe two important things about this passage: **1.** Those who reject Christ "will not see life"—meaning they won't see any kind of life at all, including a horrible life roasting in fiery torment forever and ever; and **2.** The reason people who reject Christ "will not see life" is due to God's wrath! This is why the Bible says that "It is a dreadful thing to fall into the hands of the living God" (Hebrews 10:31). This point is made in the context of this sober statement:

> **If we deliberately keep on sinning after we have received the knowledge of the truth, no sacrifice for sins is left, but only a fearful expectation of judgment and of raging fire that will consume the enemies of God.**
>
> **Hebrews 10:26-27**

Notice what will happen to the "enemies of God": Raging fire will **consume** them, not torture them for all eternity. The Greek word translated as 'consume' here literally means "to devour."

Is this immoral on the LORD's part? No, He's the author and giver of life (Psalm 36:9); none of us would even exist apart from our Creator. As noted above, God is the Lawgiver and Judge of the Universe (James 4:12) and reigns supreme over all creation. The Almighty therefore has the right to take life away, but only does so if He must.

Does "Destruction" Mean *Literal* Destruction?

Aside from the glaring examples of literal destruction we've already looked at—like weeds being burned up in fire (Matthew 13:40) and a king's enemies being slain in front of him (Luke 19:27)—Christ and the apostles plainly taught what would happen to ungodly people when they suffer "the second death." They taught that:

- the ungodly would **die** (John 11:26 & Romans 8:13),
- that they would experience **death** (John 8:51, Romans 6:23 & James 5:20),
- that **destruction** would occur (Matthew 7:13 & 2 Peter 3:7),
- that both their souls and bodies would be **destroyed** (Matthew 10:28 & James 4:12),
- and that they would **perish** (John 3:16 & 2 Peter 3:9).

As you can see, the Bible continually speaks of the eternal fate of the unrepentant wicked in explicit terms of destruction: "die," "death," "destruction," "destroy" and "perish." I refer to this as the "language of destruction." The Holy Spirit wrote the Scriptures via people of God (2 Peter 1:20-21) and the terminology that the Holy Spirit chose to use was the language of **destruction**, not the language of eternal conscious torture.

In a desperate effort to repudiate this, advocates of eternal roasting torment try to claim that the Greek word translated as "destroy" and "perish" in passages like Matthew 10:28 and John 3:16—*apollumi (ah-POHL-loo-mee)*—means "destruction, not of being, but of well-being." However, this is easily disproven because Jesus used this very word (as conveyed by Luke) to describe the **incineration** of the people of Sodom (Luke 17:29). Bear in mind that both the Old and New Testaments detail that Sodom & Gomorrah were **burned to ashes** and, even more, that this total incineration is **an *example* of what will happen to the ungodly on the day of judgment** (2 Peter 2:6). What word did Christ use to describe this incineration in Luke 17:29? Why, *appolumi*, the very same word translated as "destroy" in Matthew 10:28 and "perish" in John 3:16. Enough said.

But I Thought God Was Akin to a Cosmic Teddy Bear

Many people in the modern age have this impression of the LORD—that he's so loving, kind and gentle that he will not punish sin—but this is a lopsided view of the Creator and therefore inaccurate. Other people go to the opposite extreme and view the Almighty as some merciless cop in the sky who can't wait to utterly smash sinners and, worse, condemn them to never-ending fiery torment with no possible respite. Passages like John 3:16 and 2 Peter 3:9 offer a more *balanced* view of God, as does Ezekiel 18:32, which reveals the heart of God: " 'For I take no pleasure in the death of anyone,' declares the Sovereign LORD, '**Repent and live!**' "

What About "Hell, Where Their Worm Does Not Die"?

'Hell' in this passage (Mark 9:48) is the Greek word *Gehenna*, which—again—literally refers to the Valley of Hinnom, the perpetually smoking trash dump of Jerusalem at the time of Christ. The Lord used this incinerator as a figure for the lake of fire and the final punishment of the wicked. Yeshua said, "Their worm does not die," which the revised NIV puts like this: " 'the worms that eat them do not die.' " You'll notice that verse 48 is in quotation marks. That's because Christ is quoting the very last passage of the book of Isaiah. Let's look at this verse as it will help us to properly interpret Jesus' words:

> **"They** [the righteous] **shall go forth and look on the <u>corpses</u> of the men who have transgressed against me. For their worm shall not die, and their fire shall not be quenched; and they shall be an abhorrence to all mankind."**
>
> **Isaiah 66:24** (NASB)

The "corpses" refer to the people who have transgressed against the LORD and will be thrown into the lake of fire. Please notice that they are **no longer alive**. *They are dead.* They have been **destroyed**. They are loathsome, ashen, worm-chewed **corpses**. They will be "an abhorrence to all mankind" just as an ashen, worm-chewed corpse of a despised criminal would be abhorrent to you or me.

The fact that these transgressors are, in fact, **lifeless corpses** is backed up by verse 16 of the same chapter of Isaiah, which says they will be "**slain** by the LORD"; and verse 17, which says "they will **meet their end**." The second death is when the ungodly will **meet their end**, not when they'll meet the beginning of life in never-ending roasting agony.

The Hebrew for "worm" in this verse refers to maggots (Strong 123) and the bodies affected by these maggots are dead, which is fitting since **maggots exclusively devour dead flesh**, not living creatures. And, it should be added, maggots don't die, they turn into flies. Being that Gehenna was a garbage dump maggots bred freely and preyed upon the refuse. When corpses of animals or executed criminals were thrown in, they would be consumed by maggots or by the fires that were kept constantly burning there, or a combination of both.

Understanding the unmistakable context of the Lord's quote from Isaiah, as well as the historical facts concerning Gehenna, help us to properly interpret Jesus' words in Mark 9:48.

As for the phrase "the fire is not quenched," there are multiple references to unquenchable fire in the Scriptures and none of these passages refer to eternal torment, but rather to fire that cannot be resisted or extinguished and consumes until nothing is left. Jeremiah 7:20 and 21:12,14 are two examples. These and the other passages that mention unquenchable fire prove that such phrases refer to the **irrevocability of God's judgment and wrath**—for, when the LORD's judgment is pronounced and the fire is set to destroy, He will allow nothing to quench it until the consumption is complete (see, for example, Isaiah 34:9-11, Ezekiel 20:47-48, Amos 5:6, Matthew 3:12 and Luke 3:17).

Misguided preachers who advocate eternal roasting have had a field day with Mark 9:48, conjuring up all kinds of bizarre interpretations, including how immortal worms will forever chew on the undying souls of the damned in the lake of fire. They do this by *not* rightly-dividing the Word of God—ignoring the facts about Gehenna and the context of the quote from Isaiah. They're biased on the subject and superficial in their studies.

In response to this, I have a much less ambiguous "worm verse" that I'd like to share, which is also from the book of Isaiah:

> **"For the moth will eat them up like a garment; the worm will devour them like wool. But my righteousness will last forever, my salvation through all generations."**
>
> **Isaiah 51:8**

Just as moths eat or destroy garments, so the ungodly will be destroyed in the lake of fire. Like Mark 9:48, this is undoubtedly a figurative example of everlasting destruction. It is meant to be taken seriously, but not necessarily literally. I doubt, after all, that there will be literal moths or worms in the lake of fire devouring those thrown in. We've already deduced from Scripture that, literally, the ungodly will be consumed by raging fire—both soul and body—when cast into the lake of fire. This will result in the blackest darkness of all—absolute obliteration and extinction of being (Obadiah 1:16).

Notice how the everlasting destruction of the ungodly is contrasted with the LORD's righteousness and salvation which will **last forever**. Those who accept God's gracious gift of salvation—eternal life—will experience this salvation forever. Those who reject it have no "forever" to look forward to; they will be **destroyed like garments devoured by moths or worms**. Verses 3, 6-8 & 11 also confirm that this is indeed an eschatological passage and therefore relevant to the eternal fate of ungodly people. Why is it that proponents of eternal torture fail to ever mention this "worm verse"? I'll tell you why—it contradicts their religious position.

What About Revelation 14:9-11?

Adherents of never-ending roasting naturally view this passage as their 'ace card' on the topic:

> **"If anyone worships the beast and his image and receives his mark on the forehead or on the hand, [10]he, too, will drink of the wine of God's fury, which has been poured out full strength into the cup of his wrath. He will be tormented with burning sulfur in the**

> **presence of the holy angels and of the lamb** [Jesus]. [11]**And the smoke of their torment rises forever and ever. There is no rest day or night for those who worship the beast or his image, or anyone who receives the mark of his name."**
>
> **Revelation 14:9-ll**

As you can see, the text refers to impenitent people during the future seven-year Tribulation who received the mark of the beast and will be damned. Being "tormented with burning sulfur" refers to being cast into the lake of fire and suffering the "second death" (Revelation 20:10-15). Notice it says that "**the smoke** of their torment rises forever," which suggests that they will be burned up, while "torment" would refer to the anguish experienced while being destroyed. This coincides with what the Holy Spirit inspired David to write in Psalm 37:20: "But **the wicked shall perish**... **Into smoke** they shall **vanish away**" (NKJV).

Secondly, this passage has a 'sister text' in the Old Testament, which uses the same terminology, but clearly refers to literal everlasting destruction and not never-ending conscious torment:

> [9]**Edom's streams will be turned into pitch,**
> **her dust into burning sulfur;**
> **her land will become blazing pitch!**
> [10]**It will not be quenched night or day;**
> **its smoke will rise forever.**
>
> **Isaiah 34:9-10a**

This gives the impression that the kingdom of Edom will burn forever and ever without end, but the rest of the chapter renders this interpretation impossible. The remainder of the chapter shows that Edom would become a desolate desert inhabited by owls, jackals and hyenas. Verses 5-6 state that the people of Edom will be "totally destroyed" and slaughtered, and Obadiah 1:10 & 1:18 back this up, stating that Edom will "be destroyed forever"—consumed by the fire of God's judgment and wrath.

Notice how Isaiah 34:10 plainly declares that Edom will burn and "not be quenched night and day." This shows that the phrase "night and day" or "day or night" does not refer to an unending amount of time. The burning sulfur which destroyed Edom was not quenched "night and day" until the entire kingdom was destroyed. Likewise, the wicked people spoken of in Revelation 14:10-11 will have no rest from their torment "day or night" until the burning sulfur totally destroys them.

"Burning sulfur" is simply another name for the lake of fire (Revelation 21:8); so being "tormented with burning sulfur" is a reference to the second death. For further proof, Paul said that he worked and prayed "night and day" (1 Thessalonians 2:9; 3:10), but he did neither non-stop; and working ceased when he passed away. Acts 9:24 and Revelation 12:10 give additional support that this phrase refers to a temporary period of time.

There are other passages in the book of Revelation that use the terminology of Revelation 14:10-11, but like Isaiah 34:9-10, these passages distinctly refer to complete destruction by fire: Chapter 18 of Revelation deals with the fall of Babylon, which is the result of God's judgment. "Babylon" refers to a city that will be the governmental center of the antichrist's kingdom on Earth. Chapter 18 speaks of "the smoke of her burning" (verses 9 & 18) and of "her torment" (verses 10 & 15), and 19:3 says, "The smoke from her goes up forever and ever." This terminology gives the impression that "Babylon" will be eternally tormented and burn forever and ever, but Revelation 18:8 makes it clear that "She will be consumed by fire"—completely destroyed—just as this entire present Earth will also be destroyed (2 Peter 3:10-11). Hence, the statement "the smoke from her goes up forever and ever" refers to complete and final destruction.

These passages use the terminology of smoke rising forever and coincide with God's **total destruction of Sodom & Gomorrah**, which is a biblical "example of what is going to happen to the ungodly" at the second death (2 Peter 2:6). In the Genesis account of Sodom & Gomorrah's destruction, Abraham saw "dense smoke rising from the land, like smoke from a furnace" (19:28).

So, following the hermeneutical rule that "Scripture interprets Scripture," it's clear that Revelation 14:9-11 refers to literal everlasting destruction and not never-ending roasting torment. Adherents of eternal conscious torture who claim that the passage is their 'ace card' on the topic are guilty of being superficial in their studies and not rightly-dividing the Word of Truth (2 Timothy 2:15).

Who Will Be Condemned to the Lake of Fire?

Salvation from the sentence of eternal death is both a matter of faith in response to the gospel (faith, by the way, is simply admitting the obvious), but also a matter of repentance (Acts 20:21). "Repent" was the first word of Jesus and John the Baptist's first sermons (Matthew 3:2 & 4:17). It means to turn from what is evil by making a 180° shift; it means to change your mind for the positive which naturally changes your actions. It's a very positive thing and not negative in the least. True faith acknowledges the Creator and is willing to conform to God's will. People who say they're Christians and have faith, but are unwilling to give up something evil and continue practicing it are not walking in faith and repentance. This explains something that Paul wrote to the believers at Corinth:

> **Or do you not know that wrongdoers will not inherit the kingdom of God? Do not be deceived: Neither the sexually immoral nor idolaters nor adulterers nor men who have sex with men [10] nor thieves nor the greedy nor drunkards nor slanderers nor swindlers will inherit the kingdom of God. [11] And that is what some of you were. But you were washed, you were sanctified, you were justified in the name of the Lord Jesus Christ and by the Spirit of our God.**
>
> **1 Corinthians 6:9-11**

Notice that it's not just those who refuse to repent of sexual immorality (including adultery, fornication and homosexuality) who won't inherit the kingdom of God, its people who refuse to repent of greediness, drunkard-ness, and slander! (By the way, slander is saying something about someone that isn't wholly true, which would include gossip that naturally devolves into slander and, needless to say, puts a negative spin on a person. I'm shocked at how much gossip & slander I see in the Church, including amongst fivefold ministers and their spouses).

Two important points: **1.** Paul was talking to believers and **2.** he was referring to those who *practice* these types of things with no intention of repenting; in other words, as a *lifestyle*. We are called to turn away from sin as a lifestyle, which is what repentance is. Of course, we all miss it, even those of us who are spiritually mature (particularly in the "smaller" areas, like envy, arrogance, gossip, etc.), which is what 1 John 1:8-9 is for: When we miss it, we need to be quick to 'fess up and God is faithful to forgive us, cleansing us from all unrighteousness. This is "keeping in repentance" (Matthew & Luke 3:8). So always be sure to keep in repentance! Don't allow any sin to become a lifestyle. Be sure to throw off every weight that hinders and any sin that entangles you (Hebrews 12:1).

I want to stress that **no one has to be damned** by being thrown in the lake of fire and suffering the punishment of eternal death. Yes, "the wages of sin is death," but the **good news** is that "the free gift of God is eternal life in Christ Jesus" (Romans 6:23) "For God so loved the world that he gave his one and only Son that whoever believes in him **shall not perish** but **have eternal life**"!

At this point some might be asking 'What about the rich man and Lazarus?' That parable is relevant to Sheol/Hades, which is a separate topic from the second death, and is therefore addressed in the next chapter…

15

Questions About Sheol, aka Hades

Is the Parable of the Rich Man and Lazarus Literal?

This question refers to Luke 16:19-31 where Jesus tells the story of a rich man and poor beggar who die and go to "hell" (verse 23). Regardless of whether you take this tale literally or figuratively, it's not relevant to the eternal fate of the unsaved because the Greek word translated as 'hell' in the story is *hades*, which refers to the intermediate state of the unredeemed between death and resurrection. It does not refer to the lake of fire and therefore is not applicable to the topic of damnation, the "second death."

This story is obviously a parable since it uses symbolic language (like "Abraham's bosom," which literally refers to Abraham's chest cavity) and, furthermore, it **comes in a long line of parables**: The whole first half of Luke 16 is a parable that starts with the **same exact words** as Jesus' tale of the rich man and Lazarus; and Luke 15 consists of three other parables.

On top of this, it is a classic story of reversal-of-fortune, containing glaring fantastical elements, such as the rich man in roasting torment asking Abraham to have Lazarus dip the tip of his finger in water so he can cool his tongue—not even his hand or finger, the *tip* of his finger! Like that's going to help his agonizing condition one iota. It's as if Christ was getting a megaphone and declaring, *"This is a fantastical tale that's not meant to be taken literally!"* In truth, it's a biting satire that mimics the Pharisee's beliefs in order to brilliantly rebuke them & their ilk.

Some argue that a parable *always* reflects reality and *cannot* be fantastical, but a parable is simply a short allegorical tale that teaches a moral lesson. That's it. Nowhere does the Bible say a parable *has* to reflect reality and cannot be fantastical. For instance, righteous Jotham shared a parable in Judges 9:8-15 about trees talking to each other. Should we take that as reality? Of course not; the argument holds no water.

With the understanding that this is a fantastical symbolic story, Christ knew that religious people who fail to rightly divide the Scriptures would wrongly interpret it as a literal account in centuries to come, just as a Pharisee misinterpreted Yeshua's statement about being born-again to refer to literal physical rebirth (John 3:3-4). Please understand that the Lord didn't tell parables to reveal truth to the masses, but rather to *hide it* for those with spiritual discernment (Matthew 13:10-15 & 1 Corinthians 2:14). As such, the Parable of the Rich Man and Lazarus is **a stumbling block to those who fail to correctly handle the Scriptures** (2 Timothy 2:15). We're talking about those who are spiritually blind to some degree, usually due to staunch sectarianism.

Most importantly, taking this parable literally *contradicts* what the Word of God plainly teaches on the topic. Scripture interprets Scripture. For instance, when the *real-life* Lazarus died (as opposed to the *fictitious* one of this parable) Christ plainly said "Lazarus is **dead**," not blissfully hanging out with Abraham in some supposed nether paradise (John 11:14).

So, What Does the Bible Teach About Sheol/Hades?

Sheol or Hades involves the intermediate state of unsaved souls between physical death and later resurrection when they're judged (Revelation 20:11-15). It is "the world of **the dead**," as scholar James Strong defined it, or "the assembly of **the dead**," as Proverbs 21:16 describes it, or "the realm of **the dead**," as observed in Isaiah 14:9,15, Ezekiel 31:15,17 and 32:21,27. The verses from Ezekiel feature **the LORD Himself speaking**. In short, Sheol is the spiritual graveyard of *dead* souls located in the heart of the Earth (Matthew 12:40), albeit in the dark heavenlies or Underworld, not the physical realm. Since Sheol refers to the abode of **the dead**, it's often spoken of as synonymous with death in Scripture, e.g. Proverbs 7:27 and 9:18. Here are a couple examples from Isaiah and Psalms:

> **"For <u>Sheol</u> cannot thank you,**
> **<u>death</u> cannot praise you;**
> **those who go down to <u>the Pit</u>**
> **cannot hope for your faithfulness.**
> **19 The living, the living, they thank you**
> **as I do this day."**
>
> **Isaiah 38:18-19** (NRSV)

> **Who can live and never see <u>death</u>?**
> **Who can escape the power of <u>Sheol</u>?**
>
> **Psalm 89:48** (NRSV)

Consider those two questions in that last verse: Who can live and never see death? Who can escape the power of Sheol? Only those who are redeemed through Jesus Christ and thus have spiritual regeneration. Ever since Christ died for our sins and was raised to life for our justification, believers are redeemed and spiritually regenerated. Thus death & Sheol have no power over New Covenant believers who physically die. Instead, we go to be with the Lord in Heaven during the intermediate state in which we await our resurrection body, which is verified by several clear passages, like 2 Corinthians 5:6-9, Philippians 1:20-24, Hebrews 10:39, 1 Thessalonians 5:10, Revelation 6:9-11 and 7:9-17.

The souls of the unregenerated, however, go to Sheol at the point of physical decease wherein they are held until their future resurrection and judgment. This includes Old Testament saints who will be resurrected when Christ returns to the Earth at the end of the Tribulation (Matthew 19:28).

What Do Souls Experience in Sheol?

What do these dead souls experience in Sheol during the intermediate state? Are they tormented in fire the entire time, like the rich man in Jesus' parable? Do they chum around with father Abraham, like Lazarus in that tale? No, they're *dead* and therefore experience nothing. Solomon made this clear:

> **Whatever your hand finds to do, do with your might; for there is no work or thought or knowledge or wisdom in Sheol, to which you are going.**
>
> **Ecclesiastes 9:10** (NRSV)

The language describes beyond any doubt that Sheol is a condition of **unconsciousness**. In Sheol:

- there's neither good work nor bad work;
- there's neither positive, hopeful thoughts nor anguished, hopeless thoughts;
- there's neither knowledge of what's good and holy nor knowledge of what's evil and impure.

This is further verified in verse 5:

> **The living know that they will die, but the dead know nothing.**
>
> **Ecclesiastes 9:5** (NRSV)

The obvious reason the dead "know nothing" is because they're no longer alive and conscious—*they're dead.* This coincides with this passage from the Psalms:

> **His breath goeth forth, he** [his body] **returneth to his earth;**
> **in that very day his thoughts perish.**
>
> **Psalm 146:4** (KJV)

The Psalmist says that when an unredeemed person physically dies his/her thoughts perish. There is no mention whatsoever of a person's thoughts continuing to live on in some devil-ruled chamber of horrors. This is obviously because a dead person is no longer conscious of anything. While some translations say "plans" rather than "thoughts," the original Hebrew word, *eshtonah (esh-toh-NAW)*, literally means "thoughts."

Take another look at Ecclesiastes 9:10 above and notice that Solomon doesn't make a distinction between righteous or unrighteous people. He plainly says that **everyone** would go to Sheol during that period of time, whether righteous or wicked, rich or poor, small or great. In fact, Solomon's major point in Ecclesiastes 9 is that **death or Sheol is the common destiny of all people *before* redemption was made available through Christ's death and resurrection**. He plainly states in verse 3 that "the same destiny overtakes all." What destiny? The destiny of Sheol, death, where—he goes on to say—there is neither work nor thought nor knowledge nor wisdom.

When Is Sheol First Mentioned in the Bible?

Sheol first appears in Genesis 37:35, which is notable due to the hermeneutical law of first mention. This was the occasion where Jacob's sons treacherously sold their brother Joseph into slavery and then lied to their father by telling him that Joseph was slain by a wild beast. Jacob believed the lie and was understandably heartbroken:

> **All his sons and daughters sought to comfort him** [Jacob]**; but he refused to be comforted, and said, "No, <u>I shall go down to Sheol to my son</u>** [Joseph], **mourning." Thus his father bewailed him.**
>
> **Genesis 37:35** (NRSV)

Two simple facts can be derived from Jacob's expression of grief in this passage: **1.** Jacob ***expected*** **to go to Sheol when he died**, and **2.** Jacob **believed that Joseph was already in Sheol, that he would remain there, and that he himself would join him when he eventually died**.

The King James Version translates *sheol* in this passage as "the grave." Why? Because the verse refers to Jacob and Joseph, both righteous men of God (righteous in the sense that they were in-right-standing with God via their covenant, not that they were unflawed individuals). This is in harmony with the King James translators' policy of rendering *sheol* as "hell" when it applied to unrighteous people and as "the grave" when it applied to Hebrews in covenant with the LORD. But there's absolutely no justification for this practice; the meaning of the word *sheol* does not change depending on the spiritual state of the person going there.

Whether intentionally or inadvertently, this is evidence in the very first appearance of *sheol* in the Bible that religious people have tried to mislead the populace about its nature and who exactly went there.

As for the KJV and other translations rendering *sheol* as "the grave," Sheol never denotes the physical grave or tomb where bodies are laid to rest; there's a separate Hebrew word for this. Sheol should only be understood as "the grave" in the sense that it is **the graveyard of souls in the spiritual realm**, where **dead souls are held and 'awaiting' resurrection to be judged by God**.

Getting back to Jacob's statement in Genesis 37:35, although Jacob doesn't say anything about the nature of Sheol, it's obvious that he didn't regard it as some sort of nether paradise where his son was hanging out with father Abraham. If this were the case, would Jacob be "mourning" and "bewailing" Joseph so grievously? Of course not. It might be argued that Jacob was grieving over his own personal loss and not the destination of his son's disembodied soul. If this were so, wouldn't Jacob likely exclaim something to the effect of, "Praise the LORD that my son is now in the blissful presence of father Abraham, and I will one day go down to this same paradise rejoicing." Yet Jacob says nothing of the kind; in fact, his reaction is completely opposite to this.

Does Genesis Contain Further Insights on Sheol?

Yes, observe what Jacob later exclaims to his sons during a famine:

> **"I have heard that there is grain in Egypt. Go down there and buy some for us, <u>so that we may live and not die</u>."**
>
> **Genesis 42:2**

Jacob's son, Judah, makes a similar statement in the following chapter:

> **Then Judah said to Israel his father, "Send the boy along with me and we will go** [to Egypt] **at once, <u>so that we and you and our children may live and not die</u>."**
>
> **Genesis 43:8**

Both quotes are in reference to Jacob's sons traveling to Egypt to apprehend food so their clan "may live and not die." Obviously, Jacob and his family were in no hurry to go to Sheol to commune with father Abraham in some nether-paradise. Please notice that there's mysteriously no accompanying statement like, "...but—thankfully—if we die, we'll be in bliss with our forefathers in Sheol." Why not? Because this is an unbiblical doctrine.

This same point can be made from similar passages **all over the Bible**.

In both of these passages the Hebrew word for "die" is *muwth (mooth)*, which simply means "to die" and is used in reference to the death of animals as well as humans (Exodus 7:18). It does not mean "to separate" or, more specifically, "to separate and go to either bliss or torment in Sheol." The Hebrew term for 'separate' is *badal (baw-DAL)*, which is used in Genesis 1:4: "God saw that the light was good, and he *separated* the light from the darkness."

Needless to say, statements like "so we may live and not die" only make sense if Sheol is **the graveyard of dead souls** where souls 'rest' in death until their resurrection.

What Did Job Say About Sheol?

Job goes into quite a bit of detail on the nature of Sheol. Did he just dream up all this information or did he have Divine revelation on the subject? No doubt God revealed these truths to him. We can confidently draw this conclusion because what Job says about Sheol is in complete agreement with what the rest of the Bible teaches on the subject (taking the Parable of the Rich Man and Lazarus as what it is—a symbolic tale—and not a real-life accounting of life-after-death). Only if Job's position contradicted the rest of Scripture should we question its validity.

In the book of Job, satan argues to God that Job is devout merely because the LORD blessed him so greatly and that Job will curse his Creator if his blessings were removed. God thus permits satan to attack the man to find out. As a result, Job loses his ten children, scores of his employees (with only four survivors), all of his great wealth and even his health as he is afflicted with painful sores from head to toe.

After months of suffering, three of Job's friends go to "comfort" him, but end up judging & accusing him of some great hidden sin, which they *presume* brought about all his horrible suffering. Most of the book consists of Job, in great anguish, profoundly debating with these "friends." It should be noted, however, that much of what Job says is **directed at God Himself**. Such is the case with this passage:

> **"But mortals die, and are laid low;**
> **humans expire and where are they?**
> **11 As waters fail from a lake,**
> **and a river wastes away and dries up,**
> **12 so mortals lie down and do not rise again;**
> ***until* the heavens are no more, they will not awake**
> **or be aroused out of their sleep.**
> **13 Oh that you** [God] **would hide me in Sheol,**
> **that you would conceal me until your wrath is past,**
> **that you would appoint me a set time,**

and remember me!
14 **If mortals die, will they live again?**
All of the days of my service
I would wait until my release should come.
15 **You would call, and I would answer you;**
you would long for the works of your hands."
Job 14:10-15 (NRSV)

In verse 10, Job declares that "mortals die" and then asks "where are they?" He partially answers in verse 12 by likening death to "sleep" which humans will not "awake" from until "the heavens are no more" or, we could say, a very long time. What needs to be emphasized from these words is that **Job describes the condition of death as "sleep" from which all humans will one day "awake" or be resurrected**.

Yet he still hasn't really answered the question of *where* people go after they die. The very next verse answers this: In his anguish, he cries out to God to hide him **in Sheol** (verse 13). Why does Job pray this? Because his suffering was so great he wanted to escape it through death; and obviously when a person died—Job believed—his/her soul would go to Sheol.

One may argue that, in verse 12, Job is perhaps referring to the body "sleeping" in the grave, but the obvious focus of his words is the death condition of the soul in Sheol because in the very same breath he prays to go specifically there: "Oh that you would hide me **in Sheol**, that you would conceal me until your wrath is past, that you would appoint a set time and remember me!"

Job mistakenly believed that God Himself was causing his great afflictions because he was unaware of the devil's hand in the situation. In truth, the LORD only permitted Job's afflictions by allowing satan to attack him. Nevertheless, the fact is that **Job believed he would escape his intense suffering by dying and going to Sheol**.

Yes, Job was actually hoping and praying to die and go to Sheol, a place many religious people consider "hell" and believe to be a devil-ruled torture chamber! Obviously, **Job's view of Sheol was quite different**

from what religious tradition has taught us. He prayed to go to Sheol because he knew that Sheol was a condition of **unconsciousness**, which he described as **sleep**. Job was understandably weary of his intense suffering and wanted it to end. He knew that **in death, in Sheol, he would find relief from his misery, not an increase of it**.

Regardless of the nature of Sheol, **Job definitely believed that everyone would ultimately be resurrected from there**. In verse 12 he makes it clear that all mortals who lie down in the "sleep" of death will one day awaken, that is, be resurrected when "the heavens are no more." And, while Job prayed to go to Sheol in verse 13, it was not with the expectation that he would remain there forever. Job obviously believed that, if God "hid" him in Sheol, He would "appoint a set time and remember" him, which is when his "release" would come (verse 14). Release from what? From captivity to Sheol. So, God "remembering" him and "releasing" him are references to a future resurrection from Sheol, which is in harmony with what the rest of the Bible teaches.

Do "the Wicked Cease from Turmoil" in Sheol?

Job elaborates on the nature of Sheol in an earlier chapter where he curses the day of his birth because of his suffering. He was in essence wishing he were never born because then he would never have had to experience such agony. He then details what it would've been like if this were so:

> **"Why did I not <u>perish at birth</u>**
> **<u>and die</u> as I came from the womb?**
> **12 Why were there knees to receive me**
> **and breasts that I might be nursed?**
> **13 <u>For now I would be lying down in peace</u>;**
> **I would be <u>asleep and at rest</u>**
> **14 <u>with kings and counselors of the earth</u>**
> **who built for themselves places now lying in ruins,**
> **15 <u>with rulers</u> who had gold,**
> **who filled their houses with silver.**

[16] Or why was I not hidden in the ground like a stillborn child,
like an infant who never saw the light of day?
[17] There the wicked cease from turmoil,
and there the weary are at rest.
[18] Captives also enjoy their ease;
they no longer hear the slave driver's shout.
[19] The small and great are there,
and the slave is freed from his master."

Job 3:11-19

Job starts off asking why he didn't die as an infant. In that event, he argues, he would not be enduring all the great suffering that he was experiencing. Had he died in infancy, he believed that he would be peacefully "**lying down**… **asleep** and **at rest**" (verse 13).

Job then explains that he would have **shared this condition of sleep and rest** ***with*** kings and counselors of the Earth, ***with*** the small and the great, ***with*** rulers and slaves, ***with*** captives and weary people and, yes, even ***with the wicked!*** In this state of death, Job declares in verse 17 that "**there the wicked cease from turmoil**, and there **the weary are at rest**," and he makes it plain that there's no "slave driver's shout" as well (verse 18).

This coincides with what Job later says concerning the wicked:

"They [the wicked] **spend their days in prosperity**
and in peace they go down to Sheol."

Job 21:13 (NRSV)

He doesn't say the wicked go down to Sheol in torment; no, they go down to Sheol in peace. This contradicts the religious belief that the unredeemed go to some horrible devil-ruled nether realm immediately after physical death to suffer torments as they are goaded on by slave-driving demons in fiery pits with not a single drop of water for relief. Instead, Job makes it clear that there is no turmoil or torment for the wicked in Sheol.

Job is saying that, at death, **kings, counselors, rulers, infants, the wicked, the weary, captives, the small, the great and slaves all share the same condition**, a **condition of peaceful "sleep" and "rest," which are obvious references to unconsciousness**. No wonder Job, stripped of all his possessions, forsaken by his wife, wrongly judged by his "friends," tortured by painful sores from head to toe, mocked and made a byword by everyone, and mourning for his ten children & myriad employees, prayed to go to such a place. His understanding of Sheol was quite different from that held by many misguided people today.

Some may wonder if perhaps Job was referring to the literal grave or tomb where the body is laid to rest since there is no specific mention of Sheol in chapter 3. This idea is ruled out because Job says in verses 13-15 that, if he died, he'd be lying down asleep ***with*** kings, counselors and rulers. So, Job is referring to a common place or condition that all people shared together. Biblically speaking, this would be Sheol, the realm of dead souls, as verified in Ecclesiastes 9:10. Job would not be referring to the literal grave or tomb for the body because it is not acceptable or usual practice to bury people **together** in mass graves or tombs, then or now.

Keep in mind that this was well before the death and resurrection of Christ, hence spiritual rebirth and the consequent attainment of eternal life were yet to be manifested. For this reason, the souls of Old Testament saints could not be ushered into God's presence when they physically died. The souls of both the righteous and unrighteous went to Sheol at this time because redemption was not yet available.

What Are Some Other Descriptions of Sheol?

There are literally *dozens* of passages in the Bible that refute the false doctrine that dead souls are conscious in Sheol, whether suffering constant roasting torment or chumming around with father Abraham.

Consider the Psalms, which are "God-breathed" (2 Timothy 3:16) since all the psalmists "spoke from God as they were carried along by the Holy Spirit" (2 Peter 1:21). For unmistakable proof of this, Jesus said in

Matthew 22:43-44 that David was "speaking by the Spirit" when quoting Psalm 110:1, which of course implies all the psalms he wrote.

In other words, David's statements in the Psalms were given by the inspiration of the Holy Spirit and the Holy Spirit is God. As such, David's exposition on the nature of Sheol in the Psalms, as well as commentary by other psalmists, shouldn't be considered just "their view" of Sheol. No, it's God's view because they were "speaking by the Spirit."

Here are several descriptions:

Sheol Is Synonymous With Death

This can be observed in the first mention of Sheol in the book of Psalms (keeping in mind the hermeneutical law of first mention):

> **For <u>in death</u> there is no remembrance of you** [God]**;**
> **<u>in Sheol</u> who can give you praise?**
> **Psalm 6:5** (NRSV)

This is an example of synonymous parallelism in which the second part of the verse simply repeats and reinforces the thought of the first, just in different words. With this understanding, notice how Sheol is paralleled **with death**, not life in roasting torment.

The verse also reveals…

Souls in Sheol Cannot Remember or Praise God

David was praying for God to save his life in Psalm 6 because his enemies were trying to kill him (as indicated in verse 10). Despite his anguish, David didn't want to die; he was "a man after God's own heart" (1 Samuel 13:14 & Acts 13:22) and thus wanted to live and worship God. **He knew that, if he died and went to Sheol, he wouldn't be able to do this.**

This contradicts the prominent religious position on Sheol, which suggests that when Old Testament saints died their souls would go to a supposed "paradise" section of Sheol where they would be supremely comforted as they fellowshipped with father Abraham. If this were so, wouldn't they be able to remember God? Would they not be praising their Creator and thanking God, as long as it were possible?

Yet David makes it clear that **souls in Sheol do not and cannot remember God and consequently cannot praise their Creator either**. This suggests that those in Sheol are unconscious—"asleep" in death until their resurrection. This is corroborated by other texts. For instance:

> **The dead do not praise the LORD,**
> **nor do any that go down into silence,**
> [18]**but we** [the living] **will bless the LORD**
>
> **Psalm 115:17-18** (NRSV)

This passage shows that those who die in that era "go down into **silence**." Sheol is a place of silence because those who go there are **unconscious** and, more accurately, **dead**. There's no praising & worshipping of God nor are there horrible screams of torment. It is a condition of silence. It is the *living* who bless the Lord, the psalmist plainly states, not the dead.

Righteous King Hezekiah's prayer coincides:

> **"For Sheol cannot thank you,**
> **death cannot praise you;**
> **those who go down to the Pit**
> **cannot hope for your faithfulness.**
> [19]**The living, the living, they thank you**
> **as I do this day."**
>
> **Isaiah 38:18-19** (NRSV)

Notice, again, how **Sheol and death are spoken of synonymously**. Secondly, witness how Hezekiah makes it clear that those in Sheol are *unable* to thank or praise God, just as David and the other psalmist did.

The obvious conclusion we must draw is that, if the righteous are unable to remember God and cannot praise or thank Him, **then they must not be able to do so**. They must be either **unconscious** or **dead—no longer alive**. This is supported by Hezekiah's statement in verse 19 where he stresses that only "the living, the living" can thank and praise God, not those who go to Sheol, the world of the dead.

Here's yet another corresponding passage:

> [3] **For my soul is full of trouble**
> **and my life draws near the <u>grave</u>** *(sheol)*...
> [10] **Do you show your wonders to the dead?**
> **Do those who are dead rise up and praise you?**
> [11] **Is your love declared in the <u>grave</u>** *(qeber),*
> **your faithfulness in destruction.**
> [12] **Are your wonders known in the place of darkness,**
> **or your righteous deeds in the land of oblivion?**
> **Psalm 88:3,10-12**

This is further proof that those in Sheol are dead and therefore unable to rise up and praise God. Sheol is likened to the **literal grave** *(qeber)* or **destruction**, said to be "**the place of darkness**" and "**land of oblivion**." The psalmist plainly states that God does not show His wonders to the dead in Sheol; that the dead cannot praise Him there and that God's love, faithfulness and righteous deeds are all unknown there. What unmistakable proof that souls in Sheol are dead and conscious of nothing!

This Psalm was written by Heman the Ezrahite when his life was in mortal danger; it's a prayer to God for deliverance from death. Note in verse 3 that Heman clearly expected to go to Sheol when he died, just as Solomon, Jacob, Job, David and Hezekiah did. In the King James Version this is kept from the reader by the use of the word "grave" as a translation of *sheol*, which is likewise the case with the NIV rendering, as shown above (although the NIV provides a footnote indicating that the verse is referring to Sheol). Because of this mistranslation, the average reader is misled into believing that the psalmist is talking about the condition of the literal grave where the body is buried and not to Sheol where the soul goes. The problem with this is that it obscures the truth about the nature of Sheol to the common person and consequently perpetuates false religious ideas.

Sheol Is "The Land of Silence"

Let's examine another enlightening Psalm text by David from two translations:

…let the wicked be put to shame
and lie silent in the grave *(sheol)***.**
18 Let their lying lips be silenced,
Psalm 31:17-18

…let the wicked be ashamed,
and let them be silent in the grave *(sheol)***.**
18 Let their lying lips be put to silence;
Psalm 31:17-18 (KJV)

Notice that this passage is solely referring to "the wicked," i.e. people who are in rebellion against God—living according to the desires of the sinful nature. These are David's enemies. They have rejected his God-appointed kingship and are trying to murder him. David is actually praying for their death for **that is the only way their lying lips will be silenced**.

Observe David's description of the condition these wicked souls will experience if they die: They will **lie silent in Sheol**. The wicked do not constantly scream in torment in Sheol, but rather **lie silent**! This is in harmony with the view that Sheol is a condition of unconsciousness where souls lie "asleep" in death "awaiting" their resurrection.

Other passages likewise reveal that souls lie silent in Sheol, such as Psalm 115:17 from the previous section. Here's another coinciding verse:

If the LORD had not been my help,
my soul would soon have lived in the land of silence.
Psalm 94:17 (NRSV)

The psalmist is testifying that, if the LORD had not delivered him from his wicked enemies (referred to in verse 16), they would have killed him and his soul would have gone to "the land of silence." What is "the land of silence"? Since he's addressing the place **his soul** would go to after death we know he's referring to Sheol.

With this in mind, notice that **the psalmist does not describe Sheol as "the land of shrieking in torment" or "the land of comforts with father Abraham"** (religionists would have us believe Sheol is one or the other, depending on whether the soul is wicked or righteous respectively). That's because **neither of these descriptions is true**. Sheol is, in reality, **the land of *dead* souls where there's no consciousness of anything and thus only silence**.

Take another look at the King James rendition of Psalm 31:17-18 above and note that the passage deviates from the King James standard practice of rendering *sheol* as "hell" whenever the text referred to the wicked (and as "the grave" when it referred to saints). Why did the translators fail to render *sheol* as "hell" in this particular case since it clearly refers to "the wicked"? Obviously because the passage portrays the wicked in Sheol as lying in silence and **this contradicted their belief that wicked souls in Sheol suffer a constant state of screeching torment**.

Sheol Is "the Pit" or "Well of Souls" in the Underworld

We saw earlier in Isaiah 38:18 how Sheol/death is described as "the Pit," which can also be observed in this Psalm:

> **O LORD, you brought up <u>my soul</u> <u>from Sheol</u>,**
> **restored me to life from among those gone down to**
> **<u>the Pit</u>.**
>
> **Psalm 30:3** (NRSV)

David was thankful because God delivered him from death. He knew that, if he died, his soul (not his body) would go to Sheol.

Since Sheol is spoken of as synonymous with "the Pit," we will gain insight into its nature by deciphering what "the Pit" means.

The Hebrew word for "the Pit" is *bowr (borr)* which literally refers to a hole or pit in the ground and is used 71 times in the Bible. The setting in which *bowr* appears determines what specific type of hole or pit and, consequently, which English word is used to translate it. For instance, *bowr* is used 26 times in reference to a 'cistern,' nine times in reference to a 'well,' five times in reference to a 'dungeon,' once to a 'quarry' and once it's even translated as 'death' (Proverbs 28:17).[17]

Why "death"? Because *bowr* is a hole in the ground and that's what a grave actually is. The grave signifies death, of course—the utter absence of life.

The Word of Truth (2 Timothy 2:15) is telling us that **Sheol is like a vast pit or grave where unregenerated souls are held after physical death and before resurrection**.

Since one of the definitions of *bowr* is 'well,' Sheol could be described as "the well of souls," a pit where dead souls are held between physical death and resurrection. Like the subterranean chamber beneath the Dome of the Rock, Sheol is a dungeon—a dungeon where souls are held **captive to death** after physical decease. This explains why *bowr* is translated as "dungeon" in reference to Sheol in this passage from Isaiah:

> **21 So it will happen in that day, that the LORD will punish**
> **the host of heaven, on high,**
> **and the kings of the earth, on earth.**
> **22 And they will be gathered together**
> **like prisoners in the dungeon** ***(bowr),***
> **and will be confined in prison;**
> **and after many days they will be punished.**
> **Isaiah 24:21-22** (NASB)

[17] These figures are from the original New International Version.

The passage is referring to the day when the LORD's cataclysmic wrath will be poured out upon the whole Earth, which occurs just before the establishment of the millennial reign of Christ. Because of God's judgments, billions of people will die and every unsaved soul will be confined to Sheol "like prisoners in the dungeon." Only "after many days," that is, after the thousand-year reign of Christ, will these souls be resurrected to face judgment and suffer the eternal punishment of the second **death**, covered in the previous chapter (Revelation 20:13-15).

Verse 22 plainly says that these unsaved souls will not be punished until *after* they are resurrected from Sheol and judged; this is further evidence disproving the view that souls are punished with roasting torment while captive in Sheol. The only punishment experienced in Sheol is **death itself**, the utter absence of life. This stands to reason since it is in harmony with the biblical axiom that death is the wages of sin (Romans 6:23).

Sheol is a gloomy dungeon or prison in the Underworld where souls are confined. It is not *the* Underworld (Philippians 2:10), but rather a pit *in* the Underworld. No wonder David praised and thanked God for delivering him from this death condition. Obviously, David didn't share the view of some people today that righteous souls in Sheol are (or were) in some type of "paradise" chummin' around with father Abraham. This is a religious myth! Sheol is a dungeon, a prison, a common pit of death where unregenerated souls are confined until their appointed resurrection.

The only soul who can escape this dungeon-like pit of death is the soul that is born-again and thus *possesses* eternal life (John 3:36, 5:24 & 1 John 3:14). This is only possible because "Christ Jesus… has **destroyed death** and has **brought life and immortality to light through the gospel**" (2 Timothy 1:10). The gospel or "good news" refers to all the benefits available to humankind as a result of Yeshua's sacrificial death, burial and resurrection (1 Corinthians 15:1-4). Aside from reconciliation with God, the main benefit of this gospel is, of course, eternal life. Until Jesus' death, burial and resurrection, eternal life or immortality was not available and that's why in Old Testament times, before the ascension of Christ, both righteous and unrighteous souls had to go to Sheol after physical decease.

Incidentally, it's interesting that the original definition of the English word 'hell'—"to conceal or cover"—is in harmony with the biblical description of Sheol as "the Pit." This is evidence that the Old English 'hell' was *originally* used as a translation of Sheol because it properly gave the image of souls consigned and concealed in a pit in the netherworld until their resurrection on Judgment Day. Unfortunately, the definition of 'hell' has taken on a completely different meaning since that time, i.e. perpetually writhing in roasting torment in some devil-ruled torture chamber.

Getting back to Psalm 30, David reveals the state that his soul would have been in if God had not delivered him from death:

> [11] **You have turned my mourning into dancing;**
> **you have taken off my sackcloth and clothed me with joy,**
> [12] **so that my soul may praise you and not be silent.**
> **Psalm 30:11-12** (NRSV)

David is praising God here because he knew that, had he died, his soul would have been silent in Sheol. He well knew that a person cannot praise the LORD or tell of God's faithfulness in Sheol, as indicated in verse 9, because Sheol is a "land of silence."

Sheol Is Distinct from the Physical Grave, Yet Paralleled With It

Although the physical grave *(qeber)* and the soulish grave *(sheol)* are indeed separate terms in the Bible they are often mentioned in the same breath. Why? Because the two go hand-in-hand—if an unredeemed person physically dies, his or her soul goes to Sheol; if his/her soul is in Sheol it's because s/he physically died. Simple, right? Let's look at a few examples.

In Psalm 30:3 David says, "O LORD, you brought up **my soul from Sheol**, restored me to life from among those gone down to **the Pit**" (NRSV). David was praising God for deliverance from a life-threatening situation. On this occasion David was so close to death that he considered himself as good as dead; that's why he symbolically exclaims, "you brought up my soul from Sheol [and] restored me to life." David obviously didn't literally die, but he came so close that he spoke as if he did. Also notice that David makes it clear that Sheol is the condition and place that **souls** specifically go to after physical death, which is in contrast to the physical grave where **bodies** are housed. Take note as well that David describes Sheol as "the Pit," a synonym for Sheol.

With this understanding, consider what David goes on to say in verse 9: "What profit is there in my **death**, if I go down to **the Pit**? **Will the dust praise you? Will it tell of your faithfulness?**" (NRSV). Observe how David mentions "the Pit," which is a reference to Sheol, and then in the same breath asks, "Will the dust praise you?" "Dust" is definitely a reference to the physical grave *(qeber)* or tomb *(qeburah)* where the body is housed because dust is what (unpreserved) bodies revert to after death. The reason David refers to Sheol and the physical grave interchangeably is simply because the two, although distinct, go together.

We also see this in Psalm 88 where Heman prays for deliverance from a serious life-threatening situation. Starting with verse 3 Heman says, "For my soul is full of troubles and **my life draws near to Sheol**. I am counted among those who **go down to the Pit**; I am like those who have no help, like those forsaken among **the dead** like the **slain** that **lie in the grave** *(qeber)"* (NRSV). By saying his "life draws near to Sheol," Heman is simply expressing how close he was to losing his life in this situation. Now observe what Heman declares in verses 10-12:

> **"Do you** [God] **work wonders for the dead?**
> **Do the shades rise up to praise you?**
> 11 **Is your steadfast love declared in the grave** *(qeber)*,
> **or your faithfulness in abaddon** [destruction]**?**
> 12 **Are your wonders known in darkness,**
> **or your saving help in the land of forgetfulness?"**
>
> **Psalm 88:10-12** (NRSV)

Heman specifically mentions Sheol in verse 3 and refers to it as "the Pit" in verse 4. His reference to "darkness" and "the land of forgetfulness" in verse 12 are also references to Sheol, although they could arguably apply to the physical grave as well. In addition, he refers to Sheol as "regions dark and deep" in verse 6. He also mentions the literal grave, *qeber,* in verses 5 and 11.

The point is that Sheol and the physical grave are sometimes noted in the very same breath. Although *sheol* refers to the soulish grave—"gravedom"—where un-regenerated souls go, and *qeber* refers to the physical grave where bodies are laid to rest, both terms are parallel and signify the same condition: DEATH, the cessation of life. ***Qeber* signifies the utter absence of life in the physical realm and *Sheol* denotes the utter absence of conscious life period**.

Because *sheol* and *qeber* are sometimes spoken of in the same breath some theologians have mistakenly theorized that Sheol refers to the physical grave, at least in the context in question. Yet, Sheol is repeatedly described in the Scriptures as a place and condition where immaterial souls go, not bodies. So the idea that Sheol refers to the physical grave must be rejected.

Our conclusion is that *sheol* and *qeber* are distinct yet parallel terms in the Bible; they have separate definitions but naturally go together. Being parallel terms, they signify the same thing—death, the absence of life. Is there any life in a physical grave? No. Neither is there life in Sheol, the soulish grave. **Is a grave meant for anything other than that which is dead**? **No. The same goes for Sheol**. Both terms, though distinct, denote the absence of life.

This presents a problem for the religious view which teaches that Sheol/Hades is a nether realm where unrighteous souls exist in a state of constant torment desperately hoping for less than a drop of water for relief while Old Testament saints hang out in paradise with father Abraham. If this were so, *sheol* and *qeber* couldn't possibly be sister terms. Why? Because *qeber* would signify the utter absence of life whereas *sheol* would refer to the express opposite—conscious life in a spiritual dimension, whether in misery or bliss. They wouldn't be parallel terms at all if they represent two opposite conditions.

What Did Christ Say About the Nature of Sheol?

Jesus got word that his friend Lazarus was deathly ill and, later, discerned that he had died. Notice what the Messiah says to his disciples:

> **…"Our friend Lazarus has fallen asleep; but I am going there to wake him up."**
> **[12] His disciples replied, "Lord, if he sleeps, he will get better." [13] Jesus had been speaking of his death, but his disciples thought he meant natural sleep.**
> **[14] So then he told them plainly, "Lazarus is dead, [15]and for your sake I am glad I was not there, so that you may believe. But let us go to him."**
>
> **John 11:11-15**

Lazarus died and Christ describes it as falling "asleep," which his disciples mistook for natural sleep. So the Lord plainly informed them that Lazarus was **dead**.

Unlike the Parable of the Rich Man and Lazarus, which is figurative, like all parables, this occasion is a *historical chronicling* and Jesus says nothing whatsoever about the *real* Lazarus going to paradise to hang out with father Abraham, **which would be the case if his parable involving the *fictitious* Lazarus was a literal account of the nature of Sheol**. How does Christ describe the *real* Lazarus' condition after physically dying? He describes it in explicit terms of 'sleeping' in death. This doesn't refer to literal snoozing, of course, but to the condition of non-existence in Sheol where dead souls are housed.

The Lord describes it in terms of 'sleeping' simply because every soul in Sheol will be 'awakened' one day; that is, resurrected. This is in contrast to the "second death," which refers to being cast into the lake of fire (Revelation 20:13-15). Those who suffer the second death are never said to be 'sleeping' because they will never be 'awoken' from eternal death, which is why the Bible calls it an "*everlasting* destruction"—destruction that lasts forever with no hope of resurrection (2 Thessalonians 1:9).

Lazarus' death would've been the ideal occasion for Christ to elaborate on Sheol having a paradisal compartment for saintly souls of the Old Testament period, but the Lord says nothing of the kind. The Bible doesn't mention anything at all about the *real-life* Lazarus being in bliss with Abraham and lamenting his return to our fallen Earth after Jesus miraculously resurrects him. Why? Because it's a false doctrine based on mistaking a fantastical parable for a literal account.

Christ also described a dead girl as being "asleep" in three accounts of the same story, as seen in Matthew 9:24, Mark 5:39: and Luke 8:52. As with the case of Lazarus, this would've been the perfect occasion for the Lord to elaborate on how the girl was in paradise in Sheol with Abraham, but—again—He says no such thing. Instead, He likewise describes her condition in terms of 'sleeping' in death.

On top of this is the astounding event of "many holy people" who were raised to life when Christ was resurrected, as shown in Matthew 27:50-53. They came out of their tombs and went into Jerusalem and were seen by many. Again, absolutely nothing is said about these righteous people being resurrected from a supposed blissful section of Sheol where living souls commune with Abraham. Instead, the passage simply says this:

> **The tombs were opened, and many bodies of the saints who had fallen asleep were raised;**
> **Matthew 27:52** (NASB)

So, the Bible repeatedly describes the intermediate state of unregenerated souls in Sheol in terms of 'sleeping' in death, not being comforted in paradise or suffering constant fiery torment. It's as if God is flashing the truth about Sheol in bright neon lights in His Word, but many Christians are too indoctrinated to see it. *WAKE UP CHURCH!*

Does This Support 'Soul Sleep'?

More accurately, it supports soul **death**. When a spiritually unregenerated person dies, their body returns to the ground while the animating spirit of life returns to God who gave it (Ecclesiastes 12:7). The remains of the lifeless soul are stored in Sheol to 'await' resurrection for Divine judgment (Revelation 20:11-15). The soul "sleeping" is a metaphor: When they are resurrected from Sheol to be judged, they "awake."

What About Those Who *Say* They've Visited Sheol?

This refers to people like Mary Baker and Bill Wiese, who claim to have gone to Sheol (Hades) in a vision or out-of-body experience. These people's testimonies beg the question: Why did the LORD wait almost 2000 years after the biblical canon was completed to reveal these horrific details about Sheol? If their visions are to be believed, why aren't there similar such descriptions of Sheol in the Bible, the Word of God?

We don't need the dubious testimonies of these types of people to understand the nature of Sheol because everything God wants us to know about Sheol has already been revealed in the Word of Truth (2 Timothy 2:15 & 3:16). This is in line with Paul's doctrinal rule: "**Do not go beyond what is written**" (1 Corinthians 4:6), which explains why this chapter focuses exclusively on what God's Word says on the subject and not the dubious testimonies of people who claim to have visions or experiences that just so happen to wholly disagree with what Holy Scripture teaches.

Eliphaz argued theology based on spooky visions rather than Scripture (Job 4:12-21), but God accused him & his friends of folly in what they said (42:7-8). Those who go *outside* of Scripture and use sensationalism to prove doctrine are guilty of "the Eliphaz syndrome." If what they're saying is true, they wouldn't have to go *beyond* God's Word to prove it.

You'll rarely hear the topic of Sheol/Hades properly taught in the body of Christ due to entire sects embracing Jesus' parable as a literal accounting of life-after-death. It's a case of not rightly-dividing the Holy Scriptures due to rigid sectarianism or superficiality in their studies (2 Timothy 2:15). If this chapter has whet your interest, pick up a copy of my book *SHEOL KNOW* for further details or see the article on Sheol at the FOL site.

16

Questions About Eternal Life, aka "Heaven"

It makes sense to end this book on a positive note with questions about the nature of eternal life or "Heaven," as some call it.

What Is Heaven?

Heaven is the **spiritual abode of God** where angels dwell and other celestial creatures (Psalm 103:19 & 115:3). This is the primary definition of Heaven and it is what English-speaking people automatically think of when they hear the term.

A secondary definition is the sky or starry panorama, often rendered "the heavens"; this includes the physical universe and everything in it. For example, Psalm 19:1 states: "The **heavens** declare the glory of God; **the skies** proclaim the work of His hands." This is synonymous parallelism in which the second part of the verse simply repeats the first part in different words. In this case, "the heavens" in the first part is confirmed as "the skies" in the second. The context of the passage naturally determines the proper definition, which is the hermeneutical rule "context is king."

Do Redeemed People Go to Heaven Forever?

If by 'heaven' you mean the spiritual abode of God then the answer is no. However, it is true that the souls of spiritually regenerated people—*believers*—go to Heaven when they die to await their bodily resurrection, as shown in such clear passages as Philippians 1:23, 2 Corinthians 5:8, Revelation 6:9-11 and 7:9-15. This refers to **the intermediate state** of believers between physical death and bodily resurrection.

Where Do the Redeemed Spend Eternity?

The Bible instructs us to look "forward to a **new heaven and a new earth**, where righteousness dwells" (2 Peter 3:13). This is where we will spend eternity. The apostle John elaborated on this in his vision:

> **Then I saw "a new heaven and a new earth," for the first heaven and the first earth had passed away, and there was no longer any sea. [2] I saw the Holy City, the new Jerusalem, coming down out of heaven from God, prepared as a bride beautifully dressed for her husband. [3] And I heard a loud voice from the throne saying, "Look! God's dwelling place is now among the people, and he will dwell with them. They will be his people, and God himself will be with them and be their God. [4] 'He will wipe every tear from their eyes. There will be no more death' or mourning or crying or pain, for the old order of things has passed away."**
> **[5] He who was seated on the throne said, "I am making everything new!"**
>
> **Revelation 21:1-5**

What Exactly Are the "New Heaven and New Earth"?

"New heaven" does not refer to the spiritual abode where God's throne is located because Heaven is already perfect and therefore doesn't need restored. After all, how can you restore perfection? So "new heaven" refers to a divinely renovated physical Universe; likewise, "new earth" refers to a renovated Earth. This passage elaborates:

> **The heavens will disappear with a roar; the elements will be destroyed by fire, and the earth and everything done in it will be laid bare.**
> **[11] Since everything will be destroyed in this way, what kind of people ought you to be? You ought to live holy and godly lives [12] as you look forward to the day of God and speed its coming. That day will bring about the destruction of the heavens by fire, and the elements will melt in the heat. [13] But in keeping with his promise we are looking forward to a new heaven and a new earth, where righteousness dwells.**
>
> **2 Peter 3:10-13**

This refers to the final stage of the "final restoration of all things" (Acts 3:21), which is covered in chapter **3**. The Greek word for 'restoration' in this verse is *apokatastasis (ap-ok-at-AS-tas-is)*, and only appears on this occasion in the Bible. The root word is *apokathistémi (ap-ok-ath-IS-tay-mee)*, which means "to set up again" and "restore to its original position or condition." That's what the "restoration of all things" is about—restoring the defiled Earth and Universe to their original condition before the fall, which is the way God originally intended it to be.

As you can see, the Almighty will use fire to renovate the Earth and the "elements," which literally refers to heavenly bodies, like planets and stars. The Earth and Universe will finally be free of the "bondage to decay," with is the law of entropy (Romans 8:21). All negative things, like sin, death, pain and curses will be forever removed.

What Is the "New Jerusalem" and Where Is It?

This is the "holy city," noted in Revelation 21:2 (quoted above), which is currently in Heaven, but it won't stay there. After the Millennium and satan's final rebellion, the LORD will renovate the Earth and Universe and then the New Jerusalem will "come down out of heaven, from God" to rest upon the New Earth. This is the home city of all genuine believers, i.e. the "bride of Christ," which explains why the city itself is called the "bride" in Revelation 21:2—because the redeemed will be *in* it.

I want to stress that the New Jerusalem will not stay in Heaven where it currently is. **The Bible states very clearly *three times* that this city will "come down out of heaven, from" God to rest upon the New Earth** (Revelation 3:12, 21:2 & 21:10).

What About the "Pearly Gates"?

We've all heard references to "the pearly gates of Heaven," but in the Bible the "pearly gates" actually refer to the gates of the twelve main entrances of the New Jerusalem, not to Heaven itself. The walls of the city are said to be made of jasper and *200 feet thick* while each of the huge twelve gates are made of *a single pearl* (Revelation 21:17-18,21). Where did such huge pearls come from? I don't know. There must be a planet somewhere out there in the vast Universe with some really *big* oysters.

What's the Bible Say About the New Jerusalem?

The New Jerusalem will be unimaginably huge and glorious: The city will be 1400 miles long and wide (Revelation 21:16). That's the distance from New York to Wichita, Kansas. Can you imagine a city that big? It would take a trip of about 6000 miles just to travel around it! What's more, the magnificent golden buildings will extend into space 1400 miles. These will be some serious skyscrapers! How would you like to live on the top floor?

Revelation 21 describes this city in some detail. We've already addressed the humongous walls and the twelve pearly gates, but there's more: The main streets of the city will be of pure gold; in fact, the whole city itself will apparently be made of pure gold—so pure it's transparent!

In his book *The Revelation Record,* Henry Morris did the math and pointed out how, if say 20 billion people lived there and their homes & property took up merely 25% of the space in the city, each individual would have a cubical block of about 75 acres of space on each face! The rest of the colossal city would involve streets, parks, public buildings and the like.

What Will Be the Most Significant Aspect of Eternity?

Since Yeshua said knowing God is the most significant aspect of eternal life (John 17:2-3), I would answer: The fact that believers will intimately ***know*** God Almighty face to face (Revelation 21:3-4 & 1 Corinthians 13:12).

Yet we can know the LORD in a more limited sense in this current evil age simply by tapping into the eternal life that's in our spirits. If this doesn't make sense, consider these two facts: **1.** "Eternal life" in the Greek is *aionios zoe (ay-OH-nee-us ZOH-ay)*, which means "age-lasting life" (*aion* is where we get the English 'eon,' meaning "age"). Since the age-to-come is an eternal age, scholars render *aionios* as "eternal," hence, "eternal life." *Aionios zoe* could also be translated as "the life of the age-to-come." This is the "abundant" or "full" life that Christ said he came to give people (John 10:10). **2.** Receiving eternal life—the "life of the age-to-come"—is a **two-phase process**:

1. Believers receive eternal life in their spirits at the point of spiritual regeneration, which is why John the Baptist said: "Whoever believes in the Son *has* eternal life [present tense], but whoever rejects the Son will not see life, for God's wrath remains on him" (John 3:36). See also 1 John 5:11-12. The fact that believers presently have the abundant life-of-the-age-to-come in their regenerated spirits reveals why it's so important that we learn to put off the "old self"—the flesh—and put on the "new self"—the spirit (Ephesians 4:22-24), which means to walk in the spirit, not in the flesh. When we do this, **we tap into that full life of God and are able to manifest it in this dark, dying, lost world**.

2. Attaining eternal life is completed at the resurrection of the righteous, which is when we'll receive new **imperishable**, **glorified**, **powerful** and **spiritual** bodies (1 Corinthians 15:42-44). The fact that the believer's eternal life is *completed* at the resurrection is confirmed by Christ when he plainly stated that believers will receive eternal life "in the age to come" (Mark 10:29-30). This is verified by other passages like Titus 1:2, 3:7 and Jude 1:21.

Every believer can grow in knowing God simply by tapping into that eternal life that's in our spirits, but you have to put off the flesh to do this; it's also necessary to "throw off" every weight or distraction that hinders (Hebrews 12:1). The Bible says, "Come near to God and he will come near to you" (James 4:8). This is how you "grow in God's grace," i.e. favor (2 Peter 3:18). Think about it: You can have as much of God as you want!

What Will These "Glorified Bodies" Be Like?

We can get an idea by simply observing what the Bible says about the Lord *after* His resurrection. After all, we're going to receive the same type of glorified body He did; that is, *if* you're a believer. In light of this, we'll evidently be able to walk through solid objects (John 20:26), instantly appear out of nowhere and disappear (Luke 24:31,36-37); in other words, we'll be able to *teleport* at will. With this understanding, we'll no doubt be able to take "quantum leaps" to anywhere on the New Earth, Moon, Mars or Universe—*distances and space will no longer limit us.*

On a more mundane note, the resurrected Jesus ate fish (Luke 24:41-43).

For anyone who argues that Christ is deity and therefore our glorified bodies may not have the same capacity as His, the Bible blatantly says that we are "*co-heirs* with Christ," which means 'joint heirs' or 'joint participants' (Romans 8:17). Besides, why would the LORD reveal to us the incredible abilities of the glorified body through Jesus' actions after His resurrection if He didn't intend for us to have the same incredible capacity when we're bodily resurrected?

What's Another Significant Aspect of Life in Eternity?

Revelation 21:3-4 plainly states that there will be no more pain, crying, aging or death in the eternal age—all such maladies will have been eliminated! This makes perfect sense. After all, what good is paradise if one has to suffer pain, aging and death? The passage even says that God will *personally console us* regarding the many pains, heartaches and injustices we've experienced in "this present evil age" (Galatians 1:4).

Will There Be Nations and Kings on the New Earth?

Yes, there *will be* countries and rulers on the New Earth (Revelation 21:24). The Greek word for "nations" is *ethnos (ETH-nos)*, meaning "a race, a people or a nation that shares a common and distinctive culture." In short, peoples on the New Earth won't be look-alike drones under the supervision of the Most High. Variety is the spice of life, *Praise God!* Plus, there will be kings over these nations; that is, national authorities. And if there are national authorities there will be subordinate authorities, like governors of territories, mayors of cities and so on. Of course, there will also be authority structures in the vast New Jerusalem.

Yeshua showed who will be placed in authority positions in two parables—Matthew 25:14-30 and Luke 19:15-19. The Lord invests in every believer and expects a return on this investment when He returns. The two men in the first story who doubled what was invested in them are praised by the master and told, "You have been faithful with a few things; I will put you in charge of many things." In the second parable, the first person the king invested in is put in charge of ten cities and the second five cities. This is relevant to the Judgment Seat of Christ, which is the judgment believers undergo (2 Corinthians 5:10-11 & Romans 14:10).

Both stories are figurative of the literal truth that believers will be rewarded according to what we do or don't do with the talents with which we've been invested. Those who are "faithful with a few things" will be "put in charge of many things." This indicates a position of authority; and the second parable specifies being put in charge of cities.

When and where will faithful believers be put in charge of "many things," including "cities"? On the New Earth for sure, but other planets as well.

With this understanding, your faithfulness *now* with the few small things the Lord has put you in charge of has eternal ramifications! What has God put you in charge of? Several things: Your thoughts, your body, your talents, your service, your job, your money and those linked to you.

So, We'll Be in Charge of Things in the New Universe?

While it's true that "the meek will inherit the earth," meaning the New Earth (Matthew 5:5 & Psalm 37:29), we are also blatantly promised the "new heaven" as part of our eternal inheritance, meaning the entire new Universe (2 Peter 3:13). In other words, the New Jerusalem and New Earth will only be our **home base**; *we'll be able to explore and inhabit the unfathomable reaches of the cosmos!*

Don't think for a second that God, our Almighty Creator, formed the incomprehensibly vast Universe—the billions of galaxies and incalculable stars & planets for nothing. Be assured that the *whole Universe* will be under humanity's subjection to explore, inhabit, rule, enjoy and who knows what else? As it is written:

> **For You (God) have put everything in subjection under his (humanity's) feet. Now in putting everything in subjection to man, He left nothing outside [of man's] control. But at present we do not yet see all things subjected to him [man].**
>
> **Hebrews 2:8** (The Amplified Bible)

"Everything" in the natural realm will be put in subjection to redeemed humanity; "everything" will be put in our control. It's interesting to note that 'everything' can also be translated as "the universe," which is how the Weymouth New Testament renders it. *Nothing in the entire Universe will be outside of our control.* As stated above, we will be able to explore, inhabit and rule the unfathomable reaches of the physical Universe!

Remember, God originally blessed humankind to "be fruitful and multiply," to "subdue" and "have dominion" over all the Earth:

> **And God blessed them, and said unto them, "Be fruitful, and multiply, and replenish the earth, and subdue it: and have dominion over the fish of the sea, and over the fowl of the air, and over every living thing that moveth upon the earth."**
>
> **Genesis 1:28** (KJV)

This blessing/directive is inherent in the psycho-spiritual DNA of humankind. There's no escaping it; it's our Divine mission; it's part of who we *are*. Unfortunately, the sin nature inevitably twists this blessing and it becomes a curse, resulting in abuse, slavery, environmental raping, wars, etc. Yet, this doesn't take away from the fact that the intrinsic blessing is wholly *good* and was intended to *empower* humanity to fulfill its Divine mandate—to be fruitful, multiply, replenish, subdue and take dominion. In other words, the LORD didn't create humankind to be servants of the Earth, but to be lords over it, which is befitting since Father God is "Lord of heaven and earth," as Jesus Christ Himself acknowledged (Matthew 11:25). Keep in mind that humanity is created in God's image and believers are called to be "imitators of God" (Ephesians 5:1).

I want to stress that the LORD does *not* want us to "subdue" and take "dominion" in a negative sense. This must be emphasized seeing as how most people equate "dominion" with carnal control, no doubt because the devil naturally tries to pervert whatever God creates, commands or blesses. God's mandate was to subdue and hold dominion IN LOVE, because "God is love" (1 John 4:7-8,16). This helps make sense of this proverb:

> **Love and faithfulness keep a king safe; through love his throne is made secure.**
>
> **Proverbs 20:28**

A "king" refers to an authority figure. In our day and age, it would apply to anyone who has authority in any given environment: a father or mother, a teacher or professor, an employer or supervisor, a president or governor, a pastor or apostle, a police officer or security guard, etc. The proverb reveals the godly way of keeping one's position of authority—one's "throne"—safe and secure: Through love and faithfulness. So, when the Bible talks about "subduing" and taking "dominion" it's talking about doing so in love and faithfulness, not being an abusive tyrant.

Now, here's something interesting: The Garden of Eden was only about the size of California according to the specifications in Genesis. It was already a paradise, which is the way God created it, but the rest of the Earth wasn't. The rest of the planet had potential, but it was untamed and uncultivated, which is why the LORD empowered humankind to subdue it and take dominion. In other words, God blessed humanity to make the rest of the planet the same paradise as the Garden of Eden, which is why Genesis 1:28 above twice stresses replenishing and subduing "the earth" and not the Garden of Eden since it was already replenished and subdued.

The paradise of the Garden of Eden was God's blueprint for humankind to expand on until the entire planet was a paradise. Once 'Project Earth' was complete, they could go on to subdue and replenish every planet in the solar system, the galaxy, and ultimately the furthest reaches of the Universe! Why do you think all of these innumerable barren planets are even there? They're there for us to reach and subdue, in love and faithfulness. This is supported by Hebrews 2:8 above: God has placed *"**everything**"* in the natural Universe in subjection to humanity—*"**nothing**"* is outside of redeemed humanity's control! Chew on that.

Doesn't this remind you of various science-fiction books, shows and films—humanity uniting together and going out to the furthest reaches of space to peaceably explore and inhabit, like Roddenberry's Star Trek? These sci-fi visionaries instinctively grasp God's blessing/directive because it's part of our spiritual DNA. The significant difference is that there will be no pain, hostility, war, disease, immorality, corruption, aging or death, not to mention the palpable presence of the Almighty: All humanity will truly be united together in love, mutual respect and acceptance under the perfectly just govern-ship of the Creator of All.

If this doesn't get you excited, check your pulse.

Closing Word

You've no doubt noticed how Scripture passages are cited on practically every page. That's because this book is only meant to assist you in your pursuit of knowledge, understanding and wisdom **by means of** the Word of Truth. In other words, this work gives structure to the wealth of biblical knowledge for your convenience and spiritual growth, but it obviously does not replace God's Word as the written source of truth.

Of course, you're not obligated to agree with every jot and tittle. Eat up what you know is biblical (Matthew 4:4) and put what you're not certain about on the back burner for future consideration. This includes material that you're simply not ready for at the present time because it's too heavy or what have you.

Naturally, I've researched the differing viewpoints on every topic. If you disagree with something, that's fine. Gather the scriptural data necessary to support your perspective and weigh the positions. If you're convinced that you're right and this book is wrong on a particular topic, please write Fountain of Life and we'll honestly consider your evidence. If you can prove your position, we'll be sure to revise the corresponding articles at our site, as well as in this book (assuming it's rereleased at some point).

God Bless You Richly as You Seek & Serve! Amen.

The path of the righteous is like the first gleam of dawn,
shining ever brighter till the full light of day.

- Proverbs 4:18

Bibliography

(A person's inclusion in this list does not equal wholesale endorsement)

Altieri, Jay. Various personal insights on *sheqer* and *kazab*, unpublished.

Benner, Jeff. *The Ancient Hebrew Lexicon of the Bible.* College Station: Virtualbookworm Publishing, 2005

Brown, Francis/Driver, S.R./Briggs, Charles A. *Brown-Driver-Briggs Lexicon.* Peabody: Hendrickson Publishers, 1994

Bullinger, Ethelbert W. *A Critical Lexicon and Concordance to the English and Greek New Testament.* Grand Rapids: Zondervan Publishing House, 1975

Cameneti, Joseph. "Keys to Spiritual Maturity" (series). Believers Christian Fellowship, Warren, OH. February-March, 1996

Cameneti, Joseph. "Obtaining Your Desires II." Believers Christian Fellowship, Warren, OH. December 17, 1986

Copeland, Kenneth. *The Blessing of the LORD.* Fort Worth: KCP, 2011

Dake, Finis. *Dake's Annotated Reference Bible.* Lawrenceville: DBS, 1963/1991

Federer, William. *Who is the King in America?* Virginia Beach: Amerisearch, Inc., 2017

Geisler, Norman. *Christian Ethics: Options and Issues.* Grand Rapids: Baker Book House, 1989

Ham, Ken. *What Really Happened to the Dinosaurs?* Retrieved from https://answersingenesis.org/dinosaurs/when-did-dinosaurs-live/what-really-happened-to-the-dinosaurs/, 2007

Helps Word-Studies Lexicon. Retrieved from Biblehub.com. 1987, 2011

Houdmann, Michael S. *Got Questions? (miscellaneous).* Retrieved from https://www. gotquestions.org/, 2002-2023

Kirkwood, David. *Your Best Year Yet!* Pittsburgh: Ethnos Press, 1996

Lindsey, Hal. *The Liberation of Planet Earth.* New York: HarperCollins, 1974

LORD, The. *The Amplified Bible.* Grand Rapids: Zondervan, 1987

LORD, The. *Douay-Rheims Version. Holy Bible.* Gastonia: Tan books, 2009

LORD, The. *English Standard Version (ESV). Holy Bible.* Chicago: Crossway, 2001

LORD, The. *The International Standard Version New Testament.* Highlands Ranch: Davidson Press, 1998

LORD, The. *King James Version. Holy Bible.* Iowa Falls: World Bible Publishers

LORD, The. *New International Version (Revised). Holy Bible.* Nashville: Holman, 2011

LORD, The. *New King James Version Study Bible: Second Edition. Holy Bible.* Nashville: Thomas Nelson, 2012

LORD, *The. New Revised Standard Version. Holy Bible.* Nashville: Nelson, 1989

LORD, The. *Quest Study Bible: New International Version. Holy Bible.* Grand Rapids: Zondervan, 2003

MacArthur, John. *The MacArthur Study Bible.* Nashville: Word Bibles, 1997

Morris, Henry. *The Revelation Record.* Carol Stream: Tyndale House, 1983

Murdock, Mike. *Wisdom for Winning.* Tulsa: Honor, 1988

Peck, M. Scott. *The Different Drum*. New York: Touchstone, 1987

Peck, M. Scott. *Further Along the Road Less Traveled*. New York: Touchstone, 1993

Reagan, David. *God's Plan for the Ages: The Blueprint of Bible Prophecy*. McKinney: Lamb & Lion Ministries, 2005

Robertson, Pat. *ANSWERS to 200 of Life's Most Probing Questions.* Nashville: Thomas Nelson, 1984

Servant, David. *Heaven Word Daily.* Pittsburgh: Ethnos Press, 2009

Strong, James. *Strong's Exhaustive Concordance.* Grand Rapids: Baker, 1991

Vine, W.E. *Vine's Expository Dictionary of Biblical Words.* Cambridge: Nelson, 1985

Waren, Dirk. *ANGELS: Their Purpose, Your Responsibility.* Youngstown: Soaring Eagle Press, 2017

Waren, Dirk. *Fountain of Life Teaching Ministry.* Retrieved from http://www.fountainoflifetm.com/, 2011-2023

Waren, Dirk. *HELL KNOW!* Youngstown: Soaring Eagle Press, 2014/2016

Waren, Dirk. *How to Handle OFFENSES: Personal & Criminal.* Youngstown: Soaring Eagle Press, 2020

Waren, Dirk. *SHEOL KNOW!* Youngstown: Soaring Eagle Press, 2015

Waren, Dirk. *Solomon's SONG OF SONGS.* Youngstown: Soaring Eagle Press, 2022

Waren, Dirk. *The FIVEFOLD MINISTRY Gifts: Apostle, Prophet, Evangelist, Pastor, Teacher.* Youngstown: Soaring Eagle Press, 2022

Waren, Dirk. *The Four Stages of Spiritual Growth.* Youngstown: Soaring Eagle Press, 2015

Whiston, Lionel. *Are You Fun to Live With?* Canton: Life Enrichment Publishers, 1984

Fountain of Life

Teaching Ministry

(Psalm 36:9)

The mission of Fountain of Life is to **set the captives FREE** by **reaching the world** with the **life-changing truths of God's Word**, the **power of the Holy Spirit** and the **Awesome News of the message of Jesus Christ**.

We're calling Spiritual Warriors all over the Earth to partner with us in this mission!

Books by Dirk Waren:

The Believer's Guide to FORGIVENESS & WARFARE
Legalism Unmasked
HELL KNOW! (full and condensed versions)
SHEOL KNOW! (full and condensed versions)
The Four Stages of Spiritual Growth
ANGELS: Their Purpose and Your Responsibility
THE LAW and the Believer
The SIX BASIC DOCTRINES of Christianity
GRACE: What Is It? How Do You Grow in It?
How to Handle OFFENSES: Personal & Criminal
WOMEN in Ministry ...in God's Service
The FIVEFOLD MINISTRY Gifts: Apostle, Prophet, Evangelist, Pastor, Teacher
Solomon's SONG OF SONGS and Issues of Love & Sex
QUESTIONS & ANSWERS From the Bible

www.ingramcontent.com/pod-product-compliance
Lightning Source LLC
LaVergne TN
LVHW050532160826
845677LV00011B/2005

* 9 7 9 8 2 1 8 2 6 2 7 4 7 *